College and Character

College and Character

a briefer version of *The American College*

edited by Nevitt Sanford

abridged by the authors,
and with a new concluding chapter by the editor

John Wiley & Sons, Inc.   New York · London · Sydney

Contributing Authors

Joseph Adelson

Associate Professor of Psychology and Research Associate, Survey Research Center, University of Michigan, Ann Arbor, Michigan

Christian Bay

Research Associate, Institute for the Study of Human Problems, Stanford University, Stanford, California

David Beardslee

Associate Professor of Psychology and Director, University Computer and Data Processing Center, Oakland University, Rochester, Michigan

Howard Becker

Research Associate, Institute for the Study of Human Problems, and Editor, *Social Problems*, Stanford University, Stanford, California

Carl Bereiter

Associate Professor of Special Education, Institute for Research on Exceptional Children, University of Illinois, Urbana, Illinois

Donald Brown

Associate Professor of Psychology, Bryn Mawr College, Bryn Mawr, Pennsylvania

John Bushnell

Director of Research, State Commission for Human Rights, New York City, New York

Elizabeth Douvan

Research Associate, Survey Research Center, University of Michigan, Ann Arbor, Michigan

Joshua Fishman

Professor of Psychology and Dean of the Graduate School of Education, Yeshiva University, New York City, New York

Mervin Freedman

Research Associate, Institute for the Study of Human Problems, Stanford University, Stanford, California, and Director of Research, Department of Psychiatry, Cowell Memorial Hospital, University of California, Berkeley, California

Blanche Geer

Professor of Sociology and Education and Senior Research Associate, Youth Development Center, Syracuse University, Syracuse, New York

Paul Heist

Lecturer in Higher Education and Associate Research Psychologist, Center for the Study of Higher Education, University of California, Berkeley, California

Everett Hughes

Professor of Sociology, Brandeis University, Waltham, Massachusetts

Christopher Jencks

Resident Fellow, Institute for Policy Studies, Washington, D.C., and also an editor of *The New Republic*

Joseph Katz

Research Co-ordinator, Institute for the Study of Human Problems, Stanford University, Stanford, California

Carol Kaye

Instructor, Department of Psychiatry, Boston University Medical School, Boston, Massachusetts

Robert Knapp

Professor of Psychology, Weslyan University, Middletown, Connecticut

T. R. McConnell

Professor of Higher Education and Chairman, Center for the Study of Higher Education, University of California, Berkeley, California

W. J. McKeachie

Professor of Psychology, University of Michigan, Ann Arbor, Michigan

Theodore Newcomb

Professor of Sociology and Psychology, University of Michigan, Ann Arbor, Michigan

Donald O'Dowd

Dean of the University, Oakland University, Rochester, Michigan

Frank Pinner

Associate Professor of Political Science and Director, Bureau of Social and Political Research, Michigan State University, East Lansing, Michigan

David Riesman

Henry Ford II Professor of the Social Sciences, Harvard University, Cambridge, Massachusetts viii

Nevitt Sanford

Professor of Psychology and Education and Director, Institute for the Study of Human Problems, Stanford University, Stanford, California

George Stern

Professor of Psychology and Executive Officer, Psychological Research Center, Syracuse University, Syracuse, New York

John Summerskill

Vice-President for Student Affairs, Cornell University, Ithaca, New York

Harold Taylor

Director, Summer Program, Committee on a Friends' College, New York City, New York. Formerly President of Sarah Lawrence College.

Harold Webster

Associate Research Psychologist, Center for the Study of Higher Education, University of California, Berkeley, California

Preface

This book is a shortened and otherwise somewhat modified version of *The American College*, an 1100-page volume by 30 authors published by John Wiley and Sons in January 1962.

I was warned about the length of the original volume many times during its preparation. Who in these crowded times would plow through so many pages of writing about any subject, even the crucially important one of higher education? And no sooner was the book published than reviewers and commentators started in on the same theme. "Read it? Why, I couldn't even lift it," said a dean (who somehow managed to read it anyway). "This will be the most quoted and least read book about higher education to appear in many years," ran a review in a New York newspaper.

To friends, colleagues, publisher's representatives, and friendly critics, I want to say that I took their warnings and protests very much to heart. *Now* I am very glad to heed them; now that the authors have had their say about the details of their special fields, and now that *The American College* is available to people who have use for a book of its kind. That book and the present one were prepared with different purposes in mind and are addressed to different—but, we may hope, overlapping—audiences.

The American College contained twenty-nine chapters, each of which was prepared especially for the book and with attention to an overall scheme of organization. As stated in the introduction, the book was intended to give "a picture of the American college as a whole, a picture that conveys, we hope, the complexity and diversity of the institution and how it changes under the impact of forces in American society." The focus was on the individual student and his development under the influence of inner psychological and outer social forces.

Some reviewers of *The American College*, like some readers of the manuscript, called for a brief version or summary that would make the essential ideas of the book available to a wider audience, particularly people—usually very busy people—who were in a position to influence the policies of our institutions of higher learning. The call was for a book that college presidents could conveniently carry with them on airplanes—and then recommend to their trustees without fear of punishment. In responding to this suggestion, the authors and I have had other audiences in mind as well. There are many professional people whose work requires that they know something about students and the college environment, but who do not need the detailed and often specialized information offered in *The American College*. This book, it is hoped, will offer these professionals what they need; but we also hope that some of them will find their interest stimulated and later want to move on to the original.

Also, and above all, we have had in mind the general reader. First, he who has an immediate concern with colleges—he who is attending one now, or who is about to go, and particularly the parents of people in these categories. And second, we address ourselves to people who, as citizens, feel that they have a stake in higher education in this country, seeing in it the major instrument for the promotion of many of our highest values. It is our hope that this book will help to stimulate public discussion of higher education, providing information and points of view that have not been easily in reach of the general reader.

In preparing the present book we proceeded as follows. First, each chapter of the original was abridged by the editor with the assistance of Robert Byers and Rupert Wilkinson. The abridgment was achieved, first, by eliminating all discussion of methods and of methodological issues and by reducing to the barest minimum the scholarly apparatus—all those passages in which scholars and scientists had talked primarily to each other in accordance with the requirements of their professions. Virtually all technical terms were eliminated. Then we selected for each chapter what seemed to us to be the most important findings and more novel points of view.

These operations, and the provision of appropriate continuity, required a certain amount of rewriting. It was after this was done that the manuscripts were given to the authors. All authors have approved the versions of their chapters as printed here, although some authors approved more readily than others. Some approved what had been done and suggested minor editorial changes; some had major misgivings at first and entered into complicated discussions and negotiations usually involving a great deal of work on their part before a suitable version evolved. Some of the latter took over the entire job of abridging their chapters, in consultation with the editor. Some gave their assent to what was being done but with a minimum of involvement in the enterprise. If we consider that in most cases an author had to preside over an operation that reduced a major work of his—a labor of love—by more than 75 per cent, we can see that a lot was being asked. It is a pleasure to report that all the authors were good sports, displaying the same kind of tolerance and reasonableness that made *The American College* possible in the first place.

Two chapters from *The American College* have been omitted from this brief edition because they did not lend themselves well to abridgment. A third chapter, the concluding one, which had to do mainly with methods and strategies of research, has been omitted because it seemed to be of insufficient general interest, although a few passages from that chapter have been incorporated in the present Chapter 2. The sequence of chapters has been rearranged slightly, to make for balance among the several Parts of the book and for what, in the light of overall abridgment, seemed the most suitable order of events within a Part.

The concluding chapter has been written especially for this volume. Here I have recapitulated some of the main themes of *The American College* and of the present book and brought together some proposals for change and experimentation in our colleges. In respect to the latter I do not claim to have listed all the suggestions that the various authors have made at various places in these books and certainly not all that could conceivably flow from their contributions. I have simply included some proposals that I find particularly interesting at this time. In writing this chapter I have addressed myself to some current issues in higher education which in the light of reactions to *The American College* seem to be particularly important or controversial.

Although the present book is a fairly radical abridgment, it may be said to embody the main themes and points of view of *The American College* as a whole. Indeed it is possible that the wholeness of higher education as a field of inquiry can be better seen in this book than in the original. The perspective here is such that the interactions of the various features of the college are plainly visible. *The American College*, however, will still be preferred by those readers who require detailed information about any aspect of the college and its work and particularly by those who are interested in carrying on research in the field.

Many people have helped to prepare this book. Thanks go particularly to Robert Byers, Rupert Wilkinson, and Mary Pullman for their competent and devoted editorial work, and to some of my colleagues at the Institute for the Study of Human Problems. Christian Bay, Howard Becker, Mervin Freedman, and Joseph Katz, all of them contributing authors of *The American College*, have participated in all my problems and solved many of them for me.

Nevitt Sanford

Stanford, California
October, 1963

Contents

One

The Study of Higher Education

Nevitt Sanford

Higher Education as a Social Problem

The trouble with students, the saying goes, is that they turn into alumni. Indeed, a close look at the college-educated people in the United States is enough to dispel any notion that our institutions of higher learning are doing a good job of liberal education.

A professor in one of our great state universities arrived almost at the end of his career with the feeling that things had not gone too badly. Then he had occasion to work closely over a period of time with the organized alumni of his institution. He quickly came to the conclusion that these products of his and his colleagues' labors had no respect for learning, understood nothing of the conditions necessary to it, and were quite willing to sacrifice fundamental freedoms of the mind to the interests of expediency. Nothing happened later to rescue this retiring member of the faculty from his disillusionment.

But the failures and shortcomings of the colleges seem to be not at all discouraging to the general public, or the large segment of it that supports the colleges. It is remarkable that a culture which places relatively little value on learning or the intellectual life, and has little understanding of, or sympathy for, what professors are trying to do, nevertheless regards college—the experience of college for young people—as one of the greatest goods, virtually as one of the necessities of life.

For the great mass of our middle-class high school students, "going to college" is a future event second in importance and glamor only to securing a job or to getting married and having children. If they fail to make the grade, or leave college to get married after a year or so, they are easy targets for an insurance salesman armed with a policy that will make it easy "for the children to go to college." The situation is much the same with the parents of these youngsters, particularly if these parents have, or aspire to, lower-middle-class status or above. They are willing to make painful sacrifices to pay the necessary fees, and their anxiety about acceptance is often greater than that of the youngsters most immediately involved.

It is clear that in the eyes of the general public, college offers important benefits quite apart from those described in the college catalogues. For one thing, it seems that increasing demands for college are a concomitant of our increasing affluence and our chronic state of overproduction. Since there is little need for young people in the world of production, a practical choice is to keep them in school for as long as possible, and college is the next step after high school. In an employers' market it is a simple matter to list "college degree" among the requirements of a job, and thus create the widespread conviction that "you have to go to college in order to get anywhere these days." College, of course, has long been a major channel through which one went up in the world economically; it has now become for the middle-class young person a necessary means for holding his own.

The social benefits of college seem to be regarded as highly as the economic ones, and to be inseparably interrelated with them. For the great middle class, college has become a social necessity, while for members of the lower classes it is a prime means for social advancement.

Since colleges serve so many fundamental desires and needs of the people they are subjected to little enlightened public criticism. The recent and continuing public discussion of education, occasioned by the sputniks, has left the colleges unscathed. There have been few suggestions that the colleges might improve or reform. Rather, the question has been how can they remain as they are in the face of social change and increasing demands for admission. The colleges have their own way of putting it: "How can we maintain quality?"—few ask the natural question "What quality?" or suggest that the problem is how to come closer to the realization of stated aims.

The official position of the colleges seems to be: "We must maintain quality by increasing faculty salaries, by getting money to ensure that increases in personnel and resources keep pace with any increases in enrollment, by raising the standards for admission. And of course we must reform the high schools." The structure and functioning of public high schools have been the objects of much scrutiny and discussion, with the promise of considerable benefit to all concerned. Why have the colleges been largely exempt from this kind of examination?

For one thing, it seems that the great majority of our articulate citizens value the nonacademic benefits their children derive from college and do not really want to see things changed. They can criticize the local high school because it may not be doing enough to get their sons and daughters into a good college. To get them into that college and, to a somewhat lesser degree, to keep them there is often an end in itself.

Again, and perhaps more important, enlightened citizens have often been the victims of considerable bamboozlement. They do not know what goes on in the colleges, and have no ready means for finding out. Nor are there means for evaluating the effects of a college program. A man may be an influential critic of our foreign policy, of the conduct of the federal judiciary, or of the local city planning commission, but when it comes to policy and practice in higher education he is silent. He likes to know what he is talking about; and besides, his real problem is how to find a good college for his daughter. He picks up some gossip and vague impressions from his friends, speculates wildly about how some imagined features of this or that college will bring out the various potentialities of his daughter, and supports her in her several applications. While he is in the position of having to wait upon the college's pleasure, he cannot bite the hand that might feed him. If he has to deal with a rejection of her application, his case is worse; he does not want to be a sorehead, and even if this were his inclination he would be silenced by the notion, effectively implanted by the college, that it's all his fault anyway—for not supplying her with the right genes or with the right solution to her oedipus complex.

The chances are, however, that the serious-minded daughter of this influential citizen will be admitted to a college which through careful public relations has been able to put across the notion that it is highly intellectual, but which is in fact just like all the others and is still living on a reputation established thirty years ago. Having doubted that she was worthy of such a college the daughter reports her amazement that everybody is so friendly and helpful. The courses are "interesting."

By the time she discovers that a set of academic prerequisites and distribution requirements do not add up to a stimulating intellectual life, she has found attachments and benefits which though different from those she had looked forward to are none the less real. Her reports home continue to be favorable, which is a great joy to her father, who by now has invested so heavily in this venture that any other kind of report would be hard to take. So he recommends this college to his friends and goes along with the idea that the colleges in general are doing a good job. (It must be said, however, that if the general public has little interest in improving the colleges, many of the colleges themselves seem to have but little more.)

To understand the attitudes of the colleges it is necessary to consider that they are in an important sense corporate enterprises. Much of their activity must be devoted to surviving, expanding, and maintaining a strong position relative to other institutions. To a very considerable extent this holds for state institutions as well as for private ones. Although they appear to be riding high at present, operating as they do in a sellers' market, our colleges and universities are actually very sensitive to the wants and needs of their constituents, and are prepared to stay within certain limits set by them. It is difficult for the ordinary private college or smaller state institution to rise above the level of value and taste that prevails in its immediate community. It often has to come to terms with the demands of large donors or the state legislature.

For nationally known institutions the situation is different and more complicated. They are in competition for the status of leading intellectual center, and they attempt to further their cause by recruiting on a nationwide basis the brightest students and the most distinguished faculty members. The two go together. A distinguished faculty member is one who publishes, and typically he is more interested in research than in teaching, prefers graduate to undergraduate teaching, and has little patience with students who are not already devoted to scholarship. The constituents of these institutions go along with these arrangements—up to a point. However little they may value the intellectual life, the college of their choice must be a "good" one by educational standards in order for their sons and daughters to obtain the important "unintellectual" benefits to be had there.

The excitement about "getting into college" today is greatest among people who are disposed by reason of background and financial solvency to think of the more distinguished places. But there is a limit to how far constituents will go in supporting a leading intellectual center. Obviously our leading private colleges could not exist if they went too far in the direction of excluding the sons and daughters of people who can afford the fees and support drives for funds and who feel with some justice that such institutions belong to them. These institutions are thus under some pressure to prevent their standards from going too high, too rapidly.

The colleges' main strategy is to silence their unhappy constituents. This is not too difficult, particularly if these institutions stick together, present a united front to the public, and discourage public discussion of their inner workings. This they tend to do instinctively. If the alumni or the trustees suggest that "the intellect isn't everything," they may be reminded that our institutions of higher learning do not exist to promote athletics or the acquisition of social skills, that not everybody has a right to go to college, and that in a time of national crisis all good citizens should support the maximum development and utilization of our "human resources." The constituents do not know or cannot phrase the counter arguments, and there are few who will speak for them. The plain fact is that our leading colleges do not do enough for their large majorities of uncommitted, or vocationally oriented, or unintellectual students. These students may not be the brightest in the world, but they are bright enough for most good purposes. Alumni and friends of these colleges have every right to ask that something be done for these young people besides preparing them for the scholarly or other professions. They have this right so long as they grant the same to people who cannot afford private colleges.

This discussion is intended to underline the point that the American college, and American institutions of higher learning generally, are embedded in our culture and in our society. They are expressive of persistent trends, and persistent conflicts, in the American value system, and they have a diversity of important functions in society. This means that fundamental or widespread change in the colleges can come about only when there is a shift of emphasis in our general system of values or when there is a change in our general social processes.

Who, then, is to reform the colleges? And how is such reform to come about?

The notion that these institutions exist within a "surround" of cultural and social forces and necessarily reflect the prevalent trends is, from the point of view of social science, the beginning of wisdom; but it is not wisdom itself. There is another side to the picture. The colleges are not playthings of forces over which no one has any control. What saves them from this status is the element of rationality in our social processes; where we have knowledge of conditions and are free to use our intelligence we are able, within limits, to influence the course of events. Our colleges and universities have the functions of supplying this knowledge and developing this intelligence. It would thus be a very sad state of affairs indeed if these institutions were completely overpowered by the forces they were designed to understand and to modify.

Fortunately this condition has not yet been reached. Counter-forces to the trends that have been described can readily be observed, and we may expect these counterforces to increase in strength as the need for them grows more apparent. Things may well get better, after they have got worse.

Our professors and intellectuals are not entirely without support, and not without sanction, in their efforts to supply the necessary criticism of our society and to raise the level of our culture. They are permitted these functions by our society—the same society that would utilize the colleges for keeping the youth out of trouble, showing them a good time, and offering them social advantages. This society not only arranges for the satisfaction of diverse low-order wants and needs but it also pays its respects to ideals which have their roots in Western Civilization and in some American traditions. It expects the colleges and universities to look after these ideals, whatever else it may demand of these institutions and however many obstacles it may put in their way.

Linus in the comic strip "Peanuts" is, as every serious-minded undergraduate knows, addicted to his blanket, an unfailing source of comfort and gratification. But he wants to break himself of this habit, so he gives the blanket to Charlie Brown with the request that he hold on to it no matter what he—Linus—says or does. Then Linus immediately says he has changed his mind and that he must have the blanket back. Charlie says, dumbly, "Okay, here," and Linus screams, "You're weaker than I am." Our society suffers from addiction to practicality, power, success, social adjustment, excitement, and the gratifications of popular culture, but in a sense it has asked of our colleges and universities "Get us out of this, no matter how much we may protest from time to time."

The mandates of these institutions come from the people, but they come from the people's better selves, and they were given at times when the people were thinking well or had found spokesmen who could express their higher aspirations. The colleges sometimes seem to forget this and yield to impulsive demands for the return of the blanket; or they may try to quiet the clamor arising out of desire and fear by undertaking to return the blanket for a little while, or by offering a piece of it. Faced with a need to exist as corporate enterprises they often have to calculate how much they can give of what their constituents *want*—and still give them something of what they *ought* to want, or *do* want when fear and impulse are relatively quiet.

The crisis in higher education is chronic. The great problem today is essentially the same as it has been for a long time. It is how to do better the things that the colleges were intended to do; how to realize more fully, despite pressures from without and divided councils within, the aim of developing the potentialities of each student.

Our colleges have the task of influencing the youth of the country in directions set by the higher ideals of our culture. Although the public often has two minds about this aim, and contrives to put various difficulties in the way of its execution, the colleges still have a fighting chance to realize their objectives. For four years they have in their hands young persons who are or can be relatively isolated from the rest of society, and who are still open to influence by instruction and example.

If the colleges should achieve moderate success, that is, if a substantial proportion of their students instead of a handful were influenced in the desired way, the level of our culture would be raised. And if our culture and our society are to be changed at all by the deliberate application of intelligence and foresight, no agency has a better chance of initiating change than our institutions of higher learning.

The burden of carrying out educational policies rests mainly on college faculties, and as professionals they have the right to a major voice in the determination and reform of these policies. There is no denying, however, that when there is a movement toward reform in a college it is the collective faculty who usually seem to be dragging their feet. There have been few fundamental innovations in higher education during the past twenty-five or thirty years; and by no means all of these have been initiated by college or university faculties. College presidents, students, trustees, foundations, large donors, influential citizens, and even state legislatures, have from time to time sought progressive change only to find themselves effectively blocked by faculties. The same, of course, holds for individuals or groups within the faculty who would like to undertake new departures.

What are the reasons for this state of affairs? For one thing, the typical faculty member is by training, by inclination, and by the requirements of his position, a specialist in an academic subject. He is devoted to the advancement of his specialty by research and by teaching, and it is as a specialist that he expects to make his career. It is thus his natural inclination to see the problems of liberal education in a limited perspective.

The college administration or the governing board—or the social scientist—may view the college from a distance as it were, attempting to gauge what progress is being made toward certain broad objectives; but the teacher typically is focused on narrower, more immediate, and more personal goals. This characteristic of faculties led so sympathetic a critic as Beardsley Ruml (1959) to suggest that because each teacher is a special advocate "the liberal college faculty *as a body* (his italics) is not competent to make the judgments and evaluations required to design a curriculum in liberal education." One may be led to this conclusion either by observing faculty meetings (which are often futile rituals and sometimes mob scenes) or by examining existing curricula (which are best understood as uneasy compromises, or treaties intended to be broken). Ruml suggests that improvements will require a new curriculum-making mechanism, one to be fashioned and used by the trustees or by the president, and he may be right. One of the main theses of this book, however, is that when we know enough about higher education and have enough conviction about its purposes, we will be able to induce faculties to do what they know they ought to do.

Another barrier to reform is the fact that college and university faculties have organized themselves in such a way as to make deliberate and concerted change of any kind exceedingly difficult. This situation has its logic and its history. Although, traditionally, faculties have had the professional status necessary to free inquiry and instruction, they have always had to stand ready to defend themselves against unintellectual or anti-intellectual forces in the larger community. The struggles of American colleges and universities to withstand the demands of business, religious, or governmental groups are perennial. Even within the last decade faculties of some of our large state universities have by heroic efforts barely averted the loss of their professional status. Small wonder that the defensive stance of such faculties has not been altogether relaxed!

To resist pressures from outside, as well as to further their most immediate interests, faculties have fostered an ingroup spirit, built up traditions of faculty prerogatives, and installed the machinery of campus democracy. These are the very things that now make change very difficult, even when the impulse to change arises largely from within the faculty itself. Measures contrived for one purpose tend to be put into service for other purposes as well, until they become autonomous. Interests become vested in different parts of the machinery itself, so that the machinery persists even after the connection with its original purpose has been lost.

Faculties sometimes go so far in protecting their professional status, or in using their professional status to satisfy their desires for security and the advancement of their own interests, that they neglect the legitimate needs and aspirations of the society that supports higher learning. Faculty-governed European universities, for example, have become extremely conservative institutions; it has sometimes required acts of parliament to bring about changes in the curriculum.

One of the main barriers to reform in the colleges, however, is the lack of a scientific basis for educational practice. College teaching is constantly in the awkward position of having promised more than it can deliver. The public is told that the college experience will "liberate the mind," "build the capacity to make value judgments," and "inculcate the attitudes and values of democracy," but little evidence is offered on the degree to which these changes are accomplished. There are rival claims for different policies and programs, but the public, and indeed the faculties themselves, have little basis for a reasonable choice among them. The reason, of course, is the lack of knowledge about what kinds of educational policies or practices have what effects with what kinds of students. More fundamental than this is the lack of a generally accepted theory of individual human development in accordance with which colleges may state hypotheses pertaining to the relations of ends and means.

The major purpose of this book is to help put the resources of the newer social sciences to the service of liberal education. We might be tempted to speak of a "science of higher education" in order to accent the notion that the field may ultimately be constituted as a body of fact and theory, a discipline of sorts, in which individuals might become specialists. What needs to be further developed is the profession of higher education, a profession that has its own sanctions, its own ethics, and its own "know-how" as well as its scientific basis.

References

Ruml, B. Memo to a college trustee. New York: McGraw-Hill, 1959.

Nevitt Sanford

Higher Education as a Field of Study

Research into higher education, if it is directed to fundamental problems, soon becomes involved with questions of ends. The ends of American higher education have their roots, of course, in the American ethos, and they show a tendency to change with the social scene.

It is characteristically American that our institutions of higher learning should be as diversified as they are. They differ in every feature and dimension that marks a college—in size, standards, and curriculum; in student quality and faculty quality; in teaching methods, social organization, climate of culture, and a host of other ways. But most important, they differ in what they try to do.

A basic feature of American higher education has been its decentralization, for groups of people have always been free to start schools and colleges, in accordance with their needs and with their ideas about salvation. Consequently, virtually every conceivable objective is somewhere represented, although diversity seems to be yielding somewhat as our society becomes increasingly organized.

Education that tries to inculcate skills and knowledge, even for a social or cultural purpose, may be distinguished from education that has as its aim the fullest possible development of the individual. The former begins by asking "What do people need to know? What do they need to know if they are to live in our world and help to maintain it?" The tendency of this sort of education is to instruct, to train, to mold individuals according to the requirements of our civilization, society, and culture. To the extent that such training succeeds in its purpose, it makes people alike in various respects.

The latter kind of education does not ask what the individual should *know* or *do*, but what qualities he should *achieve*. It makes assumptions about what the individual is, with open-ended visions of what he can become, and it measures educational progress in terms of personality change—from prejudice to broadmindedness, say, or from indiscipline to discipline in thinking. It does not deny that the individual must be *socialized* and must be able to support and adapt to civilization. But it assumes that a well-developed individual can do these things in his own unique way; that as he expands and becomes more complex he becomes increasingly unlike other persons; that only a part of himself—and often a superficial part—is taken up with the mere *requirements* of life in the modern world. According to this view, the very development of the individual adapts him to his environment and makes him able to use culture in the service of his basic needs. What is more, he can criticize and help to improve society, and through creative activity he can advance civilization.

It must be remembered that students may learn a great deal without changing their personalities in any important way. Much knowledge is quickly forgotten, and a person does not change from the forgetting any more than he changes from the learning. Even when knowledge and activities that demand knowledge persist, they may be superficial in the sense that they are not used for a person's inner needs. It is here that graduate education, education in the European universities, and much instruction in our liberal arts colleges fail. They pay no attention to the student's development as a personality. Implicitly or explicitly, educators commonly assume either that the student is already sufficiently developed, or that the level of his development does not matter.

This is not to deny that official statements by college deans (and their brochures) will refer to human qualities and human development. Sometimes trust is placed in a reasonable and fairly explicit theory that the educational program will itself induce desired changes in the individual. In other instances, the educational theory is less explicit and less reasonable, as when it is supposed that the mere transmission of information will, somehow, lead to development. Even when the program of a college is heavily preprofessional, its defenders are likely to claim that it will have a generally liberalizing effect on "those who are able to benefit from it."

In fact, education may bring about changes in the person that are *not* conducive to personality development. Professional or vocational education often makes the individual identify with one particular occupation, so that his behavior is determined by external factors rather than by his genuine needs. When this happens, when a person's self-conception is largely dominated by his professional membership (as is so often the case in this country), he is likely to restrict his social behavior to the seeming requirements of that membership. Vocational choice that comes too early in the individual's life may induce a kind of premature closure of the personality, an integration or "adjustment" that, being supported by external agencies, may effectively prevent further expansion and differentiation.

Viewing the matter from the other side, however, it appears that development in the personality is very likely to favor the processes of education. The stronger and better conceived the individual's motives, the more firmly they are based on inner needs, and the better they are adapted to real possibilities, the more readily will the individual learn the facts and principles that he sets out to learn. The better his judgment, the greater his critical faculties, and the better integrated the diverse parts of himself, the more quickly will he assimilate knowledge and skills that can be shown to have relevance to his purposes.

Probably *the* central problem of educational research is to show how the curriculum, or parts of it, can be made to assist personality development. At present this problem is poorly informed by psychological theory. The use of the curriculum to develop personality is best described as "intellectual"; there is no better meaning of the word "intellectual" than this. Teachers stress their conviction that the highest development can be achieved by what they call educational means—by what goes on in the classroom and in the teacher-student relationship—rather than by extracurricular activities, psychological services, or the chance to "grow" willy-nilly in a pleasant environment. Since development through disciplined learning is likely to be difficult or even painful, and since college students often resist such development, the educator is naturally opposed to anything that might indulge that resistance by giving his pupils a chance to escape.

The fact remains, however, that a person's intellect cannot be disembodied from the rest of his personality, from his "extracurricular self." A person is all of a piece. If teaching effects any changes in intellectual functioning these will ramify throughout his personality, just as, conversely, processes already at work in his personality will help determine what happens in the classroom.

In a sense, therefore, changes in intellectual functioning beyond the mere acquisition of facts—changes that might occur through learning within an academic discipline—are instrumental to other, more general developments in the person. At the same time there is evidence that certain kinds of personality development have to happen before the individual can be expected to exhibit a genuine love of learning or taste for intellectual activity. Where the educational aim is the development of the individual, it is extremely difficult to separate means from ends, or to know what subgoals are necessary to attain more ultimate goals.

It has been said that the aims of each kind of education may be viewed in different perspectives. This becomes crucially important when we ask how successful a college is in achieving its objectives, since the question clearly depends on some means of measuring "success."

Success in college is usually measured by grades. This, from the college's point of view, represents success. But it may not be success from the point of view of the student, or of other interested people. A girl may go to college with the objective, which she shares with her parents, of finding a husband in a higher social class than her own. If she accomplishes this, she is a success from her point of view and from the point of view of her parents and her husband. Her performance in later life may well be such as to win her the approval of society at large.

Success in this latter sense is not very highly valued by educators, however. They prefer other performances although even these, from a broader point of view, may not be marks of success in attaining educational objectives. For example, educators may approve mere conformity to a cultural outlook and facility with its symbols, mistaking this for a genuine internalization of intellectual values.

We must also distinguish between success in college, as appraised at the time of finishing college, and success in later life. The two may or may not be positively associated. The distinction here is between immediate and ultimate success; it holds for different phases of the student's passage through college as well as for the college-later life relationship. The prediction of long-range success requires follow-up studies; we must confront the very difficult problem of determining whether a later performance was due to the educational experience, or whether it sprang from subsequent events.

In selecting applicants, it is one thing to choose students who are likely to graduate, and quite another to identify students who show promise of extraordinary accomplishments in life. Minimal objectives such as graduating from college are relatively easy to define and predict; whereas extraordinary performances, in the realm of creative work for example, are difficult to study.

THE ENTERING STUDENT

The student at the end of his undergraduate experience is the product of the influence of college and what he was like when he entered. Colleges attend to the latter in their admissions policies and to the former in their educational programs.

Colleges have long stressed ability and preparation, and to a lesser extent motivation, as the most important aspects of readiness for college. It is here that the mental testing movement in psychology and education has played a highly significant and influential role. Because of their success in prediction, tests of verbal and mathematical ability have for some years been widely used in American colleges and universities. As a result, much is known about the verbal and mathematical ability of students entering various institutions, and about the differences between young people who go to college and those who do not.

Colleges have widely different standards of work and, accordingly, different levels of entrance requirements. Yet even colleges that, from the nature of their main clientele, might well be designed for low-ability students, seldom turn away people of high ability. On the contrary they will seek such students so as to resemble the institutions of high prestige. Such emulation counts more highly than doing something for average or below-average students. Such success seems to depend mainly on the absolute value of the final product, rather than on how much change has been induced; and in turn, the value of the product is believed to depend most heavily on the value of the entering material.

Partly as a result of the foregoing situation, students and their families and advisors have a hard time finding out what the colleges are really like. The colleges, however, (assuming that their leaders think clearly about objectives) have special problems caused by the growing popularity of going to college. For example, there is every possibility that the range and variety of talent entering college will become progressively narrower, when colleges rely on selection devices that have worked in the past. Another *narrowing* factor, ironically enough, lies in the *expanding* volume of applicants which nearly all admissions offices have to handle. Operating in a "seller's market," the dean of admissions is tempted to select only what he thinks is the "cream"—the same "cream" every other admissions man is after.

Thus there must be new tests to distinguish between those able students who perform satisfactorily and those able students who, from the standpoint of existing tests, will not. Fortunately, we can expect that in the future much more attention will be given to personality factors other than ability, and to incentives and obstacles in the college situation itself.

THE ACADEMIC ENVIRONMENT

Fundamental to the analysis of an educational institution is the distinction between its *formal* and *informal organization*. The formal organization consists, most essentially, in all those policies and practices deliberately adopted with a view to influencing students—the curriculum, the departmental structure, the responsibilities of the faculty, methods of teaching, enrollment, attendance, examinations, grading, degrees, counseling, advising, planned extracurricular activities. In studying a college the most important questions, from the point of view of this book, have to do with whether and in what degree these various features of the students' environment contribute to his development.

The researcher might study informal organization in the same way that he would study social processes in any collectivity of people. He might, for example, be interested in friendships groups, or in the ways in which prestige was conceived and sought. The educational researcher is particularly interested in how processes in the sphere of informal organization help or hamper the attainment of educational goals. Cases where informal processes interfere with planned activity have been the subject of much entertaining, although not always constructive, literature. In a typical story some issue is debated as if all that was involved were purely rational considerations of how best to achieve some agreed objective, while everybody except those actually taking part understands that the conflict really has arisen out of the status aspirations of two groups of the faculty. Perhaps, as often, it is the other way around; the informal organization contributes in unsuspected ways to the achievement of educational objectives. And this may occur in spite of formal arrangements. For example, there might be an ill-conceived curriculum and a network of repressive requirements and regulations, and yet there may be groups of students whose members stimulate one another intellectually and succeed in reaching a high level of performance.

It is important to remember that the environment of the developing student is not limited to the college itself; even in a highly organized and relatively isolated residential institution the students are still responsive to diverse aspects of the surrounding social and cultural matrix. For example, there is the climate of opinion in the community where the college is located. If the community distrusts the college and looks upon it with hostility or contempt, it may help to unify the college society. On the other hand, college officials may be highly sensitive to town opinion. To placate powerful outsiders they might impose such unreasonable restrictions that the students feel victimized by hypocrisy.

Finally, there is the effect of the larger society on student expectations about their future. For example, where the society does not offer attractive roles for the highly educated woman, we cannot expect college girls to exert themselves to obtain advanced education. We may expect students to be more susceptible than faculty members to the climate of American culture as a whole; not only have they just left the larger society, but they expect to return to it shortly, and, unlike the faculty, they are quite uncertain about what they are going to do or be.

The teacher's environment, like that of the student, includes outside social and cultural factors as well as a complexity of forces from within the college system. Outside the college there is the general cultural climate of the day and the situation of the society. These determine the degree of mass pressure toward orthodoxy, toward conformity with popular conceptions of the teacher's role, and toward certain accents in the curriculum (such as a bias toward science and mathematics). Within the college the teacher is subjected to other forces—employment and promotion policies; demands, formal or informal, that the teacher *fit in* to a certain professional role; chauvinism on the part of his department or subdepartment. About him there exists competition of other groups; a faculty society with its rules and regulations, its channels of communication, its system for awarding status, and there is also a faculty culture which demands his allegiance. Even the physical arrangements for living are a molding force: they affect the teacher's social life generally as well as his relationship with the outside world.

But of all the pressures on the college professor, probably the greatest are those arising from his poor economic situation. Current efforts to raise professors' salaries are in recognition of this fact. It must not be supposed, however, that one can turn the colleges into happy and productive communities merely by raising faculty salaries. This act of simple justice would be but the first step toward reconstructing the professor's environment in the interests of better teaching.

STUDENT SOCIETY AND STUDENT CULTURE

The faculty's opportunity to influence students depends on such factors as the faculty–student ratio and the importance that college authorities actually attach to good teaching; on the size of the institution or community in which the student is supposed to find an intellectual home; on the amount of official or traditional sanction for sports and other cocurricular activities. It may also depend on the physical plant and facilities, with their capacity to suggest the dignity or quality of the educational enterprise; on the living arrangements for students—whether they live so far from the centers of academic activities that a sharp division is encouraged between living with friends and studying; and on the amount of time students spend on campus.

The faculty's influence depends as well on the social organization of the college—the college society—and on the culture of the college. College society as a whole is constituted of the faculty, the administration, and the students. At the same time there is always a variety of subsocieties to be observed. Although the members of these subsocieties usually belong exclusively to one another of the three groups—faculty, administration, students—there may be some overlapping. For most students, the most important subsociety is that to which only students belong. This society embraces formal structures, such as the student government and co-curricular activities, and various informal friendship or living or interest groups. Student society may promote development through offering the individual opportunities to become familiar with a variety of social roles and by confronting him with situations to which he must learn to adapt himself.

Each society or subsociety must have culture, that is, shared values and beliefs, and prescribed ways of behaving. Thus there is an overall college culture, in which faculty, administration, and students participate, and a number of subcultures. The overall culture will embrace, to some extent at least, the avowed aims and educational philosophy of the college and its ideas and standards respecting levels, styles, and directions of work; and, not unrelated to these, there may be values, beliefs, and ways in the realms of religion, politics, economics, arts, and social relations.

Society and culture vary independently. Societies of different colleges, or subsocieties of the same college, may be essentially alike in their structure but yet very different in their values and beliefs. For example, of two liberal arts colleges organized in the traditional way, one might stand for preciousness in literature and the arts and extreme conservatism in respect to political and social questions, the other for stern Protestant virtues and political and social liberalism; of two fraternities having essentially the same social structure, one might go in for athletics and dating, the other for campus politics and the values of business. And similar cultures may be found in social organizations of different types. For example, an approach to contemporary life marked by studied disenchantment and sensation seeking might be represented in an Eastern private college by a tightly cohering clique in one of the men's dormitories, whereas in a large state university the same approach might prevail in a loosely organized group of young men and women, some of whom were married to each other, who congregated upon occasion in one or another of the run-down rooming or apartment houses in the town.

Colleges aim, of course, to transmit culture, to bring about changes in the values and beliefs with which students arrive. But students do not change automatically as soon as new cultural stimuli are presented. A large factor of receptivity is involved, and this seems to be largely a matter of motivation. Perhaps the strongest force behind the adolescent individual's acceptance of cultural or subcultural norms is his need to belong to some group or to feel that he is supported by other like-minded individuals. Thus it is that the kind of culture that the college student assimilates, given some choice, depends heavily on the social organization of that college; there will be a strong tendency for him to take over values and beliefs from the group that has the strongest social appeal for him, and this will usually be a student group.

Although student culture and society are important parts of each student's environment, already in existence at the time he arrives, they also have to be considered as responses—as ways in which students in the mass adapt themselves to the college situation. We have to inquire whether, and to what extent, a separate student society and a separate student culture are necessary; whether they are inevitable concomitants of the students' common age and role or results of failure in adult leadership or of particular ways in which the larger college community is organized. Student cultures may be largely understood in terms of collective responses to problems commonly encountered. But it appears that if students are to be educated, such problems must be put in their way, and the crucial question becomes whether the responses elicited are consistent with educational goals. Here, at least, students learn rapidly, and what they learn is expressed in changed attitudes and values. Are these attitudes and values desired ones, from the point of view of the educator? Observation of some existing student cultures indicates that they may or may not be so, and that they may be so in some but not in other of their features.

STUDENT PERFORMANCE IN RELATION TO EDUCATIONAL
OBJECTIVES

Educational programs are designed on the assumption, which
may be explicit or implicit, that if students do certain things in the
right way and for a long enough time they will learn or develop
in desired ways. To encourage appropriate performances, requirements and expectations are defined, and the attempt is made to
recruit students who have the requisite abilities and inclinations.
Sometimes things go according to plan, and sometimes not.

Behavior that seems appropriate and attractive may not have the
desired implications for the future. For example, students may
meet the demands of a program of independent study by studying
independently, but instead of developing independent habits of
mind they may generate an extraordinary longing for authority
and regime. To take it the other way around, rebelliousness or
noisy complaining may be regarded by teachers or officials as a
poor way to perform in the student's role, while actually such behavior may be positively associated with future social responsibility.

Most undergraduates entering our colleges remain there for the
prescribed period—either four or two years. This means that they
adapt themselves in some satisfactory way to the college environment as a whole and attain at least minimum set standards of academic performance and general behavior. Usually they like their
college and leave with some regret and with a feeling of accomplishment. But many—perhaps 40 per cent on the average—of
those who enter a given college withdraw from it before graduation. For the student this is often a painful experience, and it is always a significant one. Nor is the college in any better position,
for it has to face the fact of its failure, either in its selection or in
its management of the student. For the private college, moreover,
the phenomenon of attrition is a continuing source of financial
headache.

Sometimes counseling will prevent a student's hasty or ill-considered withdrawal, and sometimes a college that is plagued by a high rate of attrition has to think of changing itself. But withdrawal is not always a misfortune for the student or for the college. Sometimes it is the best way to correct an obvious mistake or help a student face reality, and sometimes students withdraw before graduation because they have already gained from their college all that could be expected. Leaving college, not to enter any other, may leave a student with a sense of unfinished business that will, in some cases, make him want to go on learning for the rest of his life.

Most liberal arts colleges require that their students enter a major program of study at the beginning of the junior year. For the student, choosing a major is usually a highly significant experience. Often it is the first time that he consciously commits himself to long-range goals after giving due consideration to reasonable alternatives. The choice usually has implications respecting his future vocation, and thus he approaches, perhaps for the first time, a socially defined identity that has an aspect of being irreversible.

The official expectation is that students will choose, or be guided into, major programs in accordance with their abilities, their enduring interests, and other factors bearing on the benefit they may receive from these programs. This expectation is often disappointed, however, by irrational or nonrational processes at work in the students, and by the fact that the departments, if they are not indifferent to the whole problem, sometimes compete for the ablest students without attention to what might be done for them.

A third important aspect of performance in the role of student is academic achievement. Most of the research in this field has been concerned with the prediction of the general level of academic achievement from test scores or other indicators available prior to the student's admission to college. The aim, of course, is to improve prediction, but there is the more fundamental question of how to improve achievement. The performance of the individual student is determined not only by the abilities and dispositions that are present when he enters college but also by a complexity of factors in the college environment. When the ways in which these latter influence the student are sufficiently well understood, it may become possible to modify them in such a way as to raise the student's level of performance. This is a field in which relatively little research has been done.

INTERACTIONS OF STUDENTS AND EDUCATORS

Much of a college community's life involves interaction between faculty and administration and the students. We know well enough that students respond to an environment largely made by the educators, but we should also remember that faculties and administrations react to what *students* do. This, in turn, creates new (and often important) stimuli to student behavior, and thus there is a fresh circle of interaction.

Let us consider an example. In a traditional college of high quality a majority of the faculty believe they note a serious decline in the general level of the students' effort and performance. As the faculty dicusses this phenomenon in sessions both formal and informal, a sense of outrage builds up, and the general feeling is that there must be a tightening all along the line. Heavier work assignments, more frequent examinations, longer papers, more required reading, are thrown at the student, and classes are conducted in an atmosphere of increased grimness.

Now, for the individual student this discipline comes not from a particular teacher who knows him but from an impersonal "they." It is plain, furthermore, that some of the faculty members' stake in the new policy stems from vanity rather than devotion to intellectual aims. As a result, the students generally see the tightening up as arbitrary punishment. With a nice appreciation of their situation, they do not rebel openly; instead, they give a sort of passive resistance, although not necessarily with any conscious deliberation. In other words, they do precisely what is required but no more; they invent and share among themselves numerous devices for judging the exact nature of the requirements and for carrying them out with a minimum of effort; they establish a kind of "norm" for amount of work and make life difficult for the individual who threatens to exceed it. Particularly do they look askance at any student who "gets too close" to any of the faculty, for this tends to break up the general strategy of doing what is required by the faculty without being influenced by them in any positive way.

Since this response is very similar to the state of affairs which upset the faculty in the first place, it is likely to be met with even stricter requirements. The vicious circle becomes increasingly taut. Now the students seek ways to hold the faculty strictly to their obligations and, if possible, to embarrass them by requesting more office appointments, expecting papers to be corrected on time, asking about books they suspect the instructor has not read, remaining silent and unresponsive in class.

Some teachers do not go along with the majority; they seek to break what has become the common pattern, to "reach" the students. The students will have none of this. They have developed an effective system for handling their situation and they do not intend to be put off by any new or different methods of teaching or any appeals to their curiosity or creative impulses. They hold the deviating or innovating teacher to the pattern that has become common.

Students have the power to do this, for there are channels through which their complaints can reach the department chairman or the administration, and by now faculty morale has so deteriorated that the enterprising teacher has no assurance that his colleagues will back him up. Happily, the term now ends; the student leaders graduate, the faculty leaders take a much-needed vacation, and there is a chance for a fresh start.

Cycles of deterioration like the one just described happen with some frequency in American colleges today. It is processes like these that affect the general "atmosphere" or "climate" of a college, which in turn leave their imprint on a student who remains there for four years.

THE EFFECTS OF COLLEGE EDUCATION

Quantitative studies of change in college have been fairly numerous. Most have compared groups of entering freshmen with groups of graduating seniors; some of these have examined the same students (with the same instruments) once at the beginning and once near the end of their college careers. In a few studies the students have been examined at several intervals during college life —a system which gives more precise information about when change actually occurs.

By contrast with the amount of research done on student change, there has been relatively little inquiry into the lasting aftereffects of college. Questions which have been asked along this line have largely concentrated on (1) what in college makes men scientists or scholars (2) what are the economic benefits of a college education. Such research has little bearing on the aims of liberal learning, however much it may decide the prestige of institutions. Much more relevant are the numerous surveys where graduates are asked to say what they derived from college or what college has meant to them. Unfortunately, these last have little scientific foundation.

Since the most fundamental questions in higher education can be answered only by considering the *durable* effects of different systems, we are forced to ask why this area of research has been so sadly neglected. Here we may recall that for the consumer of higher education its general value is not in question. Going to college is the road to membership in a profession and to all the benefits of improved economic and social status. Whenever college graduates are asked in later life what they got out of college they have no difficulty in describing several kinds of important benefits. But the discrepancy between the things that head their lists of benefits and the stated purposes of the colleges is usually glaring.

There is some evidence, however, that college does make a

difference. Granted, the impact of higher education on most people is limited by the fact that their life-pattern is pretty well determined before they reach college. For many people, however, the experience may precipitate crucial changes of direction. The fact that students of personality are more inclined than formerly to attach importance to the college years augurs well for future research in this field. Just as the typical Navajo family is now said to comprise a father, a mother, two children, and a Harvard anthropologist, so the time may come when the typical college will be made up of the faculty, administration, students, and educational researchers!

RESEARCH AND PRACTICE IN HIGHER EDUCATION

By and large the colleges of today seem to welcome the study of their students by psychologists and social scientists. This is very good; it promises that our fund of knowledge about student development in college will soon be vastly expanded. Yet at the same time there is cause for uneasiness. It may be that college faculties have simply become convinced not only that this research will not harm the students but also that it involves no serious threat to the college's time-honored way of doing things. But whatever their hospitality to student studies, most colleges are resistant to change, and since their members suspect that research is an instrument for inducing change, the colleges are resistant to research into their *essential* structure and functioning.

The interrelatedness of research and action is particularly clear in the case of educational experiments. Experimentation here does not mean merely innovation but the designing of new programs in accordance with hypotheses, and the use of experimental controls to determine the effects of those programs. Such proposals or practices, however, are usually the very ones that encounter opposition from college faculties and administrators. There seem to be two main objections: (1) that it is not possible to perform a truly scientific experiment in education because it is not possible to establish and to maintain the necessary controls, and (2) that if a proper experiment is carried out it may harm the subjects.

The problems of research design involved in educational experiments of this kind are serious, but not too serious. It would not take too much ingenuity to arrange things in such a way that sound knowledge could be derived from new programs. If students are affected by the knowledge that they are taking part in an experiment, there would be a control group of students who also felt that they were taking part in an experiment. If experimental programs tend to attract the ablest students and teachers, arrangements would be made in advance for the equal distribution of talent among experimental and control groups, and so on for other "variables" that seemed likely to affect results.

The objection that experiments might harm students has more far-reaching implications. Admittedly, passage through an experimental program—say, an experimental college within a college or university—might indeed have some temporarily upsetting or painful effects on the student; he might be regarded by his fellows as unusual or queer, and he might suffer disadvantage in getting a job or applying for graduate school. One answer to this is that *any* educational program may have harmful effects—and that many of them commonly do. At present all education is experimental, for all education is guided by some kind of theory, however implicit, and the effects of particular policies and practices are largely unknown.

The main point, however, is that where education is concerned social science and social practice cannot really be separated. It is unfortunate that the word "science" so often makes people think of gadgets and guinea pigs rather than of a great humanistic enterprise that can help to free those who practice it as well as those upon whom it is practiced. In social science means and ends are inseparable. When students volunteer for studies of themselves or for experimental educational programs, they are already doing what the advancement of knowledge will permit them and others to do more often; that is, participating as free individuals in activities that can broaden experience and enrich the personality.

EXPANDING KNOWLEDGE AND THE AIMS OF EDUCATION

A curriculum that has become traditional, a way of organizing teaching that is taken for granted, a type of research that has become fashionable—these things should draw our constant critical attention. This is not because change is likely to be called for, or because change is valuable in itself, but because it is in our defense of the conventional that we are particularly likely to stray from rationality.

The rationality that we demand of ourselves is the same rationality we seek to develop in our students. Rationality is a crowning feature of the developed individual. It is the basic source of his freedom—his degree of freedom from his own unrecognized tendencies, from the pressures of the immediate social group, from the confines of a traditional or parochial outlook, and from some of the limitations of ignorance and incompetence. It is a source not only of *freedom from* but of *freedom to,* for rationality increases the individual's freedom of *choice,* and where there is rationality there is fine awareness of the world and knowledge of how to think and how to feel about its manifold aspects. As a consequence the rational individual is able to conceive and to pursue his purposes with intelligence and sensibility.

We can best guide the student's development by the force of example. Let the college demonstrate its own efforts to find the truth, especially the hard truth about itself, and we may be sure that many students will find in these a model, an inspiration to use their intelligence in trying to solve their own problems. By the same token a college that does not strive for rationality fails its students. If a college blindly defends its institutional features, or adheres rigidly to an "educational policy" whose theoretical underpinnings remain unexamined, if it makes and enforces demands whose purpose cannot be made clear to students or which cannot be justified as conducive to ultimate democratic goals, if it permits its officials to do or say, in the interest of public relations, what is not consistent with what students have been told, if it betrays the essential idea of a college or university by accepting external restraints on its freedom of inquiry, its students will become either passive or cynical and alienated from the major society and from themselves.

The highest function of social science is to be an instrument for the development of full rationality. The task of understanding the practices and potentialities of higher education does not belong only to social scientists, however; it is the charge of all those responsible for higher education. Our colleges and universities today are highly diversified, and the present trend is toward more and more specialization. Such differentiation, far from being an evil, is an essential feature of development in a college or an individual, but it increases the necessity of integration, which must keep pace if fragmentation is not to be the final outcome.

One basis for unity in the college could be its concerted attempt to find rational solutions to its educational problems. Here at least is something that all teachers can discuss together; here is an intellectual inquiry in which all can take part. The more the college becomes diversified and yet at the same time comes together in this kind of intellectual cooperation, the more it will do to make its students both as complex and as whole as they are capable of becoming.

Two
The Viability of the American College

David Riesman and Christopher S. Jencks

The Viability of the American College

Whole libraries have been filled with books on higher education in America, and much can be learned from some of them. Many have been historical studies either of a single institution or of an educational tradition. Others have been quantitative appraisals of logistic problems in contemporary higher education. Our effort here is somewhat different: it is to compare colleges not only with each other, but by a series of analogies to relate what happens in college to other aspects of our national life. We risk the dangers, and invite the stimulation, of analogies and metaphors that may sometimes appear far fetched.

Looking at colleges in terms of a theory of the labor force, we might describe them primarily as *personnel offices*, feeding properly certified employees into business and the professions. Some colleges supplement these general efforts by direct tie-ins between their educational division and local schools, their engineering division and local industry, or their business division and local commerce. All colleges inevitably participate in the informal network through which graduates of each college tend to recruit fellow alumni, or perhaps more correctly, alumni of their own fraternity or territory. Such enclaves may help explain why alumni of Harvard, Yale, and Princeton have income 30 per cent higher than graduates of other colleges—or even the fact that half the trustees of major philanthropic foundations hold degrees from Harvard, Yale, or Princeton.

But why, we may ask, should business and the professions depend on colleges for employees, and why should scholars oblige by supplying them? During the nineteenth century American higher education was not so heavily age-graded as it has become since, and college was not seen as a necessary prerequisite to the study of law or medicine. As the country has become richer and the professions stronger, however, the latter have been able to postpone choosing their apprentices, compelling the colleges to provide a litmus for measuring both intellectual and social aptitudes. This is quite compatible with the argument that the apprentice can be more readily turned into a respectable and responsible citizen, as well as a more discerning student of his speciality, if he has had the extra four years of college education.

But beyond such more or less rational considerations, the American college exists as a vast WPA project, which gives promising adolescents work to do while keeping them out of the job market —and also keeps several hundred thousand faculty members off the streets. Of course, such a comparison seems to ignore the great numbers of undergraduates who are actually in vocational programs, such as engineering, education, business administration, or nursing. Many students, however, in these apparently preprofessional programs are not actually committed to a career, but are still shopping around. Several years ago, the *Saturday Evening Post* ran an article, "Are We Making a Playground out of Our Colleges?", which reflected the attitude of many solid citizens during the depression toward the WPA. Such citizens failed to appreciate that it has become increasingly hard in our society to maintain a sense of worth without a degree; and that as the WPA provided a good deal of valuable theatre and art, so the colleges provide cultural festivals for their communities, ranging from art shows and adult lecture series to football.

To carry further the WPA analogy, it is difficult to say to what extent college, along with the rest of the educational system, trains students not only to seek work of their own devising, but also to respond in a disciplined attitude toward work *not* of their own devising, and to what extent colleges help inculcate a distaste for work precisely because of its frequently imposed and alienated quality. Certainly, quite apart from the technical skills acquired in college, the colleges do provide the locale for inculcating social and personal skills on which employers put increasing emphasis, the more so since they themselves are increasingly college trained. For this purpose the curriculum is important only insofar as it spills over from the classroom to the dining hall, from the library to the fraternity, from the teacher-student relationship to the administrator-student and student-student relationship.

One major influence of most occupations on the attitudes of the worker is to encourage him to meet certain people, and prevent his meeting others. The same thing is true of a college. In this perspective it may be helpful to view the college as a human relocation project that removes a student from parents, community, and employment to submerge him in the student culture of his adolescent peers. In the same manner a college nationalizes the student, taking him out of his ethnic, religious, geographic, and social parishes and exposing him to a more cosmopolitan world where the imagination is less restricted by preconception and ignorance.

Even in the worst colleges, emancipation from the older generation can be stimulating. Many of the Negro colleges from which lunch-counter sit-ins sprang were institutions of low standards that offered little to their students other than an opportunity to enter a sector of the "black bourgeoisie" sheltered behind the wall of segregation.

COLLEGE AS AN INITIATION RITE

College is an initiation rite for separating the upper-middle from the lower-middle class, and for changing the semi-amorphous adolescent into a semi-identified adult. All studies of taste and opinion suggest that one of the great cultural cleavages in our society is between those who have been to college and those who have not. To go to college is to join what commencement orators call "the fellowship of educated men," and what Vance Packard more sceptically dubs "the diploma elite." In part, this transformation is a matter of faith.

By standing as the watchdogs of the upper-middle class, the colleges have greatly circumscribed the range of behavior common among the national elite. Furthermore, precisely because

college is now the gatekeeper to the upper-middle class, as well
as a decisive influence on its styles of life, every minority group
of any standing in America has an interest in preserving or creating colleges which accept its own members and suit its own particular needs. Nevertheless, as American nationalism, the national
economy, and the mass media reflect an increasingly uniform
color, colleges tend to copy one another to make sure that their
programs remain acceptable as certificates of respectability.

Occupational Interest Groups

In the Colonial Period some of the zeal that went into the
founding and maintenance of the first American colleges came
from the fear of educated immigrants that their children, born
in less urbane surroundings than their European parents, might
revert to barbarism. This fear evoked an effort to perpetuate the
educated classes, which in most areas meant both the ministry and
the class of gentlemen.

This pattern of mixing occupational and social training still
persists. Hundreds of colleges have been founded to provide some
community with theologically orthodox leadership that could
not be conveniently recruited from colleges elsewhere. As the
theological and geographical schisms that generated the new colleges faded, they could no longer count on recruits and patronage
from those who once thought their ideological specialization important; and so most such schools have expanded, sometimes to
train men of several faiths, but more often to train laymen who
at least nominally hold to the college's beliefs. Such expansion
has produced alumni of less religious commitment, who have in
turn opened their college to new cadres of unbelievers or indiffer-
ents. Equally important is the fact that religious sects have tended
to upgrade themselves socially, in part through these very colleges. As a result a pulpit that at first needed only a smattering of
Biblical passion eventually demands a man with a liberal education who can converse with the now-educated parishioners. Once
the facilities for such liberal education are provided, they can

seldom be supported solely by future preachers. Nevertheless there are today over 500 purely theological seminaries, of which perhaps half are not part of a larger educational enterprise.

Even so, in the last century the need for ministers has inspired fewer new colleges than has the need for teachers. During the late nineteenth century, state normal schools spread across the country to provide teachers for the ever increasing primary school population. As the demand for secondary teachers caught up with the demand for elementary teachers, normal schools became teachers colleges, with liberal arts divisions. Conversely, liberal arts colleges added education units in order to cash in on the single biggest source of potential college students. Today the majority of teachers come from liberal arts rather than teachers' colleges.

With this distinction of purpose abolished, the former teachers' college is likely to feel that it is distinguished only by low prestige and low standards, and must, therefore, move with all possible speed to emulate the liberal arts college program. Once a liberal arts curriculum is established, the teachers' college becomes suitable for the education of students headed for other careers, so that even in its clientele it resembles the liberal arts college.

In arts and sciences there are today perhaps three dozen universities that turn out almost all doctorates. Yet none of these universities has seriously considered abolishing the B.A. degree, or eliminating undergraduates. Some have merely neglected the undergraduate, some (Columbia and Chicago) have set up semi-autonomous undergraduate divisions, and some (e.g., Harvard) have merged graduate and undergraduate instruction as much as possible.

As the academic profession itself (i.e., the college and university teachers) rises in power and prestige, it becomes a serious competitor with law, medicine, and engineering for talented students. Hence the graduate schools of law and medicine, and perhaps particularly the schools that insist on four years of college from their applicants, may have an increasingly hard time holding their own.

Of course, the preparation of school and college teachers was

only one need that led to the creation of colleges. Some of the
presently leading institutions have grown from the demand for
trained engineers, agriculturalists, veterinarians, and technicians
of every sort. Congress was moved in 1862 to pass the Morrill Act
providing for the training of such men and women in what were
often called Colleges of Agriculture and Mechanical Arts. In relatively new states these land-grant colleges often attracted an increasingly wide cross section of students not envisioned by their
founders. This magnetism was enhanced in such states as Minnesota, Wisconsin, and Nebraska, which combined the technical
college with the state university. The same rapid growth did not
occur in states like Massachusetts which had a tradition of private education and were long unable to see what legitimate functions a public institution might serve beyond those specified by
Congress.

Because of the widespread influence of the Morrill Act all but
about 50 of the nation's 100 schools of agriculture and 200 schools
of engineering, are under the aegis of a comprehensive college
or university that lends the facilities and prestige of the liberal
arts to technical programs. Although all efforts at vocational
training have been increasingly permeated by the liberal arts,
thereby elevating the vocations to more dignified positions, there
is a seemingly endless cycle of new occupations whose practitioners want colleges oriented in their direction. One recent area
of rapid growth has been business education, sometimes under the
auspices of local magnates who want recruits, but more often
sponsored by colleges which want to attract and retain local students to whom the liberal arts seem irrelevant and difficult.

True, in the most selective colleges there seems to be an increasing tendency for students to avoid business careers altogether.
Nevertheless, the majority of upper-middle-class college graduates consider business quite respectable—an attitude that is strengthened as executives are exposed to, and even influenced by, such
academic values as breadth of view, scepticism, and the ability to
master complex chains of information.

The spread of the degree-hierarchy has encouraged many occupations requiring even less technical expertise than business to seek a certificate which will set them off from mere high school graduates. For many, this distinction has come from the two-year A.A. degree awarded by the junior colleges. But although these institutions were often founded to provide such terminal vocational programs, they have rarely been content to tie themselves to middle-level occupations. Today only one junior college student in three takes a vocational program, whereas the other two begin a transfer program that would, if completed, allow them to spend only two years away from home for the B.A., instead of the usual four years.

The junior college has grown so fast in recent years that it is now proper to speak of the junior college "movement." Many of the nation's junior colleges are supervised by local boards of education. Some use the buildings of the local high schools, and most have recruited their faculties largely from secondary school teachers. Thus the junior college may become, in its academic temper and its conciliation of local powers and felt needs, a near-automatic, upward extension of high school to the thirteenth and fourteenth grades—an easy option for students who are not yet prepared to make the final decision about college or whose families cannot afford the sacrifices that going away to college might entail.

Some junior colleges have been tempted to retain gifted students by expanding their programs, improvising a bachelor's degree that succeeds in holding students who would be better off elsewhere. If, on the other hand, their B.A. becomes established, the college is likely to neglect those seeking a technical degree in two years even though these may remain the great majority. But partly because the junior college faculty without Ph.D.'s fears for its status and security if the institution upgrades itself, and partly because of a genuine commitment to general education for the many, most two-year colleges remain two-year colleges.

Elsewhere, technical curricula which could be mastered in two or three years now include general education. This means not only that the program gains social eclat by taking four years and awarding the B.A., but also that entrants are entitled to think of themselves as professionals. In addition they can feel at least casually familiar with culture and other marks of social sophistication.

Such shifts have been partly justified by vocational arguments. The liberal arts for example, are supposed to teach engineers to communicate verbally with one another, thereby making them better engineers. An important consequence of liberalizing the engineer is to help make his occupation a possible career for upper-middle-class students, whose parents have been to college and who are therefore likely to regard a little culture as a sine qua non of any collegiate program. Such students have traditionally taken a liberal arts degree and then gone into law or medicine or business. But as the number of students from college educated families grows, and as the prestige of the business world falls in the better colleges, new professions must be found to supplement law and medicine as high-status pursuits. By coming to terms with culture, engineering and applied science, architecture, and various forms of civil service are attempting to fill this role, hoping to combine the economic rewards of business with the intellectual appeal of science, as medicine (and law, in another sense) have long done.

One difficulty is that as technical colleges add liberal arts programs, the combination, although undoubtedly producing better employees and citizens, may keep out some of the traditional socially-mobile recruits who believe they can only afford a four-year meal ticket and have no time for "cultural bull." The men at the top in business, however, increasingly insist that they prefer recruits initially trained in the liberal arts. They do so partly because this has become a fashion, but also because they realize that the scientific revolution has outdated technical skills almost as fast as it has required them. Many employers have discovered that their technicians must be rapidly replaced by younger men who know more recent developments. Older men must therefore be given administrative positions that require the ability to organize one's fellows instead of the material environment. Hence the liberal arts.

At the same time, on the lower levels of businesses that put specific job descriptions in the hands of campus recruiters, the demand often remains for the "tech" graduate. If and when these often gauche technicians are ultimately promoted to managerial posts, many businesses find they have to retrain them, and even then they often discover that men with a purely engineering background cope badly with administrative problems whose intricacies seem to defy purely rationalistic analysis.

Thus, although in a sense we can proclaim the decline of the liberal arts, noting that two bachelor's degrees out of three are outside the arts and sciences and that at least four in five are vocationally oriented, we must also realize that these officially preprofessional programs conceal much study that has only indirect relevance to the students' future work. In fact, if we examined the academic training of influential Americans in 1900 and 1960, we would probably discover that today's elite spends far more time studying at least nominally liberal subjects. To be sure, many more would also have had vocational training, but it seems paradoxical to assume, as many humanists do, that liberal subjects are worse off when men study engineering than when they leave school after the eighth grade or after high school. It is true enough, however, that few American institutions can claim academic purity. That colleges must serve many masters offends those who want institutions to serve a single clear-cut purpose and who perhaps correctly fear that what they most deeply care about cannot survive in pluralistic competition.

Religious Interests

Today there are nearly 700 church-related colleges scattered across the country. About 400 (not including ones that have wholly left the fold) remain Protestant or Protestant-related, whereas nearly 300 are run by Roman Catholics. The Catholics, for all their late arrival in the college-founding business, have now nearly caught up with the Protestants. Although the Catholics are theologically more uniform than the Protestants, competition and jealousy among their various Orders have resembled the rivalry among Protestant sects and have contributed in the same way to the multiplication of the Church's colleges. Contrary to popular opinion, there is no comprehensive plan for Catholic education in America, and many colleges have no better reason for existence, than, let us say, the desire of Franciscan Fathers not to let the Jesuits capture all the talented local youngsters, or perhaps the conviction of the Dominican Sisters that the local Sacred Heart College is snobbish or intellectually radical.

The ties of the major Protestant denominations to their colleges have become increasingly attenuated, and subventions from the churches, although still of great importance especially in the small institutions and in the South, seem less and less able to assure solvency. No less important, the merger of Americans into a kind of ecumenical Protestantism, impatient of sectarian distinctions, has lessened the monopolistic position of any given Methodist, Presbyterian, Baptist, or other college over a particular flock.

Such monopolies survive only in the more other-worldly sects, such as the Adventists, whose tiny colleges barely stay afloat on the piety of the constituencies and the poverty of their faculties. The better established, church-related colleges increasingly compete for the same students and endowments as nonsectarian institutions. Often they can only be distinguished from the latter by such archaisms as compulsory chapel, a few ministers on the Board of Trustees, and a tenuous connection with a mission college in the Middle East or Africa.

Whatever the osmotic pressure of the Congregational tradition at Oberlin, the Episcopalian at Kenyon, the Quaker at Swarthmore or Bryn Mawr, for all practical purposes these and similar colleges live today in the secular world of the private institutions, seeking good students and faculty from everywhere, people with every shade of belief and unbelief.

Comparable forces have been at work on Catholic education, but the Catholic colleges will not necessarily become secularized either *de facto* or *de jure*, as so many of the Protestant-founded ones have done and are doing. Catholic higher education (like Catholicism generally) copes with secularization by incorporating parts of it. Thus the architecture of Catholic colleges, where they are not the converted mansions of the once-rich, is generally meant to be imposing rather than ascetic—even though it is seldom avant-garde and about as tasteless and imitative as American collegiate architecture generally.

What is striking here as elsewhere is the historical ability of the Church to expand and to hold within its orbits such conflicting departures and desires. The flood of newly college-conscious students who are attracted to or satisfied with the traditional type of Catholic college has not blotted out all attention to the small, self-conscious, intellectual minority who want these colleges to become more cosmopolitan. Yet the long-run future remains opaque. With the possible exception of the Mormons, who have brought to higher education the same enormous communal zeal as to other activities in the state of Utah, no religiously-oriented culture has so far managed to grapple with modern industrial society in the United States in a way that is satisfactory to the most sensitive and talented. The campuses where religious interests seem most intensely intellectual (as distinguished from devotional) are often the secular ones where Tillich and Niebuhr, Berdayev and Barth and Buber, Bernanos and Father Darcy, are read and discussed.

On a Catholic campus the very presence of Churchly religion may somewhat minimize the search for personal insight that characterizes the religious concern of some Protestants and Catholics today. Many lukewarm Protestants, like many lukewarm Jews, discover in secular colleges that their sect is a remarkable historical and intellectual achievement that can provide a frame of orientation, if not of devotion.

Geographic Interest Groups

Geographic and religious interests have sometimes worked together in generating new colleges. Thus, when the Connecticut ministers founded Yale, religion was only the symptom of a broader difference and jealousy between Massachusetts and Connecticut. Likewise, when the Amherst divines revolted against Unitarianism a century later, they may have succeeded less because of their theological orthodoxy than because they represented the underprivileged western half of Massachusetts against the dominant Bostonians.

In general, however, the provinces are becoming more cosmopolitan, and so are their colleges. In many Midwestern colleges the cadre of self-conscious intellectuals, usually said to come from "New York," is growing in both numbers and influence. We are developing a national market for college recruiting. From all directions students are solicited who would once automatically have attended either the nearest denominational institution, their parents' school, or the state university. And, as this process robs the local institutions of their presumptive customers, they in turn are forced to expand their orbits of recruiting to a regional if not national scale. Just as many local brands of food have given way to the chain store brands, so students everywhere are gradually becoming conscious of the fact that they might apply equally to Cornell, MIT, Harvard, Michigan, Stanford, Oberlin, or Haverford.

Feminine Interest Groups

Although Oberlin admitted women in 1837, three years after its founding, and although the Universities of Iowa and Cornell also did so quite early, throughout the nineteenth century women's higher education continued to be regarded by many in both sexes as debilitating to mind and body. Today, women are the most numerous if not the most influential minority seeking higher education—they constitute one-third of the college population.

Only in the intellectually laggard institutions has the notion that women are the "opposite" sex led to an effort to create an equally opposite form of education. In some of the Southern women's colleges this has meant an emphasis on social skills and gracious living, and in the Catholic women's colleges, which constitute more than half the nation's 276 feminine institutions, a similar emphasis on "learning to live together" is often evident. Sometimes, especially in coeducational colleges, the quest for distinctively feminine training produces programs in home economics which, indeed, can become highly scientized and difficult—a kind of "women's engineering."

As the most obvious distinctions that once held women within narrow boundaries evaporate, so too the feminist counterattack of the "Seven Sister" colleges tends to disintegrate, and it is not easy to see what form the women's colleges, or feminine programs within the coeducational ones, can take in the future. At present, the most talented women college students hope to get married but see little way of linking their college work to their image of a future life. Caught between old and discarded goals and new and as yet undiscovered ones, it may be hard for the best women's colleges to maintain their present enviable standards of academic instruction, particularly as the ablest Ph.D.'s increasingly want to teach in the big universities and don't need to begin their careers as talented teachers of girls.

Professionalism in College

The interest groups we have described help shape higher education in America. Few groups have been happy with the compromises they have had to make for the survival of a college, and still fewer have been pleased to discover that, having labored together, they bring forth progeny with a life of their own. Once a college is established, those nominally in charge become more interested in the college's survival than in the welfare and contentment of the interest groups that fathered it. Metaphorically, a college gradually comes to have more respect for its peer group of other colleges than for the public that stands *in loco parentis*. The academic profession itself gradually becomes the dominant though never the sole voice in the operation of the college.

In theory this professionalization is wholly praiseworthy, for if academicians are truly professional educators, they presumably are able to serve the interests of competing interest groups better than these groups serve themselves. The difficulty, however, is that there is no such profession of higher education. The only aspect of college life that has been professionalized is research; professional scholars are often only trained as educators on the job and do not consider this their principal function.

To be sure, there are professionally committed teachers dedicated to producing the right kind of alumni rather than to the equally important but different task of "pushing back the frontiers of knowledge." But there are no graduate schools that offer an academic equivalent to the clinical years in medical school. There are no professional standards governing classroom activities comparable to the standards governing research work. There is no effort at evaluation of teaching by outsiders comparable to the evaluation of research. There are hardly any graduate schools that make a serious effort to induct graduate students into teaching, in contrast with throwing them as underpaid auxiliaries into large introductory classes to sink or swim, haze or be hazed.

And, of course, if the teaching situation is amateurish if not worse, the overall operation of colleges is frequently chaotic and improvised without being creative. Despite efforts, notably at the Harvard Business School, to give some minimum of training to college administrators after their selection, the management of higher education has not been professionalized. This reflects partly the envy and resentment that college faculty members, along with other Americans, share against "bureaucrats"; but such disdain has not prevented bureaucracy in the pejorative sense, but only professionalization.

The colleges themselves, in their relations to their customers and each other, behave like small businesses before the entry of rationalization or union pressures. On a national scale, there are hardly any policies for getting the right teachers and students to the right colleges, and then to the right classrooms. A few private and public commissions have made notable efforts to look ahead at the prospects for higher education, but most faculty members are unaware of their findings. Few colleges can be said to *plan* their future programs, let alone to support research on the development of the adolescent intellect in college—one reason why this book was written. In sum, it seems fair to say that the academic profession has superseded competing interest groups in the field of higher education without doing anything systematic to implement the legitimate aims of the latter.

It is important and proper for scholars to argue that politicians have no business investigating the political opinions of students, but this does not mean that the political naiveté and indifference of many students is no business of the scholar; indeed, one reason why the politicians have to be fought off is that the campuses most apt to encourage political responsibility are the radical ones. Similarly, the academicians rightly denounce vocationalism as shortsighted, but they seldom take seriously the legitimate interest of the employer in hiring graduates who enjoy work, know what they are good at, and are eager to find out what they do not yet know.

THE COLLEGE AS A SUBCULTURE

In describing college as an initiation rite, we have employed a variety of metaphors such as "personnel office," "WPA Organization," and "relocation project." All involve comparisons with other American institutions. A college is not only an institution but also a subculture through which some students pass for a few years, and to which faculty and administrators are likely to dedicate their adult lives. To the extent that a college is a subculture with its own idiosyncratic customs and concerns, an anthropologist can study it in much the same way that he studies a primitive tribe or a modern community.

Of course no college is immune to outside influence, for students have parents, and close to a quarter of American undergraduates are also married. Furthermore, most students have had jobs, and all have future occupations. Even among the faculty, aspirations and friendships often extend beyond academia, if only because no American is immune to messages from the mass media which are frequently at odds with the ideas and attitudes that the college culture purveys.

Political Environment

Any sizeable educational institution can be seen as a vast relocation project that upsets normal ecological expectations, disrupting typical patterns of taxation, land use, housing, and local business. These competitive strains and disruptions have been one source of the frequent political attacks on the colleges, combining ideological differences with economic complaints. (The latter, it should be added, are usually without realistic basis—witness the charges about tax-exempt property.)

The leadership in a small town will often join together against the liberals and other deviants at the college and in alliance with those faculty members who, through Rotary or sports or ideological ties, have become integrated into the business-minded community of Main Street. On the other hand, the sort of small-town hegemony Veblen satirized is rare today, and open Philistinism and open Veblenism are vanishing phenomena. The environment of a college is, in a sense, a series of front organizations lying between the inner core of discipline-oriented faculty members and the outer rings of community-oriented alumni (and employers of alumni). The trustees face both ways. In the wealthier private institutions, where to be a trusteee is both an honor and a considerable responsibility, the president and higher administration have an opportunity to educate the trustees as they are co-opted, and to use them as the first line of defense against outside attack as well as against insolvency.

Like any other organization faced with multiple constituencies, the colleges have set up public-relations departments in an effort to control or at least moderate the image they present to their public. Naturally enough, these departments also serve to remind faculty members of the tigers—or the customers—at their gates. Public relations activities both create and stem from the increasing awareness of all university personnel (including students) that they may be watched, and that a "foolish" speech or donation may bring repercussions. Inevitably, the president of a university, like the president of a nation or corporation, becomes the chief public relations officer of the enterprise—an activity that, combined with fund-raising, takes him increasingly away from the more discipline-oriented phases of his work, just as it has taken the presidents of other corporations away from their industries into negotiations with Congress and other publics. As a result, the president, deans, and other ancillary nonteaching personnel often become scapegoats for faculty resentment and feelings of deprivation and insecurity.

In the graduate schools and elite colleges the faculty can look to its own outside publics for protection. The professional organizations of the various academic disciplines, the agencies that accredit colleges, and the general intellectual public all offer some support. But in the weaker and less prestigious institutions, as we have suggested earlier, the academic freedom arm of the American Association of University Professors is less able to help than it should be. In church-related colleges, the relevant Protestant ministry may be either a bulwark or a fifth column, depending on the denomination, the issue, and the history of previous incidents.

Social Environment

The place of environment in studying a college, however, extends beyond geography and politics. In the broader sense, what proves important is the range of publics from which the college recruits its faculty and student members. This depends on the impressions of the college that are current in various academic and adolescent circles. The brand-name imagery of a college, like that of a car, is a complex thing, and little research has been done in this area.

As competitive free enterprises, individual colleges have not been willing or able to do much in the way of explaining themselves. Their catalogues are seldom designed to help the high school student distinguish one institution from another, or tell what any of them is like. A few colleges have attempted to put useful information into the hands of applicants by such devices as supplying the high schools with College Board scores of entering freshmen. But the majority of colleges have feared that this, or any other form of honesty, would be misunderstood or misused by the applicants. If the median Scholastic Aptitude Test score is high, the college fears this may scare away those students with low scores but special aptitudes that the college wants. If the median scores are low, the college fears that it will freeze its mediocre image and thus obstruct its hope of getting better students.

Most colleges resist consumer research not because they do not want people to know what they are like now, but because they fear that their shortcomings, if generally recognized, will become fixed in the public mind, and hence be irremediable. Most secular colleges want to change faster than the natural evolution of their constituency allows. Such colleges are supported in their ability to attract new constituents, according to new images of themselves, by the fact that applicants for perhaps a hundred American colleges outnumber the places available.

All colleges seek the freedom to acquire new clientele even when, like Reed, their few applicants are mostly the traditionally "right" ones for the college, or when, like a few of the most sought-after institutions, their admissions officers sometimes feel they could pick as well by lot as by free choice among the many highly qualified applicants. Graduates of evolving colleges often discover that their sons cannot gain admission and that "their" fraternities are now inhabited by liberals and semi-intellectuals who want to open the club to those Jews or Negroes who, by the newer liberal-intellectual college standard, may be the elite rather than the dregs.

Yet, although college officials are anxious for as much leeway as possible in picking their freshmen, they have shown very little consistency or planning as to the actual formulas used for selection. These formulas represent a compromise between pressures from alumni, faculty, parents, and high schools more often than they reflect any fairly empirical determination of what combination of students will best produce mutual development and learning.

The foregoing, however, are problems of surfeit, based on the success of the brand-name and the attraction of students whom most colleges would be glad to have. The majority of institutions have no image whatever, other than the local coloration provided by one of the interest groups described in the preceding section. Many institutions, especially but not exclusively the new ones, are seen by both high school and college students as essentially similar —just plain "college." Students choose these imageless institutions because they are convenient or because they offer some half-desired occupational training, or for other unformulated reasons. Yet such colleges, or at least several hundred of them, are rapidly acquiring new constituencies, often faster than they can handle them.

There are deans whose greatest headaches are caused by conflicts between the avant-garde students from "New York" who run many provincial college newspapers, and the fraternity boys, often from small towns, who still typically dominate student government. Faculty members find themselves in equally difficult positions as they overflow the traditional elite into the newer public colleges. These colleges, having grown up overnight, possess no outstanding academic image, either positive or negative, and they provide a kind of ambiguous respectability while the faculty looks for a more congenial community.

Such colleges may fear that consumer research would scare away the talent they hope to attract and ruin their chances of becoming something better, but in fact good college applicants are multiplying so rapidly that many mediocre colleges will soon become much better no matter what the public thinks. Perhaps the fear of consumer research is actually based on the desire of many colleges to go on fooling themselves.

The difference between the 750,000 students who enter college in a year, and the 350,000 who graduate, like the difference between the two-thirds of junior college students who plan to transfer and the one-third who actually do so, might be taken as an index of American optimism. Like the rate of small business failures, the differential is highest in California.

Even in the selective colleges, however, there is always a small group of intellectually well-equipped students who select themselves out after having been selected in. Frequently they enter the army or work for a year, and then, confidence restored or illusions about "life" dispelled, they reenter and graduate. The combination, however, of careful admissions screening and students' faith in the B.A. as the carte blanche to happiness has greatly reduced the attrition rate in such selective colleges.

In the women's colleges, by contrast, nearly half the entering class may drop out before graduation. Some marry and finish their baccalaureate elsewhere; others work to support husbands through college. Certain public colleges use their freshman year as the real basis for selection; thus in many state universities less than half of those who begin the year finish it. Some of these dropouts certainly find other colleges that will allow them to earn a B.A. Others probably transfer to a junior college and settle for the A.A. Still others may join the ranks of the academically fed up, raw material for the forces of anti-intellectualism and political reaction. Whether such people resent a college more if they flunk out than if they are refused admission we do not know, and their overall impact on the social environment is equally difficult to appraise. Furthermore, if the behavior of many alumni is any index, there are numerous degree holders who feel as bitter about their college as one would expect the rejects to feel.

SOME EVOLUTIONARY APPROACHES

The mere fact that colleges themselves believe in evolution and play follow-the-leader makes an evolutionary perspective relevant. In a culture so "linear," metrical, and evaluative as America's it is understandable that academic institutions should seek to rank themselves along some scale, just as backward countries now tend to do.

Economic Hierarchies

Like tribes that depend on hunting and gathering there are at least 500 institutions without accreditation, struggling to survive without visible means of support, scrounging for private gifts or public appropriations while staving off creditors with promises, gaining subsidies from an ill-paid faculty that lacks the connections to find jobs elsewhere, and getting the same from students in a similar fix. At the other extreme, only a handful of universities have undergone what we might call the academic revolution, which introduces them to the affluent world of foundations, expense accounts, teaching assistants, offices, secretaries, and other luxury items. Even those are usually beset by optimism, and they must make annual struggles to balance the income from tuition, taxes, and philanthropy against the outgo for buildings, professors, and the ever-rising costs for ancillary services such as landscaping, guidance, and administration.

Among the 600 public institutions, taxes are the most important source of revenue. Tuition, even for out-of-state residents, is quite nominal. These institutions also seek support for research from government agencies and foundations, but only a few, such as Berkeley, Minnesota, and Michigan, have produced alumni who are generous with buildings, professorships, and the like.

Among the 1200 accredited private colleges, tax money may play a minor role, whereas tuition and philanthropy provide the main support. In practice, of course, the difference is less than it

appears, for legislatures in many ways resemble recalcitrant phi-
lanthropists, and public institutions must cajole the reluctant law-
maker with the same coyness that private colleges exhibit in court-
ing their alumni, or that church-related colleges show in trying to
boost the subvention.

A crucial difference between public and private institutions is
that the public institution knows a few hundred men it must court,
whereas the private institution has thousands of potential benefactors and only a few dozen actual ones. In the legislature on the
other hand, every vote counts for one, despite the tendency of
crucial men, and the lobbyists around them, to make or break the
annual budget.

In general, colleges are increasingly divided into the "haves" and
the "have nots." The "haves" attract able applicants and make
them feel that attending college is a privilege that will in large
measure be responsible for their future success. As a result, their
alumni are likely to be both successful and nostalgic, and to be
generous with Alma Mater, either as donors or legislators. Moreover, such alumni tend to gravitate to positions where they can
ask mutual favors of one another on behalf of educational and
other philanthropic goals. In this, as in all respects, the majority
of "have not" colleges are caught like backward countries in a
self-perpetuating poverty. Unable to attract gifted students and
teachers in large numbers, they can seldom produce alumni or
research that would bring solvency. Instead, they breed an atmosphere of mediocrity in which the talented minority feel alienated from their college. Nevertheless, since self-made men in
America are often not ashamed of the fact, one or two graduates
who do succeed in the world may come to the rescue of their Alma
Mater, putting it, along with themselves, on the map.

Organizational Hierarchies

In college as in other societies, however, the evolutionary scale
is more than a matter of economics. It is also a matter of social

organization. There are perhaps a dozen huge graduate universities, primarily concerned with research and the training of researchers, which play the same role in the academic world that the metropolises play in the American nation. These universities shape and are shaped by the various academic disciplines, just as the metropolises shape and are shaped by various industries. Both universities and metropolises look largely to one another rather than to the provinces for examples of what can be done next. It is even tempting to make specific analogies between the private monoliths (Chicago, Columbia, Cornell, Harvard, Pennsylvania, and Stanford) and the older centers of commerce, or to compare the public superstates (Berkeley, Indiana, Michigan, Minnesota, Illinois, Texas, UCLA, Wisconsin) to newer industrial complexes. These institutions produce the most influential Ph.D.'s and most of the research, and they have most of the surplus money that can be directed into experimentation and luxury.

Similar in name only to these universities are about a hundred demi-universities both public and private. They produce many M.A.'s and an increasing but still small number of Ph.D.'s, and they are really indistinguishable from perhaps 200 "complex colleges" that have a whole variety of preprofessional undergraduate programs to supplement their liberal arts divisions. Such institutions may, of course, have substantial numbers of graduate students—mostly terminal M.A.'s.

Often, however, they will let go from the teaching staff an M.A. who is a good teacher in favor of a Ph.D. who is an indifferent or vindictive one, because the doctorate looks better in the catalogue if not in the classroom. Furthermore, since the more ambitious institutions want not only Ph.D. holders but also professors who will become widely known beyond their classrooms, there has developed a kind of arms race, in which one or two showpiece departments are built up to do nationally-known work, subsidized where possible by foundation or government money. Such symbols often conceal the lack of supporting resources, or infrastructure, that might be used to solve the problems of the students or the local community instead of the problems scheduled by the national disciplines.

By the same token, the faculty acquired for this showpiece purpose comes from outside the community and remains loyal to the discipline rather than to the institution. Their readiness to pack up and move on to a better department may stimulate improvement of their present institution, or it may merely give them a temporarily privileged status at the expense of less mobile faculty. The conflicts that ensue between itinerants and home-guarders bear some resemblance to the struggles in many middle-sized cities between the itinerant executives brought in by national corporations, and the traditional local elite.

To attract scholars and enter the big league, an institution needs not only research money but also graduate students. Imported scholars want graduate students as research assistants and apprentice-colleagues. Graduate students grade, test, and instruct the undergraduates face-to-face, thus saving the professor's time and protecting him from having to confront often stultifying indifference to his academic interests.

By working for nominal wages these teaching assistants also help to subsidize their professors, and the college can therefore keep a balanced budget while paying decent wages and giving relatively light teaching loads to the top-rung scholars. By acquiring its own graduate students, furthermore, a university may eventually save itself money in another way, for these students will come to regard the school as "their" university, and may not follow the pattern, set by professors trained elsewhere, of leaving whenever a better salary or department is offered.

The majority of American colleges are still too far from the world of scholarship and science to worry about such problems—just as the majority of towns are still too far from being wholly industrialized to worry about city planning. They are provincial and often unspecialized, with teachers handling a variety of subjects, and students usually taking a fairly limited repertoire of general courses, plus some preprofessional training. Very often, these colleges will resemble one-industry towns, relying on a single program (in teacher training, for example) to carry the college both economically and otherwise. When such resources vanish, as sometimes happens in both colleges and towns, the college may fail unless enterprising leadership can quickly generate alternative sources of students, funds, and respect.

Subcultural Pressures

We have already referred to the distinction between the institution-oriented and the discipline-oriented faculty member. If the professor is an alumnus of the college where he teaches, he may feel a special loyalty to it. This may engender parochialism, but it may also produce a concern for the problems of his institution, instead of merely his department.

The administration is also likely to play a critical role in evolving the college toward university status and thus toward the destruction of administrative initiative at the hands of a powerful and contemptuous group of scholars. Despite this last point, college presidents are familiar with the social and economic advantages of the next upward stage of evolution and, unlike many of the faculty, are committed to their particular institution. Even when the president or dean hopes to move to a bigger college, he knows that his best maneuver is to make his present institution as prosperous as possible and thus to get a reputation as a builder.

At a lower level, however, the administration may become involved with the students, and with protecting or manipulating them. Deans in the big universities are likely to include knowledge of student life in their discipline, and to use this as a counterfoil to the contempt with which the faculty transfixes them. Where deans outrank professors, however, they do not need to rely on support from minority groups like students. Such men, supported by institution-oriented faculty who hope to become deans, are likely to wield their power openly, manipulating faculty and simply coercing (rarely defending) students.

The students also determine the rate of evolution by forming various subcultures, which produce different kinds of alumni and different public images. Very little effort has been made to map these subcultures, or to channel students into the ones that seem most likely to encourage growth and productivity, as opposed to failure and departure. A few colleges, with Sarah Lawrence and Bennington in the vanguard, have elaborate and self-revealing admissions forms that make possible highly individuated initial guidance of students, assigning them to advisors and roommates in a genuine effort to create optimal matchings. Others ask entering students in a very off-hand way to say what "types" they will and will not accept as roommates. Still others assign roommates and freshman advisors on a random basis, despite the often crucial nature of these decisions for the individual's career in college. In freshman orientation week, such places ask neophytes to "buy" a variety of courses, sports, and extracurricular activities —a procedure often more like a country fair than a serious introduction to an intellectual or even social community.

In the larger institutions, such decisions as whether to take athletics seriously, whether to join a fraternity, and what field to major in, are made on the basis of the networks of the peer culture. Despite the relative precocity of which we have spoken, many students do not flounder productively—sometimes because the ideology of independence makes them feel that they ought to stand on their own feet and not consult anyone. Few large colleges, moreover, have done much to bridge the gaps, caused by age and occupation, that prevent faculty members from doing a great deal to understand, let alone influence, the choices college students make. It is true that a few colleges, such as Yale, have tried to make their advising systems more effective by mixing resident graduate students with freshmen. Yale has also, along with a few other institutions, sought to provide students with ancillary psychiatric guidance and to make advice from this quarter seem unthreatening and "normal." Although these efforts reflect sympathetic concern for the casualties attracted to or created by higher education, the psychiatric services can also become a center for obtaining a fuller understanding of basic dissatisfaction with the overall pattern of college life—dislike for impersonality, suspicion of alienated learning, etc. Not all the evolution that occurs in the collegiate world needs to be blind.

But evolution can, so to speak, be overdirected, and at some colleges with extensive personnel services, students may be well advised to avoid the guidance department. In an effort to help students make only right choices of department or occupation, it is possible simply to confirm existing tendencies both in the students and in the institutions to which they are sent. Yet it is only by allowing students to make apparently wrong choices that a college can encourage them to change, becoming something they are not, instead of confirming themselves as they are.

Only a few advisers have the gift of helping students discover their potential rather than their visible abilities, encouraging them to try things at which they now look inept but may do well. Yet many students who have chosen a college for the wrong reasons profit immensely from their blunders, and many whom any judicious adviser would have told not to study physics, or not to enter the law, have been so changed by the experiences of entering these fields that they become immensely successful. As a result they may even have helped to change what law is, and what physics is, and hence recruitment to these fields in the future. Yet some of the enormous suffering that is the uncreative price of occasional anarchy might be alleviated if choices were less irrevocable.

There is no doubt that the authors are extremely sensitive to the unnecessary suffering and misdirection of effort that colleges, like all other human institutions, can bring about. In the *Vanishing Adolescent*, a book written with a similar animus, Edgar Friedenberg describes the damage done to youngsters at a Midwestern high school. But he also portrays the way in which one of the students, whom he calls Stanley, was able to ride the school to his destination as if it were the Pennsylvania Railroad, relatively unaffected by such of its purposes that were not his.

There are students like Stanley in every college who pursue their interests because they are talented enough and tough or pliable enough to do so. By the same token, whatever the deficiencies of higher education as an organized system, these scarcely excuse students' lack of ingenuity and their readiness to assume that their own actions could not possibly make any difference. Given the chaos and confusion of purposes, the cross pressures from customers, the mixed motives of faculty members and administrators, the very idea that American colleges and universities form a hard and fast system needs demolition.

A few years ago one of the authors sought to explain the organization of American higher education to a group of Russian youth leaders and student editors who refused to believe that anything could be so planless and lacking in central direction, if not from the ministry then from some hidden elite. Nevertheless we must insist that there is no plan; there are only osmotic pressures that bear unevenly throughout the landscape, and models that are imitated at different levels of excellence and ambition.

We have portrayed here some of the gaps separating the ideals of higher education from the institutional practices, but the ideals have their own weight and an individual dedicated to them can exert enormous leverage if he wishes. He can still more easily resist current pressures by creating a niche or enclave for himself. Periods of reformation in higher education can always succeed periods of acquiescence.

Three
The Entering Student

Elizabeth Douvan and Carol Kaye

Why People Go to College: Motivational Factors [1]

Boys often phrase college aspirations as vocational aspirations: they say that they plan to go to engineering school, forestry school, theological seminary, college and medical school, or law school. Half of all boys' college plans are couched in specific vocational terms. By contrast, girls' college plans are not specifically tied to vocational ends, except for girls who say they plan to attend teachers' college.

And in fact, many of the girls who intend to go to college have vocational aspirations that do not require college training, a discrepancy we virtually never find in the occupation-education plans of boys. For many girls, then, college is obviously an end in itself. Enrichment from further education may promise a better life, greater capacity to meet and realize pleasure from the challenge of adulthood, or a chance for social mobility, but specific vocational or utilitarian advantages occur only to a minority of adolescent girls.

Girls' phantasies about college are not simple in content. The dominant theme is a social-sexual one, but other themes—travel and geographic mobility, transformation of the self, social mobility, and a general sensuous longing for experience and the exotic—figure in their thoughts as well. The dream of college apparently serves as a substitute for direct preoccupation with marriage; girls who do not plan to go to college are more explicit in their desire to marry, and have a more developed sense of their own sex role. They are more aware of, and more frankly concerned with, sexuality. Admittedly, in answer to the question "What do you hope to get out of college?" 70 per cent of freshmen girls

[1] Dr. Douvan and Dr. Kay have based their observations on interviews with 1045 boys and 1925 girls who represent the national population of children in school. Their studies were carried out at the University of Michigan's Survey Research Center and were sponsored by the Boy Scouts of America and the Girls Scouts of the U.S.A.

polled at a major Midwestern university included among their hopes the happy encounter with "the man for me," or the desire to meet boys and have a lot of fun. But they also mentioned the desire for personal metamorphosis, a search for status and a different life style, and the wish for unusual and exotic experience.

Boys who plan to attend college have greater autonomy vis-a-vis their parents and are more self-reliant in issues involving values and personal controls than those who do not intend to go to college. The difference is particularly striking in working-class boys. Apparently in this group the decision to seek a college education signals intense motivation and a high degree of personal integration. Among girls we find no comparable differences. The college-bound are no more independent of parental control or self-reliant than other girls, nor do they reveal strong conscious annoyance with parental authority or active resistance against it.

Our analysis so far has tended to obscure differences that exist *within* the population of boys—or girls—who expect to enter college. But important differences of orientation and motivation within each group do exist. In the college group two patterns are of special interest: the youngster who has serious intellectual goals that he expects to realize through college, and the one who sees college primarily as a mechanism for crossing class lines.

The first is an unusual pattern, but it nonetheless serves as the ideal in this field. The social mobility pattern is more common, and it fits a strong traditional conception of the purpose of higher education. The number of young people using college as a means of mobility has increased since World War II, and it will probably continue to grow in the post-Sputnik era, with its emphasis on utilization of talent. In fact, the two motivational types are not easy to separate, for adolescents with high academic motivation are also often those who will use college to gain access to a higher social class.

Aside from this and verbal facility, we find only a few characteristics on which the academically motivated distinguish themselves from other college candidates; they are somewhat more con-

versant with phantasy, they have particularly close family relationships, and they are often from small rather than large families.

There is one other important difference among girls—judged by
traditional concepts of the female character, the academically-
oriented are less feminine. Aside from these features, they are
much like other adolescents who plan to attend college: in their
activities, social development, relationships with contemporaries,
values, and independence in forming values.

Among boys the desire for higher social status is accompanied
by a seriousness of purpose, a willingness to postpone gratification, a highly developed internal morality, and values of individualism and individual competence. Boys who have these traits approach college with a well-established desire to learn.

For girls the picture is more complex. Some socially mobile girls
have serious academic or vocational interest in college; the mobile
group holds such goals more often than the relatively immobile
upper-middle-class girls who plan to enter college, but the connection between values and the desire for status is not nearly so
clear for girls as it is for boys. We can say, however, that when
we look only at those girls who view mobility as an individual
achievement in itself, we find status aspiration and attitudes related
as they are for boys.

The Choice of School

If we know little about *why* people choose a college education,
we know even less about *how* they select a particular school. We
are learning to understand the conscious standards that parents
and students apply in judging and selecting schools. But we do
not yet know who influences their choices, where they get their
information, and what kinds of unconscious motives enter into
their choice. At this point we must be content merely to draw
attention to the various decisions implied in the choice, the forces
and agents that may have affected it, and their range of importance.

People choose colleges for many reasons, but before defining
the major factors involved, here are four cases that can tell us

something of how the decision is made, and at the same time will set in relief the problems involved in any study of the process.

Case A. An urban lower-middle-class boy who chooses the men's Catholic college in his own city. His parents, European immigrants, support the idea of college, yet are torn between wanting their son to better himself, and fearing the rejection his decision may hold for them. The boy is attractive and has already risen a little in the social scale. He chooses the college for two reasons. First, lack of money (and perhaps emotional ties within his family) requires him to live at home. Second, of the two local schools, the Catholic men's college has the greater prestige: it is a private school attracting students from the whole country as against a public institution enrolling a more provincial group. Also, a number of his upper-middle-class friends in high school are Catholics bound for the college, and as a casual Catholic himself, and a yearner after social mobility, the boy's decision is strongly influenced by these considerations.

Case B. The brilliant only son of a wealthy businessman, winner of a National Merit Scholarship, who chooses a small Midwestern college of high academic standing. In doing so he turns down two top Eastern private schools and another small Midwest college. His parents, highly sophisticated people, who helped him with his applications and enabled him to visit the schools, would prefer one of the Eastern schools, but do not actively pressure their son. Family friends express surprise at the boy's choice, because in this social group it is generally assumed that a boy only chooses outside the Ivy League when he cannot get in. The boy himself is quietly pleased with his choice, explaining it on the grounds of the school's excellent faculty and curriculum in his "major" field.

Case C. A middle-class girl from a small industrial city who chooses a Big Ten university. A serious, conscientious student, who has done well at high school, she has nevertheless been consistently rejected by her parents as the shy and awkward member of the family. The parents regard education highly, and fancy the opportunities for mobility that college provides. But although their two older children have entered distinguished schools they have never encouraged the college plans of this their third child. Consequently, the girl has gained from one close friend in high school much of the love and affection denied her by the parents. The friend is a warm, attractive, popular girl who might not have chosen this girl for a companion except that they are both middle-class girls in a school that serves a mainly working class area. And so the two girls have become very close.

When the time comes to choose a college, the friend's parents urge their daughter to select a major university in a neighboring state—an excellent choice for this outgoing, social girl. But the shy one, dependent on her friend's company, makes the same choice, a decision that seems destined to cause the separation she means to avoid. Her friend will almost certainly enter a highly rated sorority on campus, while this girl, lacking social skill and assertiveness, is likely to be accepted by a less popular sorority, if, in fact, she is pledged at all. Girls sometimes manage to retain close friendships despite differences in affiliation, but it is the exception rather than the rule.

Although we do not necessarily predict maladjustment and misery for this girl—the range of environments in this school are broad enough for her to find, perhaps, a group into which she will fit happily—we think that there are other schools whose dominant values would better support her and relieve her of "going it alone" in finding a happy milieu.

Case D. The son of a college teacher, a boy with medium talents, who chooses an obscure school of agriculture and mining in the far West. He has made a poor showing in high school, and would not be able to enter the major university at which his father teaches, or any school of comparable quality. His idea of applying to the local teachers' college clearly threatens his parents' status in the community; if he goes there, the fact of their son's undistinguished ability would be brought into the open. So the alternative is suggested—a technical school of agriculture and

mining in a distant state. Although it is no higher academically
than the teachers' college, it has the advantage of "going away to
school" prestige, and its very distance blurs status characteristics.
Also from the standpoint of prestige, it enjoys the advantage of
not including any technical reference in its name. The choice,
therefore, fits in with the boy's relatively poor academic performance; and if it does not entirely save his parents' "face," it does
something to mask it.

These cases suggest that we investigate at least two kinds of
psychological factors that affect a person's choice of school:
(1) the standards by which the individual appraises an institution,
for example, geographical area, academic quality, prestige, cost
and religion; (2) sources of influence, for example, the opinion
of teachers, counselors, close friends and relatives, and, particularly, parents. In fact, parents are so important they should really
be considered as a separate factor.

Although parents and students make every effort to find the best
school for the students, their efforts are not always successful—
witness the number of students who do not complete the four
year course. This failure suggests that something goes seriously
awry in their choice process. Even discounting the large number
of transfers that occur because of the move from junior college,
the rates seem to reveal that choices are frequently based on inap-
propriate or transitory needs. The shopping around that occurs
after adolescents are already in college causes many of them a great
deal of loss and unhappiness. Although this may lead to developmental gains in some cases, surely some of the grief might have
been prevented if students had received more careful advice when
they were making their decision. The question arises, how do students who stay in college differ in the way they choose schools
from the students who drop out? Such a question is both important and relatively easy to investigate.

T. R. McConnell and Paul Heist

The Diverse College Student Population

The Center for the Study of Higher Education of the University of California, Berkeley, has made extensive studies of the composition of student bodies in a number of colleges and universities. It has also compared the selection standards of different colleges and universities. An important premise underlies these studies. In short the premise declares that the measured intellectual ability of students is only one factor affecting academic achievement. A whole range of other factors enters into the picture—student interests, goals and attitudes, student personality and certain characteristics from the vast realm of an individual's social and cultural background. Together these components affect not only academic performance, but the climate of a college, its general culture, and its student subcultures.

VARIATION IN SCHOLASTIC APTITUDE

A question of great interest in recent years is what proportion of high-school graduates at various levels of ability should go to college. To many the question is two-edged; they are concerned about too few in the upper levels of ability and too many from levels of lesser ability attending college. In a much-quoted report Wolfle (1954) showed that only 53 per cent of the top one-fifth of high school graduates entered college, but that 17 per cent of the lowest one-fifth did so. A report by Educational Testing Service (White, 1954) indicated that in the Cleveland Area 40 per cent of the students with IQ's above 115 did not enter college immediately following graduation from high school.

To estimate the selectivity of American colleges, the Center at Berkeley studied the aptitude test scores [American Council on Education Psychological Examination (ACE)] of students entering 200 institutions—a representative sample of the more than 1800 colleges in the United States. The average ACE total score for the 60,539 students in the sample of 200 schools was 104.4. The average scores for *institutions* ranged from a low of 37.5 to a high of 142.2, or from the first percentile to over the 90th percentile.

Diversity within student bodies is as striking as the diversity among institutions. In over 85 per cent of the schools in the sample the difference between the lowest and the highest ACE score found among entering students was as great as 80. At a conservative estimate it would be safe to say that many teachers in the great majority of the colleges were facing classes whose IQ's varied by more than 50 points.

We may conclude that almost *any* high school graduate can gain admission to some higher educational institution without going very far from home. The kind of college that will accept him, however, will vary greatly according to his ability.

These findings, very briefly summarized, raise some important questions.

1. It has been suggested that each institution should select its students from a narrow range of measured aptitude. But since only a small number of highly selective colleges are relatively homogeneous in student ability, how could such pairing of students and institutions, even if it was desirable, be carried out? Would such a distribution stimulate students from every level of ability to fulfill their potential more completely than they would in a diverse student body? Which is more important—to have a narrow range of ability among students, or to have in each institution enough students of high ability to stimulate each other? What is the effect on his motivation when a student of high ability has to compete with other students equally capable, or nearly so, and has to adjust, perhaps, to getting C's when in high school he received mostly A's? On the other hand, what is the effect on a student's motivation when he finds himself mentally outclassed by most other students in his college?

2. Institutions whose student bodies have relatively low-ability

scores generally enroll a few students of exceptional capacity. Should these students have been advised to enter a more selective institution or should they be advised to transfer to another college now? If it appears that the presence of a few exceptional students in a student body of below average ability represents mismating of student and institution, how can this be avoided? Is the stimulus of a student with high ability—supposing he performs reasonably well in an environment with low general demands—sufficiently valuable to ordinary students and to members of the faculty to justify him remaining?

3. If an institution chooses to be highly selective in scholastic aptitude should it be similarly selective on other grounds, such as social and cultural background, the *kind* of intellect a student has (for instance, theoretical or empirical), attitudes, and values? More particularly, would a student whose interests and values are characteristic of engineering students do well at a college with many free-thinking liberals, even if his scholastic aptitude scores were adequate? Alternatively, would an intellectually and socially unconventional student perform successfully at a college with students drawn almost entirely from a single, conservative religious denomination?

Before asking the last group of questions, however, we should ask how much students of the same college vary in non-intellectual ways, in their interests, values, attitudes, readiness to learn, and social backgrounds.

DIVERSITY OF ATTITUDES

How diverse are expressed attitudes at the time of entrance to college? Are there differences among institutions in students' attitudes, as well as in their interests and aptitudes? Can the members of a large and complex university be broken down into different groups on the basis of their basic attitudes? To what extent do those who choose various academic majors differ in attitudes and opinions? Inquiry into these questions to date has only produced tentative conclusions.

A study reported by E. Nelson in 1938 may be considered a pioneering attempt in the study of attitudes. Nelson was mainly concerned with changes in attitudes over a number of years, but some of his findings dealt with differences among students at a particular time. His study of 3754 students at eighteen institutions, —public, private, Protestant, and Catholic—showed that in the late 1930's the student bodies of *all* these schools were essentially conservative, and the women were more so than the men.

In recent years, J. S. Coleman has been gathering information about the opinions, preferences, and attitudes of precollege adolescents to determine their major values, especially those concerned with academic achievement. He describes what appears to be the pervasive atmosphere of most high schools—one which tends to inhibit learning. Attitudes unfavorable to intellectual development are well learned by the majority of pupils in three or four years, and are carried on to college and university environments.

The Center for the Study of Higher Education has investigated the educational and intellectual development during college years of a large sample of National Merit Scholarship winners and near winners, whose measured ability places them in the top 1 or 2 per cent of all high school graduates. During their freshmen year they answered a questionnaire about their attitudes, and the replies indicated rather uniform attitudes from field to field. As a group, however, the women were always a little more conservative than the men. The men in engineering and the women in the humanities were somewhat less in favor of unrestricted scientific investigation than were the other groups. But, asked whether the best government is the one which governs least, more women in the humanities took a "liberal" position than did those in the natural sciences and mathematics. Men in both the humanities and the "nonphysical science" group responded in the liberal direction more often than did other male groups. On the whole, attitudes on items such as government provision of medical care and college teaching of religious values seem to be unrelated to choice of academic major, especially for very able students.

From findings such as these an important question evolves. After four years' time in a college or university, what will the same students think and believe? Will their attitudes be even more uniform, but still showing a liberal tendency? How durable, in fact, are the alterations wrought at college?

Educational Goals

The National Merit scholars were also queried indirectly about their attitudes toward education. Before entering college they were asked to choose from a list of possible educational goals those they thought the ideal institution should emphasize. Their reactions varied strikingly according to the type of college they went to. The following table illustrates this contrast.

Primary Educational Goals	PERCENTAGES IN TYPES OF INSTITUTIONS			
	Public	Private	Catholic	Protestant
1. Vocation training	50	25	17	25
2. General education and appreciation of ideas	38	60	40	53

A rather similar study, conducted at Cornell, produced fairly similar results. It was found that students at Wesleyan, Yale, Harvard, and Dartmouth most often checked "basic general education and appreciation of ideas" as an educational goal, and they least often stressed vocational training. Conversely, men at the state universities checked vocational preparation much more frequently than those at the Ivy League colleges.

One point to be made here is *not* that students whose vocational goals are foremost should go to state universities rather than private, but that faculties in the public institutions who want to interest students in ideas face a challenge and problem different from that confronting their brethren in the private colleges.

Personal Traits

In measured personality traits, how do college entrants compare with high school seniors? Differences between students at these two levels have been illustrated by data from the California Personality Inventory, one of the most widely used instruments, and the Omnibus Personality Inventory, an instrument assembled and constructed at the Center for studying student growth and development.

Both tests indicate that, as one should hope, the college student possesses a greater interest in academic and intellectual activities than does the high school senior. The college student does have the greater readiness for education and further personal development, and it might be said that in general he seems further along on a course of development that continued education should foster. Whether these attributes spring from age or from selection is not yet known.

Turning to comparisons of different colleges in terms of student personality we may note some findings of further research conducted at the Berkeley Center. This dealt with students who were attracted to colleges and universities where a large proportion of graduates later earned their doctorate. A group of students of superior ability, male and female, entering these productive institutions were compared to a group of equally able students entering less productive schools. The authors found that students who entered the former institutions were more genuinely interested in learning, more theoretically inclined, more flexible in their thinking, more tolerant of ambiguity, and potentially more original and creative. Thus the kind of personalities recruited in the first place by certain institutions is itself a key factor in scholastic achievement, along with the impact of the institution.

Do student bodies of average scholastic ability have as many different "types" of personality as more able groups? At the Berkeley Center freshman classes from two colleges situated within the same county were compared. The average academic ability of both classes was virtually the same as the national freshman average. Only in two respects—first, degree of interest in reflective thought, and secondly, liberalism vis-a-vis conservatism— did these two freshman classes appear similar. On all other measured characteristics they seemed to be distinctly different. In one college many more students were theoretically and aesthetically minded, had a more complex outlook on their environment and were more impulsive in their every day behavior.

CONCLUSION

Far too little is known about the relationship between the personality characteristics students bring to college and their academic achievement, either in the conventional sense of grades and persistence, or in the more subtle sense of independent thinking and creativity—qualities seldom reflected by academic marks. Even less is known about the relationship between personality and the attainment of personal effectiveness. But the first step in making these studies is to *know* the entering student, to know him as an actual or potential scholar, to know him as a person and to see him against his background and against the college environment and its subcultures.

The assessment of such psychological characteristics as attitudes, interests, aspirations and values is becoming more and more accurate; so much so that there may no longer be legitimate reasons for confining information about the new student to a narrow range of attributes such as scholastic aptitude test scores or high school grades. A minimum program of assessment, including academic aptitude and achievement, biographical information, social and cultural background, and a few relevant personality characteristics will provide a meaningful description of the student body as a whole, and the student subgroups that are found on most campuses. By supplementing such data with measurement of beliefs, opinions, and attitudes, a way can be found to spot changes in behavior that occur during college years and to analyze the factors that impede or facilitate these changes.

References

Coleman, J. S. The adolescent subculture and academic achievement. *Amer. J. Soc.*, 1960, 55, 337–347.

Nelson, E. Radicalism-conservatism in student attitudes. *Psychol. Monogr.*, 1938, 50, (4).

White, R. C. The potential and probable supply of college students. *Coll. Admissions* (ETS), 1954, 1, 12–23.

Wolfle, D. *America's resources of specialized talent.* New York: Harper and Brothers, 1954.

Joshua A. Fishman

Student Selection and Guidance

Today the American secondary school and the American college
frequently pursue quite separate, if not antithetical, educational
programs. They may serve very different clienteles, different both
geographically and socially. Many colleges want to select their
freshman class from applicants all over the country (and, in some
cases, all over the world), with widely varying family backgrounds
and cultural traditions. The price that the colleges pay for this
diversity, however, is that these applicants arrive presenting credentials from secondary schools that vary widely in scholastic
content and quality. The high schools agree only in their opposition to any form of dictation from colleges about curricular
matters.

Presented with this kaleidoscope of grades, courses, and curricula, American colleges rely on selection and guidance techniques that maximize descriptive impartiality but do little to suggest what ought to be taught at the high school level.

CURRENT FINDINGS

A review of all college guidance and selection studies completed during the decade 1948 to 1958 shows that this area is one
of the most intensively investigated in the entire field of educational research. What is the upshot of all this inquiry? Unfortunately, it can be summarized quite briefly. The most usual way
of predicting college performance is to look at high school grades
and scores on scholastic aptitude tests.

As going to college becomes an increasingly universal American
experience, more and more information will become available concerning the high schools and the communities from which college
applicants come to any given college. This information will permit those colleges that so desire to refine continually their use of

test scores (and/or high school averages) as predictors of intellectual performance in college.

This "improvement" can come about by "correcting" or weighting the high school average and the test scores, of applicants coming from particular high schools, on the basis of the college performance records of many previous applicants from the same high school, on the basis of many applicants with similar community and school characteristics, or on the basis of many applicants with similar social and cultural characteristics. There will also be an even stronger urge than that already felt today to use personality and other nonintellectual measures in addition to high school grades and aptitude-achievement test scores. So far, however, this has not proved successful. Why?

THE UBIQUITOUS HIGH SCHOOL AVERAGE

To a much greater extent than is commonly realized, high school grades are influenced by relatively nonintellectual factors such as personality, adjustment, and motivation. Frequently, indeed, school grades merely reveal how closely a student's personality resembles the generally preferred personality of the middle-class academic world. High school grades, like scholastic aptitude test scores, also indicate important social characteristics. As a result, the simple addition of a nonintellectual test to our selection or guidance battery does not accomplish much. The added personality test simply measures the same factors that grades measure and yields no improvement in prediction.

The same is true at college. Since college grades reveal many of the same personality and social preferences revealed by high school grades, it is scarcely surprising that high school grades should be the best predictors of college grades. What *is* surprising is that educators and even social scientists should value grades purely for what they say about intellect.

In fact, high school grades are the summary of a life story. It is easy to forget this, but we must not let the crudity and simplicity of our index mask the subtlety and complexity of real life. Through practical necessity our experimental designs must simplify nature, but we must not then reify our simplification.

ALTERNATIVES TO PERSONNEL SELECTION

The rising tide of college-going in American life must not lead us to an inflexible reliance on personnel selection devices to accomplish all our ends. Even industry, which has provided the model for personnel selection, at times shows awareness that it owes something to society besides an exclusive dedication to maximizing profits—and to producing profit maximizers.

Similarly, American higher education owes something more to society than a continual pursuit of the "safest" cream that can be discovered at the secondary school level. Of course, given our great institutional and cultural diversity, it is certainly justifiable and desirable for *some* colleges to adopt this approach exclusively. Another approach also has merit, however—one based not only on personnel selection but also on deliberately changing individuals and their educational environments. Let me merely outline its broadest features here.

THE NEED FOR NEW THEORETICAL FOUNDATIONS

To understand the relationship between intellectual and non-intellectual factors in student performance, and to use the latter predictively, we must identify the differences, both in behavior and environment, between high school and college. Of course there are similarities between the two settings, but these similarities, we must remember, are already being used to predict intellectual achievement; this is simply the same as saying that college admissions men assess applicants at least partly on high school performance.

Now if both the individual and the environment are the same in high school and college, no new nonintellectual predictors are needed, since we have already noted that high school grades are a composite measure of *both* intellectual attainment, and nonintellectual adjustment to the environment. If, however, there *are* differences between the two settings, and if these differences can be attributed *primarily* to changes within the students themselves (e.g., impulse expression, social maturity, self-questioning, complexity of outlook, etc.), we need separate, nonintellectual predictors, that is, ways of assessment that consider the student's personality.

In the same manner, if there are differences in total setting between high school and college that can be attributed primarily to differences in the two *environments* per se (e.g., religious auspices, coeducation, rurality-urbanity, institutional-size, etc.), separate predictors that take into account institutional contrast are needed.

Furthermore where *both* developmental and environmental differences, as mentioned previously, obtain, both individual nonintellective predictors and institutional predictors are called for. On the other hand, we must recognize that not all differences in personality and environment between high school and college can be allowed for in predicting how an individual will turn out at college. Individual changes due to protracted illnesses, deaths or other major dislocations in the immediate family, serious financial reverses, etc., cannot be predicted. There is a counterpart to such random individual change in random environmental change. "Falling in with the jazz-group (or the chess-nuts)," finding four out of five professors in the freshman year to be "liberals" or users of the "nondirective" instructional approach, discovering two geniuses from one's home-town in the tough physics course—such unforeseeable phenomena may form part of the individual's college environment. All of these can be treated only via "*post*diction" (guidance and counselling) rather than via *pre*diction. Postdiction is certainly as important as prediction (many would say it is more important) for it takes the initiative in a way that mere prediction does not. It involves helping students to change, and planning environmental change, for the purpose of attaining desirable academic outcomes. We must admit, however, that we are quite far from having sufficient knowledge of either individual or institutional differences for the purpose of effective guidance.

The social psychologist's greatest contribution to education may well be to persuade those concerned with predicting absolute standards of ability to forget about it. For a while at least, it would help to think less of *level* than of *kind*—kinds of students, kinds of high school environments, kinds of college environments. Too much of our present emphasis on prediction has entailed a rigid, absolutist view of what constitutes "ability"; let us instead consider how different kinds of students make different kinds of uses of different kinds of college environments.

I am quite confident that ultimately we shall return to prediction; our own research proclivities as well as larger social pressures will push us in that direction. Nevertheless, if we set prediction aside for a while in favor of some basic theory and research, we may ultimately return to it with greater understanding and flexibility than we now possess.

Nevitt Sanford

Freshman Personality:
A Stage in Human Development

At no stage can the development of a man's personality be defined simply by either his chronological age or his academic status. The proposal here is that a stage of late adolescence intervenes between adolescence proper and early adulthood. Certain high school students and college sophomores as well as freshmen are included in this stage, and it may be that not all juniors and seniors have passed beyond it. But because the phase is often *connected* with age, as it is with going to college, the freshman is more likely to be at this point than are other categories of older or younger people.

For most freshmen the main crisis of adolescence is over, and controlling mechanisms are again in the ascendant. But the controls developed for the purpose of inhibiting impulses are still unseasoned and uncertain; they are likely to operate in a rigid manner, to be overdone, as if the danger of their giving way altogether were still very real. Thus the freshman tends to be like a convert to adulthood, an enthusiastic supporter and imitator of adult ways who knows what it is to backslide—which he sometimes does.

The achievement of *flexible* control, an arrangement in which there is genuine freedom of impulses because there is little danger of their getting out of hand, still lies ahead. Nevertheless, impulses are now sufficiently inhibited or contained so that the young person can turn his attention to other matters. He is now ready to concentrate on his relations with the world about him—to improve his understanding of that world and to find a place within it.

This picture of the freshman's psychological situation is essentially that of an authoritarian personality. He inhibits impulse by being morally strict, both with himself and with others. He is ready to meet stiff requirements, to work hard, to conform with what he takes to be the prevailing standards of behavior—and he is inclined to be somewhat intolerant of those who do not.

An element of perfectionism, of striving for purity of thought and action is characteristic of the freshman. Needing, and finding, moral heroes, he is apt to demand in them perfection. When, in fact, his idols are shown to have feet of clay, or at least some human weakness, our freshman is unprepared for the discovery. Indeed, one of the hardest things about growing up in contemporary America is that at just the time when a young person most needs models of private and public virtue he is likely to become aware of corruption in high places, organized immorality in some of our major institutions, inconsistencies in our economic system and our sexual mores, and meanness in people close at hand whom he thought he could admire. If the young person is not to remain in an authoritarian stage of development he must learn to see things as they are, develop an articulate individual power of judgment, and become able to criticize what he judges to be bad.

If he does this, however, he courts new danger: that he will reject the existing order out of hand, and become totally alienated from the society and values represented by his parents and his community. If this happens while the young person is still emotionally as well as economically dependent on his parents, and before he has had time to develop a value system based on his own experience, we get one type of modern "beatnik."

Closely related to the freshman's authoritarian propensities is his uncertain self-esteem. He does not know what he can do, how good he is, or what to think of himself. Just as he looks to authority or the social group for guidance in the matter of moral values, so does he look to external sources for definition and measurement of himself, and these sources give conflicting testimony. On the one hand he is happy to remember his parents' faith in him, the accomplishments of high school and the plaudits received there, and, perhaps particularly, the fact that he was chosen for admission to his college. On the other hand, he suspects that he is now playing in a different league, and he knows that the major tests of life still await him. In his uncertainty, he vacillates between overestimation and underestimation of himself. His inclination is to stick to patterns of behavior that have been rewarded in the past and to display such confidence as he can muster.

Vulnerability to other people's appraisals makes the average freshman highly susceptible to the influence of his fellow students; their approval or disapproval can make or break his self-confidence. In this situation it is often a good thing that he is given academic grades, and is told about the results of tests of ability and achievement. Bad news may be better than no news; better, that is, than uncertainty or than his gloomy imaginings. Freshmen flourish best not when they are given no grades, but when they are given searching and hard-hitting analyses of their performances accompanied by intelligible and realistic pictures of what they can become.

To understand the freshman's developmental stage is to know how he might be changed and what the college might do to bring about desirable development. Effective teaching does not deliberately call a student's attention to his private motives or mechanisms; instead it undertakes to show the student something of the variety and complexity of the social world of which he is a part; it tries to show him the inner feelings and motives and mechanisms of people in general; it seeks to broaden self-awareness by inducing empathy with many kinds of people—real and fictional —and by confronting the student with some of the deficiencies of his old, automatically adopted values, so that he experiences conflict and has to make decisions.

The nonacademic college environment may also provide important stimuli to individual development. The student is placed in many situations that require new responses. In the relative anonymity of the college society, he can be free of his home community's limiting expectations and can be himself in a variety of new social roles. That he may do so at a time when he must seriously consider future roles but does not yet have to commit himself to any one of them is a great advantage of the college situation.

A person can only throw himself into the most challenging and enriching experiences possible when he feels fairly sure of himself, sure that repressed impulses will not capture him, sure that he will not be made to feel worthless in the eyes of others. To get the most from experiences such as going abroad, getting married, entering into a vocation, and having children—and to do well in such roles—the individual must, in a sense, lose himself; that is, he must permit himself to be enveloped by the situation's demands. It is this process that further expands and differentiates the personality. Losing oneself in this way means forgetting to be defensive, doing without external supports for self-esteem, and abandoning behavior that merely served to reassure. Such freedom can exist only where a basic stability underlies the person's self-conception. He will not gladly "lose" himself in new experiences unless he feels that his essential identity can survive such experiences—can survive them and assimilate them.

Concept of the Developing Person

The arch-problem for the student is to know how to wait, how to tolerate ambiguity and the open question about himself while he prepares for the future. The problem is not easy for he is constantly tempted to take short-cuts to maturity: neglecting the paths to full development by imitating adult behavior and prematurely fitting himself into adult roles. It is for the college, therefore, to help him to wait.

The college may greatly improve its work by regarding the student as a person in transition. If it really did so, a different view might be taken of "the junior year abroad." It might be remembered that many college juniors are still in an authoritarian stage of development, and that when people in this stage go abroad they tend to experience only what they have experienced before and to become confirmed in their preexisting outlook. Again, the college might take a less approving view of student marriages if it considered that, for many students, marriage is more an attempt to establish a suitable self-conception than the expression of a well-formed personality's natural bent.

To help the student wait, however, the college must do more

than simply view him as a developing person. It must convince the student to see *himself* as a person-in-transition, and to accept happily what he sees. The college must in effect tell him, "You are going to change. It is all right, therefore, for you to feel uncertain about your future; what matters is that you enter fully into those activities that can develop you." In other words, what we need is a stronger definition and greater social acceptance of the role of *student,* so that those who occupy this role may more comfortably and easily be what they are—developing persons.

This, it must be granted, goes against a strong trend in American culture, which smudges the boundaries between stages of development and permits younger people to define themselves as miniatures of older people . . . social dancing at 10, beer and high-powered cars at 16. Yet if we are to have an education that develops people, we must somehow build into our culture the concepts of the developer and of stages of development.

Four

The Work of the Teacher

Joseph Adelson

The Teacher as a Model

Discussions of the good teacher are likely to leave us more up-lifted than enlightened. The descriptions we read generally amount to little more than an assemblage of virtues; we miss in them a sense of the complexity and ambiguity that we know characterizes the teacher's work.

Here are some paradoxes to help us begin: a teacher may be a good teacher yet not serve as a model to any of his students; he may inspire his students and yet fail to influence them; he may in-fluence them without inspiring them; he may be a model for them and yet not be an effective teacher; and so on.

These paradoxes make the point—an obvious one but generally overlooked in the more solemn and global discussions of the teacher—that charisma, competence, and influence do not neces-sarily go hand in hand. A great many college teachers, perhaps most of them, are "good" teachers, good in the sense that they are conscientious and devoted, that they are lucid, articulate, and fair-minded lecturers, and that more often than not they succeed in illuminating the subject matter. Their students learn from them, often learn very much; yet these teachers do not ultimately make much of a difference in their students' lives beyond the learning they impart.

At another extreme we have those rare teachers who stir and enchant their students, and yet who may be spectacularly inept in teaching subject matter. I think now of a former colleague of mine, in some ways a truly great man, who is so ebullient, erratic, and distractible, so easily carried away by the rocketing course of his thought, that his students, even the bright ones, just sit there, be-numbed, bewildered, and finally enthralled. They know they are close to a presence, and they are willing to suffer incoherence to join vicariously in that demonic enthusiasm.

What we must do, plainly, is to recognize the pluralism in teaching, that is, the many styles of influence and the many modes of connection that bind student and teacher to each other. Teaching styles are so diverse that they can be categorized in a great many different ways. The grouping I want to try out was suggested by the work of Merrill Jackson, an anthropologist who has been doing a cross-cultural study of the healer's role. Three of the distinct modes he documents can also be found in the college classroom.

The Teacher as Shaman

Here the teacher's orientation is narcissistic. The public manner does not matter. This type of teacher is not necessarily vain or exhibitionistic; he may in fact appear to be withdrawn, diffident, even humble. Essentially, however, he keeps the audience's attention focused on himself. He invites the student to observe the personality in its encounter with the subject matter. He stresses charm, skill, and mana in the self's entanglement with ideas.

When this orientation is combined with unusual gifts, we have a charismatic teacher, one of those outstanding and memorable personalities who seem more than life-size. The charismatic teacher is marked by power, energy, and commitment; by power we mean sheer intellectual strength or uncommon perceptiveness and originality, by energy an unusual force or vivacity of personality, and by commitment a deep absorption in the self and its work.

Generally, all of these qualities are present to some degree. Energy without power turns out to be mere flamboyance; power without energy or commitment is likely to be bloodless, arid, enervating.

The Teacher as Priest

The priestly healer claims his power not through personal endowment, but through his office; he is the agent of an omnipotent authority. Do we have a parallel to this in teaching? I would say it is the teacher who stresses not his personal virtues, but his membership in a powerful or admirable collectivity, for example, physics, psychoanalysis, or classical scholarship.

The narcissistic teacher to some degree stands apart from his discipline, and seems to say, "I am valuable to myself." The priestly teacher says, "I am valuable for what I belong to. I represent and personify a collective identity."

It is difficult to generalize about this mode of teaching since the teacher's behavior toward the student varies so much with the nature of the collectivity. It is one thing when the collectivity is coterminous with a subject matter, and another when it is an enclosed or beleaguered sect within a discipline (e.g., the various "schools" within sociology and psychology).

Collectivities differ in their openness, their degree of organization, their status vis-a-vis other groups. Some are easy to enter, whereas others are closed; some are loose and informal, bound by common interest and camaraderie, and others are stratified and formal; some are marginal in status, whereas others are secure, entrenched elites. Other differences involve the teacher's status in the collectivity: the undergraduate teacher may proselytize, seeking recruits among the promising students; the graduate-professional school teacher will first indoctrinate, then examine, and finally ordain the recruit.

There is no question of the potency of the priestly mode of teaching. It achieves its effectiveness for a great many different reasons. Teacher and student are generally in a close relationship to each other. The student is encouraged to model his activity after the teacher's, very much as in those charming experiments on imprinting, where the baby duck follows the decoy. We also find a good deal of close coaching, both of behavior and ideology. In most cases the teaching is both positive and negative—that is, the student not only is trained to develop new behaviors, but is also required to eliminate competing or discordant responses. Generally the student is given an unambiguous ideal of character and behavior. He may be allowed, as part of the strategy of training, to feel uncertain whether he is meeting this ideal, but the ideal itself is usually clear-cut enough. In some instances the collectivity offers an encompassing doctrine, and the student is exhorted to reinterpret his experiences in the vocabulary of the doctrine, and when this is not the case, the training itself demands so complete a commitment of time and energy that the student's ideational world narrows to include only the collectivity and its concerns. The teacher customarily enjoys a great deal of power in relation to the student, which reenforces the latter's dependency. The student's tie to the collectivity is further reenforced by his close association with peers—rivals, fellow-aspirants, fellow-sufferers—who share his trials, sustain him in moments of doubt, restore his flagging spirits, and keep alive his competitive drive. Finally, this mode of teaching is effective because it offers to the student a stake in a collective, utopian purpose, and also in promising such tangible rewards as power, position, money, and intellectual exclusiveness. Less obviously, but quite as important, the collectivity makes its appeal to the student in helping him to resolve internal confusions. His participation allows a distinct identity choice, it supports that choice by collective approval, and it reduces intellectual and moral ambiguity.

The dominance of this mode of teaching in the graduate and professional schools, although regrettable, is probably inevitable. It is more disturbing to note its steady encroachment in undergraduate education. For many college teachers the introductory courses have less value for themselves than as a net in which to trap the bright undergraduate, whereas the advanced courses increasingly serve only to screen and socialize students for what the faculty deems "the great good place," namely, the graduate school. Furthermore, academic counseling at the freshman and sophomore level frequently produces a guerilla warfare between disciplines, each seeking to capture the promising talents for itself, and without too much regard for the student's needs and interests. If matters are not worse than they already are, it is not because the disciplines have any genuine concern for the undergraduate or for liberal ideals of education, but because the leviathans have managed to neutralize each other's demands. Even so, the pressure of required courses and prerequisites serves to force the student into premature career commitment, while the onerous demands on his time (especially in the laboratory sciences, but also and increasingly in other fields) keep him from trying anything else.

The Teacher as Mystic Healer

The mystic healer finds the source of illness in the patient's personality. He rids his patient of disease by helping him to correct an inner flaw or to realize a hidden strength. The analogy here, and perhaps it is a remote one, is to the teacher I will term altruistic.

He concentrates neither on himself, nor the subject matter, nor the discipline, but on the student, saying, "I will help you become what you are." We may recall Michelangelo's approach to sculpture; looking at the raw block of marble, he tried to uncover the statue within it. So does the altruistic teacher regard his unformed students. This type of teacher keeps his own achievement and personality secondary, and he works to help the student find what is best and most essential within himself.

At this point we are uncomfortably close to the rhetoric of the college brochure. This is what colleges tell us they do; and yet we know how very rarely we find altruistic teaching. Why is it so rare? For one thing, it is a model-less approach to teaching; the teacher points neither to himself nor to some immediately visible figure, but chooses to work with his student's potential and toward an intrinsically abstract or remote ideal. Also, this mode of teaching demands great acumen and great sensitivity, that is, the ability to vary one's attack according to the student and to the phase of teaching, now lenient, now stern, now encouraging, now critical.

The reason that the altruistic mode is so rarely successful lies deeper than these, however. The mode is selfless. It demands that the teacher set aside, for the moment at least, his own desires and concerns to devote himself without hidden ambivalence to the needs of another. In short, the teacher's altruism must be genuine, and altruism, as we know, is a fragile and unsteady trait, all too frequently reactive, born out of its opposite.

If the teacher's selflessness is false, expedient, or mechanical, if it comes out of a failure in self-esteem, or if it gives way to an underlying envy—and in the nature of things, these are real and ever-present possibilities—the teaching at best will not succeed, and at the worst may end in damaging the student.

TEACHERS AS NEGATIVE MODELS

This reminds us of what might otherwise escape our attention, that the teacher may sometimes serve as a negative or anti-model. Here the student uses the teacher as a lodestar from which he sails away as rapidly as he can, seeming to say: whatever he is for, I will be against.

Teachers who exercise this power of revulsion are, in their own way, charismatic types; indeed, the teacher who is charismatically positive for some will be negative for others. He breeds disciples or enemies; few remain unmoved. If we follow a student's development closely enough we generally discover both positive and negative models; the decision to be or become like someone goes hand in hand with a negative choice of identity and ideal.

Value Changes

An even more important topic on the negative side of modeling concerns the teacher whose value changes—the disappointing model. I would not have thought this to be so important since it does not come up in casual conversations on modeling, but close interviewing brings to light frequent mentions and examples of disappointments in the model.

In the main, students learn to be realistic about their teachers, enough so that they are spared any strong sense of disappointment. Indeed, they manage it so well that we are likely to remain unaware that even the "normal" student undergoes at some time some crisis, however minor, concerning the clay feet of an intellectual idol.

The student's response to disappointment depends not only on his susceptibility but also on the type of flaw he discovers in the teacher. It makes a difference whether or not the failing is role-relevant. It puts a greater strain on the student when the model's fault involves role-performance than when it is unrelated to how the teacher does his work. In the latter instance the student can more easily compartmentalize his image of the teacher.

Moral Failure

Probably the most difficult type of failure for the student to accept is a moral one. By "moral" I do not mean, primarily, the teacher's living up to conventional standards in pleasure-seeking; rather I mean such qualities as integrity, fairness, ethical sensitivity, courage. The student is not overly demoralized to discover that his model's personal qualities are not quite what he thought or hoped they were, that his teacher is not as intelligent, penetrating, or perceptive as he first appeared to be. It is, in fact, part of the student's maturation that he learn to tolerate such facts, just as the child learns to give up his belief that the parents are omnicompetent. But a moral failure is not so easily accepted, and if it is serious enough in nature, is likely to be a disheartening or even a shattering experience.

The teacher's life is as filled with moral tension and ambiguity as any other, but the moral dimension is most visibly operative in areas that do not affect the student—for example, departmental politics. Consequently, moral issues do not ordinarily become problematic in the teacher-student relationship. But when they do, we become intensely aware of their tacit importance.

Those of us who were at the University of California during the loyalty oath troubles had a unique opportunity to observe how the moral qualities of our teachers, ordinarily taken for granted and so overlooked, could assume overweening importance in a moment of moral crisis. It was an uncanny time for us; with one part of ourselves we lived in the routine of things, concerned with courses, prelims, dissertations; and all the while our inner, central attention was elsewhere, held in a fretful preoccupation with the morality play in which our teachers were involved. We wondered how things would turn out, of course, but beyond and deeper than that, the intimate compelling question was whether our models would behave honorably.

They did not, not most of them; although for a time we kept ourselves from recognizing this, largely by allying ourselves psychically with the very few who acted heroically while ignoring the very many who did not. It taught us, on the one hand, that moral courage is possible, and on the other, that it is uncommon. All in all, it was a quick and unpleasant education. Perhaps it is just as well for all of us, teachers and students alike, that serious moral examinations occur so rarely.

Joseph Katz

The Classroom: Personality and Interpersonal Relations

A great many college professors do not have an extended interest in exploring the ultimate effect of college education. This lack of interest is so striking that it cannot be explained simply as neglect. Nor can it be attributed merely to a hesitation to engage in self-study. It stems, rather, from a deep-lying philosophy—from the college teacher's conviction that the subject matter he teaches has absolute worth, quite aside from its effect on his students. Such a conviction is not free from half-conscious doubts, but it has strong roots nonetheless.

Characteristics of the College Teacher

The college teacher sees himself as offering knowledge of the world as he has grasped it. In presenting that knowledge, he regards any modification of it as a regrettable concession, a dilution which must be kept to the minimum. To resort to a metaphor, when the college teacher looks at himself he sees himself as a vendor standing at his stall in the fair of knowledge, confident in his specialty, and hopeful that those who can appreciate it will come and taste. In fact, each teacher's specialty gives him a primary focus in which to organize his life and make it meaningful. He is little trained, and often little disposed, to see the college student, who is not a specialist, in the student's own perspective. He is likewise ill-prepared to make the vital distinction between, on the one hand, advancing and preserving knowledge and, on the other, the process of educating others.

College teachers are highly professionalized in regard to the subject matter they teach. As educators, they are not professionalized. They do not know what the effects of their teaching are, for they lack systematic ways of gauging those effects. It follows that they have no reliable means for future improvements. Despite all this, given the influence that college teachers have or might have on their students, some sensitivity to human interactions may well come to be regarded as part of the teacher's job. But alternatives to increasing teachers' awareness need to be explored, too, for example, the careful placing of different kinds of students with appropriate kinds of teachers.

As a group, teachers share certain characteristics with the rest of society, and they have certain characteristics peculiar to themselves. One of the latter attributes is their ready acceptance of subordinate status. Ironically, the current agitation for higher salaries comes largely from outside the college faculties who themselves have only mildly supported it, even though griping about low pay is a staple of faculty conversation. Another general characteristic of teachers is a sense of separation from the rest of society. College teachers tend to view students as belonging to an alien, even a hostile culture. Their definitions of student recalcitrance vary; they may view it as a social or political phenomenon, as a purely anti-intellectual position, or even as an aesthetic reaction.

John Dewey has stated that one of the university's functions is to criticize the established order. But this critical function must be distinguished from the sense of social alienation that, in greater or lesser degree, seems to be a particular mark of faculty culture. This sense has been strengthened by the treatment college teachers have generally received from their administration as well as from their students. Indeed, faculty seem to feel at times that their situation is one of outright rejection, and the worst thing about it all is that many teachers implicitly accept this situation—if their passive response to it is any indication.

Let us turn now to the part the teacher plays in the classroom. He arrives in the classroom unprepared, not in his own knowledge, but for communication. The college teacher has probably never once analyzed systematically a single classroom hour to find out how effectively he can communicate. Instead, he relies on examinations, comments by students, and faculty remarks on what students have said. Some teachers occasionally pass a questionnaire around. Above all, there is the behavior of the class itself, quiet or restless, attentive or bored. But the skill and aptitude required to evaluate class reaction, and to differentiate individuals and groups in the class, are frequently lacking. Such clues as there are must be filtered through the teacher's anxiety, vanity, obtuseness, or optimism; and as a result they tend to confirm initial prejudices.

The Process of Becoming Deadwood

It is obvious that much here invites stagnation. The students are always of the same age group, between 17 and 21. They arrive in the professor's course with the same ignorance and naiveté as the class the year before, and instead of going on where he had left off the previous season, the professor has to start all over again. From time to time, he will meet a student one year out of college and the student with some wonder will ask: "Are you still teaching such and such course?" From the student's point of view this is a most reasonable question; for he has gone on to other things, with or without using what he heard in the course. The professor is still there, and will be there for decades to come.

The classroom, then, seems to offer insufficient challenge and stimulation to keep a teacher intellectually and emotionally alive. What is so frequently talked about as undergraduate apathy has its equivalent in the "deadwood" attitude which many college teachers share to a differing extent. The "deadwood" process is a special case of demoralization caused by conditions of work. This demoralization stems, in part, from ignorance about what is achieved in the classroom. Without a clear evaluation of the classroom process, almost anything seems to be acceptable, and in the end nothing seems to make much difference.

The absence of any mechanism for supervising or assessing the teacher is presented, in the prevailing ideology, as a condition of freedom and independence in teaching. But it has an unrecognized side effect in that it deprives most, if not all, teachers of a firm sense of accomplishment and a firm sense of mistakes from which to learn. Without assessment, teaching leads almost inevitably to a cycle of repetition. Only detailed, sophisticated, and continuing assessment can make the teaching experience a cumulative thing and thus instruct the instructor.

Strange as it may sound to the outsider, institutional devices for keeping the learning process alive for faculty are extremely underdeveloped on most campuses. The prevailing note is often one of isolation. Teachers are separated not only from their professional colleagues nationally, but even from departmental colleagues locally. When college departments get together in meetings, most of them spend less time discussing ideas than they do administrative questions, evaluations of students for grades and degrees, and planning who will teach what course.

It might be suggested that where people in a department can no longer spark each other, such devices as regular seminars attended by invited colleagues from elsewhere and periodic residences of "visiting firemen" might be of some value in counteracting intellectual isolation. Another source of learning may be colleagues in the other departments. Therefore colleges that have no graduate school attached are missing a unique opportunity. Where there are no graduate departments the faculties, because of their much lesser specialization, have an intriguing opportunity for investigating how knowledge and methods from differing fields can best be pooled. Here indeed there is open to the faculty a novel research function, quite beside the effect of interdepartmental learning on teaching and teachers. Finally, there could be more external devices, beginning with the stipulation that no professor repeat the same course too many times. Teachers might frequently give courses in departments other than their own, and the visiting and exchange system between schools could be organized on a systematic basis, enabling teachers to become acquainted with a variety of institutions and colleagues. A system of circulation may work as well for the college as for the carp pond.

The Classroom as the Teacher Sees It

Given the absence of clear-cut goals and of measures of progress toward them, college teachers are inclined to resort to magical thinking. Some, for instance, will assert that uncouth students benefit from simply being in a classroom; if the immediate results are meager, they are glossed over by reference to supposed long-range effects. In any event, the more cynical among teachers will see the value of college less in the subject matter of courses than in the discipline and self-denial learned incidental to obtaining a passing grade. Still more cynical ones see college as a convenient episode before entering father's business and the like.

It is a chastening experience for a professor to interview graduates several years after they left college, or to read a dossier of interviews conducted with students while they were still at school. Few indeed are the references to the classroom. Mention of teachers' personality characteristics, though rare too, is more frequent than reference to the content of courses.

It is not to be inferred from this that the influence of subject matter is a negligible one in American colleges. But the evidence indicates that, both in and after college, students do not tend to talk readily or at any length about their classroom experience, about the great and exciting ideas to which they have been introduced in course after course.

The problem is not fundamentally different from the one the Lynds posed concerning the Middletown high school in the 1920's. They wondered why, in a society where going to school is so highly valued, the academic contents of education are considered the special province of grinds and freaks, and why the athlete rather than the scholar is likely to be idolized.

Part of the answer lies of course in our popular culture. The American college curriculum, born of and shaped by the needs of a small, European, intellectual and managerial class, rests in the custody of teachers who tend to identify with that European class. It is presented, however, to youngsters who grow up in an adolescent world where the emphasis is on jobs, cars, sports, the fabulous intricacies of dating, and other adolescent adventures. And the adult society into which they grow is perhaps even less friendly to the values held by the colleges.

The Classroom from the Student's Point of View

Like the teacher, the student arrives in the classroom insufficiently prepared. Typically, he arrives after having been shuffled through a rather soulless and bureaucratic process of registration that is concerned with credit points, prerequisites, corequisites, grade point averages. He is herded into a frequently uncomfortable classroom, often assigned a seat, his attendance is checked, regular assignments are given, as well as frequent quizzes, tests, exams, and papers. His written work may be read not by his teacher but by arrogant or timid graduate students on whose desks there is always a groaning pile of unfinished blue or white books. Objective tests may be a further step in making learning impersonal. The whole process is recorded and presided over by the IBM machine which is increasingly taking the place of the registrar, who in the past was often a friendly human to whom students could turn in the process of grade-getting.

The students' individual evaluations of the entering teacher express a wide range of attitudes—from seeing the teacher as a representative of reality to seeing him as a representative of unreality, with the corresponding attitudes to his subject matter and his ways of presenting it. The members of the class will have common concerns about a teacher, with obvious variation in intensity. How is he going to grade? Is he going to work the class hard or not? How is he going to present his material, and what learning effort is he going to call forth from his students? A student's evaluation of his teacher is continuous. An initial liking of the teacher's quality as an entertainer may give way to the realization that this goes on at the expense of learning. For some students a course, and its teacher, jell only when review is made before the final examination. In retrospect, even years after, a course may be seen as hollow, which at the time it was taken seemed subtle and profound, an illusion created by the teacher's verbal agility or his seemingly meaningful obscurity.

One of the meanings of "good teacher" is that he is one who presents his subject matter in a clear and well-organized manner. Although some students like this kind of teacher, others may not. They feel he is too close to their level, and too pat. They may prefer the teacher who seems confused and to whom they have difficulty catching on. (This will tend to be the reaction of students who wish to learn rather than merely to pass the course.) Thus it is not so much the teacher's preoccupation with research as its lack of vitality that tends to interfere with teaching. Part of the criterion of good teaching is the degree of challenge, of opportunity for growth it provides.

Transference in the Classroom. It is frequently held that a teacher's enthusiasm is *a* major, if not *the* major, factor in arousing the enthusiasm of his students. The student's reaction to the teacher's enthusiasm is only one facet of a more complex and underlying phenomenon—the transference and countertransference relationships between teacher and student. (I borrow the term "transference" from the clinic. It needs to be redefined for the classroom.) The college teacher is a special transference object for his students. He is an "in between" object, in between parents and the adult relations the student will establish in and after college. College itself, for large numbers of students, means living away from home for the first time and thus is transitional between adolescence and adulthood. Teachers thus may become "associates" in the student's mind in his rebellion against his parents. As I have indicated, this is a role to which teachers often lend themselves readily, being frequently permanent rebels themselves. But teachers pay insufficient attention to the transitory nature of the student's rebelliousness. When the rebelliousness wanes, it is likely, therefore, to be replaced by renewed identification with the parent recently rebelled against. College teachers then are likely to throw up their hands in despair over students and alumni. All their efforts

seem to have been wasted. Yet what they missed was the opportunity to help the student find secure identities other than the traditional ones when he was seeking a new equilibrium. Other students react to teachers more as if they were their parents, and then
the brunt of rebelliousness against the parents will be experienced
by the teachers too. In other students there is a pre-rebellious at-
tachment or compliance. College teachers tend to take these very
varied reactions at their face value; that is, they see them as "objective" responses to themselves and their subject matter and then
adopt "objective" ways of dealing with them.

The intensity of the transference naturally varies with the
school and with individual students. Transference may be at a
minimum where the classroom is regarded as a nuisance in the
pursuit of socioeconomic advancement or of fun, as with the girl
attending a large university who exclaimed, "I love school, but I
hate classes!" But wherever learning takes place, the transference
reaction also has a certain intensity and calls forth all the variety
of manipulative, erotic, compliant, defiant, passive, aggressive, and
other reactions. These reactions both facilitate and interfere with
learning. Moreover, they color the learner's intellectuality to a
very significant degree. One wonders, for instance, whether the
blandness, or even sterility, of some work exhibited in professional
journals and meetings does not have a major root in the often very
frustrating transference situations of graduate school life.

Teachers, of course, do not do the only teaching on our college
campuses or even the main part of it. Students teach themselves and
each other, and this teaching, in and out of the classroom, is worthy
of detailed study. Communication among students varies from
classrooms where students function as individual units to classrooms where much concerted action is possible. Isolation of particular students is often a marked phenomenon. A most striking
phenomenon is the underdevelopment of direct communication
between class and teacher. The establishment of more conscious
and direct channels of communication and creating the atmosphere for such communication would seem to be beneficial for

teachers and students alike. As has been indicated, teachers are sensitive to certain cues from their classes, but to others they are not sensitive, and they too rarely seek to create new ones.

Classroom Types. It will be very desirable to develop a theory of classroom student types. First there is the student type mainly oriented toward passing the course. The second type is distinguished by his greater involvement or tenacity in scholastic matters. This is the student who seeks to control knowledge; on closer inspection he does not so much wish to know as he wishes to control. A third type is the curious student. Somewhere in the spectrum of this type falls the student whose curiosity can address itself realistically to subject matter and the problems and questions from which subject matter springs. In a fourth student type, strong personal orientation to the teacher predominates. The personal element is so strong as to put relation to subject matter in the shadow, so that it does not become an object of interest in its own right.

The fact that the college student is an adolescent, or recently was one, means that his intellectuality, even his whole personality, has a transitional character. Parents seem to know this better than teachers. They are apt to think of college as a "phase" whereas teachers are likely to cry "betrayal" when yesterday's student shows up as alumnus. College teachers, by seeing college as a phase, could help students utilize their rebellions and gropings more effectively, so that the college phase would be more fully a stage in development and less of an episode. Teachers may unwittingly make college more episodic by an emphasis on the discrepancy between the school and the outside world.

W. J. McKeachie

Approaches to Teaching

Teaching is the heart of higher education. The effectiveness of administrative organization or of curricular plans depends on whether they facilitate good teaching. In turn, the ultimate criteria of effective teaching are changes in students, changes toward whatever we want higher education to produce.

This brings us to the problem of *motivation*. We know that student learning and memory are closely tied to motivation. Students will learn what they want to learn; they will have great difficulty in learning material which does not interest them. Much as we would like to teach only students who are eager to learn, most of us have to recognize that not all our students will be deeply interested in everything we like to teach.

One of our primary problems, therefore, is how to motivate students. At this point the psychologist's interest in learning usually stops; yet, to be useful, the principle of motivating students must be supported by information on what students' motives potentially are. We know, for example, that most of our students are taught by their parents to want to do well in school. Thus we can count on some motivation for achievement. We know, too, that most of our students want to be liked. This motive, however, may work against us as well as for us. In some colleges students who want acceptance by their classmates avoid any conspicuous display of academic achievement. Many students suffer from real conflict between the need to get good grades and the need to be well liked.

Many of our students, thus, have conflicting motives. One common conflict is between independence and dependence. This means that students are likely to resent the teacher who directs their activities too closely, but they also are likely to be anxious when given independence. As a result of this conflict some students disagree with the teacher not from any rational grounds but simply as a way of expressing emotions.

Let us consider the case of our most potent motivational device—grades. If a student is really interested in learning, grades represent an expert's appraisal of his success; if he is interested in getting into professional school, good grades are the key that will unlock graduate school doors; if he wants to play football, grades are necessary for maintaining eligibility. The majority of students are motivated to get passing grades, if only to remain in college.

Most professors are a little embarrassed by this state of affairs. We regard grades as one of the necessary evils of teaching. We try to discount grades when we discuss the organization of the course, and we try to arrive at grades in such a way that we can avoid trouble with disappointed students. But we frequently fail to *use* grades to bring about the sort of learning we desire.

Because grades are important to them, students will learn whatever is necessary to get the grades they desire. If we base our grades on memorization of details, students will memorize the text. If they believe our grades are based on their ability to integrate and apply principles, they will attempt to do this too. In short, motivation depends a great deal on how the curriculum is *organized*. A teacher's job is not done when he interests his class; the amount they learn also depends on the amount he teaches, but the relation between the two is not a simple one. At a certain point it may well be that the more we teach, the less our students learn.

Several years ago some teaching fellows in psychology were arguing about how to present the nervous system. One group argued that since students would not remember all the details, they should omit them and teach only the basic essentials that everyone ought to know. Another group agreed that students would forget much of what they learned, but drew different conclusions: "if they are going to forget a large percentage, we need to teach much more detail than we expect them to remember." The combatants agreed that they would try their ideas in their own classes and compare the results on the final exam. The outcome was clear. The students whose instructor had omitted details were clearly superior to those whose instructor had given them the whole story.

Fortunately it is possible both to teach more and have it remembered better. The magic formula really is "organization." We can learn and remember much more when our learning fits into organization. Teaching that helps students find a framework within which to fit new facts is likely to be much more effective than teaching that simply communicates masses of material in which the student can see no organization. The ideal class would begin with a problem that was so meaningful that the students were always just a step ahead of the teacher in approaching a solution.

"Feedback," and active learning

If we expect students to learn skills, they have to practice, but practice doesn't make perfect. Practice only works when the learner learns the *results* of his practice, that is, if he receives feedback. One of the chief advantages of teaching machines is that the learner finds out quickly whether his response is right or wrong. Nevertheless, feedback is probably more important in learning new and superficial responses than in learning the real content of material.

A number of experiments have demonstrated that *active* learning—learning which demands student initiative—is more efficient than passive learning. One reason for this may be the improved opportunities for feedback in active learning. For example, discussion techniques may help develop intellectual skills because students actively do the thinking and there is an opportunity to check their thinking against others. On the other hand, a danger of "student-centered" or "nondirective" discussions is that the results are not apparent. Students may make comments, express opinions, and participate actively, but this does not guarantee that their opinions are any more informed at the end of a semester than they were at the beginning. Of course not all feedback has to come from the instructor, but in order to learn students need to test out their ideas in a situation in which the results are evident.

This brings us back to the question of motivation. To develop motivation we need to pose problems that are within the range of our students' abilities. Studies of childrens' desire to achieve indicate that parents can develop such motives by encouraging the child to do well and by setting standards that the child can attain. Thus, to inspire and help students to think critically, experience in solving problems within the student's ken is essential. This by no means implies that the student should never experience failure or criticism, but it does mean that he should be faced with problems that will, more often than not, be soluble.

It is a common misconception that a student's motives are fixed. We can teach students to enjoy learning for its own sake. Although we must make use of existing motives to create initial satisfactions in learning, we need not be limited by those motives.

TEACHING METHODS

Large Lectures vs. Small Discussions

One attractive solution to the problem of teaching more students is to replace some of our small discussion classes with larger lecture classes. This is often justified by the several studies that have found no significant difference in effectiveness between lecture and discussion.

The studies that have found differences, however, make surprisingly good sense. Two studies have found differences favoring the lecture method, but both of these used tests of knowledge of subject matter. Five experiments have found significant differences favoring discussion over lecture. All five used measures other than the usual final examination of knowledge.

Here as elsewhere there is no simple answer to the question, "What teaching method is best?" As this research indicates we have to counter the question with, "Best for what?" If our most important objective is transmitting information, we should probably use lecture (or reading) rather than discussion. If on the other hand, we are primarily concerned with teaching critical thinking, a change in attitudes, or other complex objectives, discussion appears to be the method of choice.

This conclusion is also supported by the recent experiments on class size carried out at Miami University. Large classes were virtually as effective as small classes in transmitting information, but small classes were more effective in producing changes in psychological misconceptions, problem-solving in marketing, and attitudes toward the courses.

Types of Discussion

One of the difficulties in evaluating comparisons of teaching methods is that a wide variety of kinds of teaching may be included under one label of "lecture" or "discussion." Discussions, for example, include everything from formless bull sessions to highly organized question-answer sessions. Fortunately there are a number of experimental studies comparing different styles of discussion. These too tend to come out with negative results, but once again there are occasional, significant differences, and these are consistent.

In eleven studies, marked differences in attitudes, in ability to apply concepts, or in group membership skills have been found between discussion techniques emphasizing freer student participation and those with stricter control by the instructor. In these studies the difference favored the more student-centered discussion.

Our consideration of lecture and discussion methods may be summed up by the phrase, "Examine your goals." College catalogs speak in glowing generalities about skill in the use of the intellect and preparation for personal responsibility. Knowledge is an important ingredient for achieving these goals, but to promote the fullest intellectual development we must use methods which give students an opportunity to practice thinking for themselves. Before committing ourselves to one pattern of instruction we need to analyze the specific aims of each course and the way in which various teaching techniques and aids can best achieve each objective.

Television

The most widely publicized solution to the problem of teaching greater numbers of college students has been the use of closed-circuit television to enable a single teacher to reach several class-rooms. Although some experiments were not well enough designed to permit evaluation of their results, there are probably more good comparisons of television and live instruction than of any other college teaching methods. The results are also much more consistent than are any other comparisons. Of the thirty college experiments in which there were adequate controls, twenty-four indicated greater learning in the "live" class than in those taught by television. Most of these differences were not statistically significant by themselves but their consistency *is* statistically significant.

Independent Study

One of the most appealing methods of solving the impending faculty shortage is to reduce the number of hours in which teachers and students meet.

Unfortunately the potential advantages of giving students independent study do not seem to have been achieved in most experiments. Not only do students not learn any more; they also fail to develop independence.

Encouraging results, however, were obtained in experiments on independent study at the University of Colorado. Here students continued to meet their instructors in weekly classes and were free to consult them whenever they desired. Actual reduction of contact hours was only about 10 per cent. With this fairly high degree of instructor supervision, students discussing problems in student-led discussion groups were superior to their conventional classmates in making difficult applications, in learning new materials, and in curiosity.

Independent study thus holds promise, but it is still no panacea. What is more, there is another factor which complicates the simple decision to inaugurate independent studies on a large scale. Evidence from studies at Michigan, Antioch, and Oberlin suggests that some students are better able to profit from independent study than others. Unfortunately there are no reliable ways of identifying these students in advance. Moreover, even if we could pick them out, we do not have well-tested methods of training students to do independent work. We still need more research.

Teaching Machines

Another hope for saving faculty time is the teaching machine or programmed book. When presentation by teaching machine or programmed system is compared with the usual textbook approach, the programmed material tends to be superior for retention but inferior in speed of learning. Programs which provide special review or "skip" sequences for the poorer or better students sometimes tend to improve learning as compared with rigid "linear" programs; whereas the kind of intellectual response elicited does not seem to make much difference in the sort of learning required by most college courses. Thus it may well be simply a waste of time to require the student to write out the answers to questions. In fact it appears that learning proceeds more rapidly if the materials to be learned are presented in statement rather than question form. (Whether or not this is all a reflection on the "fact-feeding" nature of most college courses does not affect the teaching machine's efficiency at serving courses as they are.)

Little research has been done to determine what kinds of students learn well or poorly from teaching machines. We might expect that the practice of writing programs so that every question is answered correctly by every student would be boring to most students, particularly to those with strong achievement motivation. (And indeed one study shows that the latter type of student is most highly motivated where the truth is uncertain.)

SUMMARY

When we ask what teaching method is most effective, we need to consider four factors:

1. Effectiveness depends on one's objective. Lectures, for example, are effective for teaching knowledge but not for teaching critical thinking.

2. Effectiveness depends on the instructor. Some instructors are enthusiastic about television; most are not.

3. Effectiveness depends on the student. A type of student who profits from one method may do poorly when taught by another method that is effective for another type of student.

4. Effectiveness depends on the subject matter. Some material may be especially fitted for teaching machines or another method; other material may not.

THE ROLE OF FACULTY ATTITUDES

What can we say about the work of the teacher? Clearly it is not possible to detail in a few summary statements the "best" methods of teaching. Nevertheless, recent research suggests that the choice of teaching method employed does make a difference educationally. The precise effects of any one method will, of course, depend on the student, the course content, the instructor, and the overall "climate" of the college. To analyze such complexities would obviously be a task for a giant computer.

In the absence of the data necessary for such an analysis, we must, as in other frontier areas, depend on expert judgment. Unfortunately, most studies of teaching fail to report the reactions of teachers themselves, except for television where reactions are generally negative. Faculty comments on teaching methods are extremely important, however, *quite aside from* their possible validity as expert judgments, because the effectiveness of a method surely depends on the competence and enthusiasm of the teacher. If the teacher is important, his very enjoyment of the method becomes a critical factor. Even if we found that a particular method was superior to any other when used ideally, this author would still be dubious about urging its widespread adoption if teachers using it become bored or dissatisfied.

What are the satisfactions in teaching? Certainly one is the pleasure of seeing a student develop. Another is the pleasure of intellectual interchange with young people possessing questioning minds and fresh ideas. A less laudable but equally real satisfaction is the acquisition of disciples who respect and admire us.

These satisfactions are difficult to secure without close and sustained personal contact with students. To know students well enough to see their progress, we must have small classes, not only because they permit more individual interaction with students but also because they let the instructor use term papers, essay tests, and other evaluation methods in a way that gives him greater understanding of what the student is thinking.

Moreover, if the satisfaction of *seeing* students develop is important to the teacher, we must create opportunities for contact between instructor and student over a period longer than a one-semester course. One advantage of the small college over the large university is that the student in a small college not only is more likely to come into contact with his instructor outside the classroom but also is more likely to elect later courses from the same professor. And in a community where professors know most of the students, professors are more likely to discuss students with other professors. In a large university, by contrast, the professor may teach a student one semester and never see him again. He is very unlikely to discuss the student with other professors because he does not know which colleagues know the student.

If the size of a college is important to faculty-student relationships, it is also important to the quality of education students receive from each other. On the one hand, the large university with a diverse student population offers its members the chance to gain breadth, tolerance and new perspectives from their contacts one with another. On the other hand, large size is likely to reduce intellectual exchange between students. Granted, there is nothing to prevent the student at a large college from discussing with a friend interesting problems raised by his professors. But he is probably more likely to do so if he lives near another student concerned about the same things; and in a large college the statistical chances that another student in the same class will be in the same living group are smaller than in a small college. Students in a large college with many courses, even those students in different sections of the same course, have few common intellectual experiences. As a result it is difficult for them to communicate about intellectual problems outside class, and the common concerns which become the basis of social communication are football, the student newspaper, dating, and dormitory food.

With such barriers to inter-student education, the professor misses the good feeling one experiences when he finds that his teaching has provided an intellectual stimulus reaching far beyond his classroom. Of course there are also satisfactions in teaching a large class, as there are in teaching by television. One can gain a very satisfying sense of power from knowing that he is communicating ideas to a large number of students. Where the lecture is televised, the "Master Teacher" can get satisfaction from carrying through a well-planned lesson without interruption. And where "live" audiences are concerned, the roar of laughter to a joke well-told can be music to a lecturer's ear.

All are real satisfactions but they seem less directly related to the goals of education than the satisfactions that come from observing student development. What *would* a college be like if the pleasure its faculty got from teaching was mainly that of the good performer?

As colleges increase in size to cope with a growing student population, there is a natural tendency to automate educational processes for the sake of increased efficiency. In industry, assembly-line methods have long been effective. Yet in recent years firms have found that workers are even more efficient if instead of performing one specific, repetitive task their jobs are enlarged enough to provide variety and interest. Although there is little likelihood that college administrators will intentionally insist on uniform teaching methods, increasing class size indirectly limits the professor's choice of teaching methods, reducing his ability to select the methods best suited for his objectives and reducing his satisfaction in teaching.

That the teacher should enjoy his teaching is doubly important —important not only because his enthusiasm may spread to his students, but because his interest will inspire him to keep on improving his methods. These important effects are quickly lost when teaching becomes so routine and impersonal that it is no longer fun. By contrast, the motivated teacher, responding to feedback from his students, can develop his skill continually. And as knowledge about teaching accumulates, his rate of improvement should increase.

Joseph Katz and Nevitt Sanford

Curriculum and Personality

Despite its central place in the college program, the curriculum has rarely been systematically investigated. There is, of course, a vast literature on the curriculum, but most of it describes existing programs and proposals for reform rather than the effects of the curriculum on students.

It seems to have been almost universally assumed by educators that the college curriculum, as presently constituted, defines the goals of achievement for the student and that the nature of the curriculum is to be largely determined by whatever is the present state of the "body of knowledge." This assumption usually implies (1) an identification of the "body of knowledge" with the curriculum of the graduate school, a very debatable identification, and (2) only very limited attention to the role of such knowledge in the whole *development* of the student. It is usually very glibly assumed that the better the mental capacities of the student, the more he will assimilate of the "body of knowledge," and that the more he absorbs, the better for him.

PRACTICAL AND IMAGINATIVE FUNCTIONS OF KNOWLEDGE

Knowledge performs for man two main functions—the practical and the imaginative. In its practical function knowledge acts in the service of man's survival and his successful mastery of the environment. In this attempt at mastery it confronts two worlds: the outer world, comprising both nature and human society, and the inner world of impulses. The attempt to understand these inner and outer forces has always characterized the pursuit of knowledge. It has not always taken a form, however, that contemporary canons of scientific inquiry would approve of.

The other side of the intellectual pursuit has been an imaginative extension of the real world. "Poetry" originally meant "making," and here as elsewhere intellect has served in the making of new worlds. This imaginative extension of reality has really served two quite different purposes: (1) the enrichment of reality by lifting the person beyond sensuous and practical immediacy, and (2) the provision of a vehicle for withdrawing from reality. The fundamental difference between the two purposes is that the second is served at the expense of the individual's vital and essential relations with reality, whereas the former is not.

Since imagination is necessary to master the real world, there is no clear distinction between the practical and the imaginative dimensions of knowledge. The phantasies of the prophet or the plans of the architect—even when they seem to defy gravity—have often become tomorrow's reality. Thus imagination seems to be both a dependent and an independent entity in the make-up of human personality. In its dependent function it serves the purposes of mastering reality. In its independent function it is close to being, and perhaps is, a primary need. Even the most prosaic task can scarcely be performed without some admixture of imagination.

If we are interested in freeing the imagination, opening the individual to experience, and encouraging creativity and spontaneity, we have no recourse but to free the individual's impulse life. And here lies a central problem for the educator, because modern schools, and perhaps even colleges, are largely concerned with suppressing a student's impulses, while building up to the highest degree possible his self-control. Much of this is necessary, but the fact is that unless a person's impulses are freed in certain directions—including the direction of phantasy—he will lack the spontaneity with which creative imagination is intimately linked. The educator's job, therefore, should be to show the student that his childhood impulses can indeed find gratification in the world of literature and drama and art, and in creative activity in science.

At the same time we must recognize that knowledge of facts may be acquired now and stored, only to bear fruit later in some fresh insight or some creative achievement of the individual. Much college education, indeed, is based on the assumption that such acquisition of knowledge may eventually serve the individual. Surely this does happen, but it is easy to overestimate the frequency of such occurrences.

CLASSROOM PRESENTATION

In discussing the effects of curriculum, we need to distinguish between content and mode of presentation. Although mode of presentation is related to subject matter, quite different subjects may have similar modes. It would certainly not be easy to teach English as one teaches, say, chemistry, but it could be done if the teacher were determined. Some ways of teaching favor the development of personality while others have the opposite effect.

Modes That Hinder Development

Let us first concentrate on the modes that hinder development. Many of these methods serve a common ideal of discipline and hard work, although in practice they may be more lenient. With the birth of the sputniks, however, and the unprecedented mass influx of students seeking college degrees, discipline has been tightened.

To enforce *external* discipline, the grading system can be used as a stick. Likewise, the "weekly quiz," demanding the regular collection of tidbits of knowledge, ensures that work (of some kind) goes on unabated. Idleness is the archenemy of any compulsive system, and the students are kept so busy that on many campuses it is becoming harder to make an appointment with a student than with a professor.

A further common characteristic of teaching methods hostile to real development is the emphasis on "right" answers. The student gets the notion that there is only one answer or at best a very limited set of right answers, to any one question, that the teacher is in possession of these answers, and that he expects the student to produce them.

Impersonality is a third factor hindering development. In interviews with students we have found that students almost universally link their most significant educational experiences to teachers with whom they have had some personal relation in and out of the classroom. Even in a class of 100 or more students, learning seems to be aided a great deal if the student can establish some sort of personal relationship with the professor. This is easier to do when the teacher's own personality is very vivid. And if a student plans to enter the professor's field of specialization, anticipation of a professional bond with the teacher may well make the student feel a personal relationship, even though, from the professor's standpoint, no such relationship exists.

Development is also hampered by a purely abstract approach to the subject matter. This has been given much attention, and many teachers and programs have tried strenuously to tie subject matter to concrete events, particularly events which may crop up in the student's own future experience. When this is done, however, it often means that the teacher implants a stereotype of what the student's future will be, rather than drawing on the student's very real, *present* experience and his current interests.

Excessive emphasis on method of inquiry per se and excessive pigeonholing of subjects represent two other enemies of development. The importance attached to method becomes excessive when a student is taught more details of method than he needs for his level of inquiry. Such excess is due both to the sophistication that procedures have achieved in all fields of learning and to the purism of many teachers, particularly teachers who are at the same time researchers. It is likely to leave the student at first frustrated and then either indifferent or intransigent.

Pigeonholing springs in part from the fact that universities have departments, and departments govern the curriculum. Only occasionally will teachers report, with agreeable surprise, that a student has related something from another course. Apparently students tend first to segment information from the rest of their personality, and then to segment departments of information from each other. The knowledge taught the student by outside agents—course lectures and required reading—is seldom really connected with the student's own spontaneous thought. As a result he feels that he can remember his "course material" more easily if he leaves it in the compartmentalized form in which he received it. Pigeonholed and temporarily forgotten, it is only to be drawn upon when the schoolroom bell rings for it again.

Modes that Assist Personality Development

The pursuit of objectivity is a major factor in developing personality. Yet perceptions of reality that are undistorted by wishes and anxieties are one of the hardest things for the human organism to acquire. The emphasis on objective evidence that pervades much of our college teaching is an important antidote to distortion. Intellectual mastery—particularly when a college student discovers his ability in a subject hitherto unknown to him —may become a basis for revision of his self-image and of much of his inner and outer life. Furthermore, by broadening his knowledge of what human experiences are possible, the individual can be stimulated to fresh experiences of his own.

The pursuit of objectivity requires joint attention to the student's impulse and to his thought. Otherwise the two will neither combine nor balance; and the individual will be in effect two men, an emotional man dominated by impulse and an intellectual man dominated by thought. This, in fact, is the life story of many a liberal.

We have so far spoken of the pursuit of objectivity and logic as an individual experience. It can also be a social experience— learning with and in view of others. Our school setup tends to make the curriculum competitive, by contrast with many extracurricular activities which are cooperative. Under certain circumstances classroom learning can impress upon the student *both* the fundamental otherness of his fellow and the communication that is possible with him. We do not mean a superficial other-directedness, but rather that community which thrives best when its members have achieved their own distinctively separate identities. In contrast, present classrooms are characterized by a high degree of isolation of students from each other, an ironic corollary of students' failure to develop individually.

Another ally of the developing personality is learning to think by hypothesis. Hypotheses begin in hunches and require free association of ideas as a necessary condition. A man can only produce hypotheses if he is willing to relate subjects that superficially may seem quite *un*related. Some teachers maintain that it is precisely this profusion of phantasy that needs to be disciplined. But when they argue thus, what they really have in mind is not the result of phantasy per se but woolly, vacuous abstractions that have lost any clear and logical connection with the impulsive hunch that prompted them.

THE CURRICULUM

Content: The Freshman Curriculum

It is in the freshman year that the failures of today's curricula are most glaring. Typically, freshmen arrive on the campus filled with enthusiasm, in eager anticipation of the intellectual experiences they are about to have. By the end of the year not a few have dropped out and a large proportion of the remainder are ready for what in the Eastern colleges is known as the "sophomore slump."

At Vassar it was found that the "sophomore slump" occurred in the spring of the freshman year. This at least was a period of considerably reduced academic interest and effort, accompanied by a dawning awareness that college was not coming up to advanced billing, and that the exciting experiences would have to be postponed until a girl entered her major program. At Berkeley, on the other hand, one did not hear of a sophomore slump. Perhaps students enter with smaller expectations or fewer illusions than in other liberal arts colleges; or perhaps the game of getting good grades or staying in college to graduate, whichever the aspiration, is played with the same coolness year in and year out. Listen to the talk on the campus:

> I wanted to take 10-B this fall so I could get into 116 next year but the only section I could fit into my schedule was filled; so I'm going to take 7-A and get that out of the way. Did you know that you could substitute 24-C for 22-D and count it toward your natural science requirements? Freshmen can take it with permission of the instructor. That's where all the Phys. Ed. majors go.

We are dealing here, of course, with the common or traditional type of curriculum, drawn up with a minimum of attention to how students learn, but a maximum of concern with how knowledge may be organized on paper, and how the departments' privileges may be represented. There are so many breadth or distribution requirements, so many prerequisites for courses that the student thinks he will want to take later, that for many students the whole freshman year is taken up with "necessary evils," and for most there are no courses that can be regarded as ends in themselves.

The point is sometimes made that existing arrangements serve well to "weed out" inferior students. At some state universities, indeed, there is weeding out with a bulldozer. But nobody knows how many potential learners go out along with the unable and the indifferent; nor do we know to what extent remaining in college is a matter of gamesmanship or capacity to adapt oneself to conventional pressures.

Existing programs are easy to criticize. What is to be done? We suggest that, where the foremost concern is with the development of personality, the major aim of the freshman year should be to *win* the student to the intellectual enterprise. With full recognition of the fact that for many it is now or never, every effort should be made to capture the student's imagination, to give him a sense of what it means to become deeply involved in a discipline or subject, to learn things that make a difference in his life, to be a member of a community that is devoted to the pursuit of truth.

Most essentially, the student must be shown that college edu-

cation is a means for the expression of his impulse life, an opportunity for gratifying his natural curiosity, and not merely a
set of painful tests designed to make him more appreciative of
his college degree. As educators we should ignore conceptions of
what freshmen "ought to know," whether the concern be with
their preparation for more advanced courses or with a suitable
sampling of organized knowledge. We should concentrate instead on giving these students experiences that set in motion the
development we want.

Each course should be conceived as an end in itself. To repeat
a point, it should be designed first and foremost to develop the
complete personality, and to do this the freshman course must be
geared to the freshman's stage of development. Subject matter
has a crucial role to play, but the results that we seek will have
little to do with "how much is covered."

There is irony in the fact that when we teach elementary courses
we tend to look ahead to the advanced ones, asking ourselves what
information is likely to be required, and supposing that we can
impress the teachers of these advanced courses with how much
our students know. Yet when we teach advanced courses, we frequently assume that very little has been learned in the elementary
ones; and so, to make sure of "proper coverage," we proceed to
teach what all the students have had before.

The relation of high school courses to college courses, and
college courses to graduate courses, is much the same. We have,
for example, little notion of what undergraduate courses make the
best preparation for graduate work in psychology. There is nothing, in fact, to suggest that undergraduate psychology is best;
indeed, some psychologists prefer students who have had little
or no psychology but much literature, philosophy, mathematics,
and biological science.

A Comparison

In discussing the psychological functions of course content, it
must be remembered that the official titles of college courses give

only the crudest idea of what particular teachers actually *do* in any particular course or section thereof. Broadly speaking, however, we can say that literature courses hold more appeal for the impulse life than does, for instance, chemistry. It goes without saying that chemistry can, and should, involve highly creative work, but for this to happen extra effort must be made to encourage spontaneous impulse.

We might range subjects by their proximity to the life of the imagination and in such a list we would proceed from subjects like English, to sociology, to physics. This is not an evaluative ranking, but simply an indication of proximity to direct appeal to impulse and feelings. Ideally, a student would broaden his impulse life through subjects that evoke impulse; at the same time he would turn analyst and become more aware of his impulses by his contact with behavioral science and would sharpen his hold on reality by contact with natural science.

Once the teacher of any subject grasps the theory of personality development, he may devise his own ways of using his course material for the student's development.

The group of subjects that can most easily free the impulse life consists not only of literature but also the arts. Let us concentrate for the moment on literature. Let us assume, furthermore, that literature will be taught in the proper way—that the teacher will have his students understand characters before judging them. The student's natural inclination, of course, is to judge characters in literature, as well as elsewhere, by the values that he brings to college. If his anxiety is so great that he cannot tolerate any change in these values, he will not do well in literature.

If, on the other hand, he discovers that *anything* can be done in the imagination, that everything that he has so far imagined has been done by somebody, and that those who did these things can be understood, he is bound to admit into his own scheme of things a broader range of human potentialities. These potentialities he can see as present in himself as well as in others.

The point about literature is not simply that it releases fundamental impulses to be expressed in their original fundamental form—this could hardly be called freedom. Instead, it gives the individual some of the very thing that made the creation of that literature possible. It supplies a vehicle for transforming the impulse life in such a way that it meets the requirements of reality and of conscience, *but meets them just barely*. If such transformation occurs through the study of literature, it will affect the individual's performance in his other courses and his life generally. In other words, change wrought by education in one discipline ramifies throughout the personality and affects ways of responding to any discipline.

We spoke earlier of the need to challenge a student's *cognitive structures*—his ethical principles, his concept of the world and himself—with which he enters college. These structures undoubtedly derive mainly from family and community; many have been taken over automatically and have not been the object of the student's own thought and experience. Here it would seem that the study of philosophy, comparative religion and the history of ideas is nicely calculated to provide the necessary challenge, for one of philosophy's principal aims is to instill the notion that all systems of beliefs and concepts are tentative and flexible, and that at various points they have their equivalents in other systems. In the same manner, by studying comparative religion the great variety of beliefs which have called forth men's emotion can be examined. Such study can bring about understanding where the student might have felt strangeness or even repugnance before.

Of course the values and beliefs with which students leave college are often not very different from the values and beliefs with which they enter college. There is, however, the possibility that these values and beliefs are now held in a different way, that they have a firmer basis in the subject's own experience and thought, and hence a different relation to other processes of the personality. It might also be expected that, regardless of what his values and beliefs at the moment actually are, he has the means for improving his decisions in this area as time goes on.

Let us now turn to mathematics and natural science. As they are so often taught today these subjects help to maintain within the individual a defense mechanism, playing into the hands of the conventional, the restrictive, the suppressive functions of a personality. Study in mathematics and science can all too easily help turn out a well-disciplined, well-controlled, well-behaved young lady or young man who grimly accepts the formulas, memorizes a mass of factual material, and hands in meticulous lab reports. But things do not have to be this way. The teaching of science can convey a spirit rather than simply facts or precise techniques: it can lead the student along side avenues of curiosity as well as immerse him in one discipline.

Science, after all, is out to upset the existing order of things. It is essentially daring and unconventional. Its rules and discipline derive out of its own processes and needs and have nothing to do with conventional morality. Many young people who choose science, however, hope thereby to capitalize on their prematurely organized consciences. When science is chosen for this reason, when its discipline is used to support the suppressing and controlling functions of the personality, it is not likely to free the individual later on. Would it not be better both for science and for society to recruit those students who demand freedom, who are passionate and curious and out to discover and to change the world? Only then, having found such students, should we teach the necessary disciplines.

CONDITIONS OF CURRICULAR REFORM

It is seldom realized just how potent the curriculum can be in developing personality. The modern curriculum's failure to realize this potential stems from the fact that its high priests make no sophisticated attempt to contact the student's impulse life.

To revise the curriculum we must obtain at least four conditions: (1) Clearer articulation than we now have of different approaches to teaching. (2) The development of a *curricular science*, a continuing process of experimentation guided by theory. Needless to say, the prescriptions pointed to by such experiments would be useless if they were not constantly injected into the curriculum. (3) Self-examination of teachers. (4) Recognition that any curriculum will have a different impact on different students.

Adequate redefinitions of the curriculum, therefore, will have to wait for the future, but a beginning can always be made on the basis of past experience and present institutional patterns. The field is wide open to the exercise of imaginative and experimental skills.

Robert H. Knapp

Changing Functions of the College Professor

About a quarter of a million Americans today are engaged in college and university teaching. They constitute a professional class, impressive both in numbers and in its potential influence on the shaping of American civilization. Nor is that number and influence likely to decline in future decades. The Federal Office of Education estimates, perhaps rather generously, that present numbers may well double in the next decade.

The rise of this profession in recent years has been sensationally rapid. At the turn of the century the country had about 20,-000 college teachers; even the college student population was less than today's teacher population. Forty years later Charles Beard could observe that college professors "represented a larger proportion of the population set aside for scholarly pursuits than had been the case since the dissolution of monasteries and convents." In short, a vast and historically unique professional class had emerged in American society.

The college professor in America has been asked to perform three quite disparate functions: first, original research; second, the imparting of knowledge; and third, the inculcation of values and the development of character. According to time and circumstances, the relative weight of these functions has varied, but even so, most of the paradoxes and vicissitudes of the profession have resulted from the inherent difficulty in mixing all three. In the long run the character-developing function of the American professor has declined, whereas his research and informational functions have grown apart to form two quite distinct callings.

During the seventeenth and eighteenth centuries, and the first half of the nineteenth, the central focus of the American university remained relatively unchanged. It maintained a clear commitment to "classical" education, placing heavy emphasis on Greek, Latin, history, theology, and other subjects particularly germane to the clerical calling. The professor in this phase of development was, by all modern standards, an intellectual generalist who might at once profess natural history, ethics, and theology while remaining a Latin or Greek scholar.

In the latter half of the nineteenth century, however, several new factors appeared that had profound effects on the professor's role. The first of these was the rise of state-supported institutions, stimulated particularly by the Morrill Land-Grant College Act of 1862. This development can be seen as a sort of secularization process; higher education now became deeply concerned with technology, science, and other practical affairs, while the older clerical and classical emphasis was largely superseded. Closely related with this change was the rise of natural science, in itself a major trend. Finally, there was the emergence of the elective curriculum whereby students gained some freedom to choose courses. Originating at Harvard but quickly spreading elsewhere, the elective system went hand in hand with the rise of science, the crumbling of the old classical domination, and the growth of departmentalism.

These, then, were the main developments affecting American higher education during the late nineteenth century. Although they did not strike every institution equally, their impact on the college teaching profession was to be immense.

And what after the turn of the century? First, as we have already noted, there was a clear decline in the character-developing function so vital to American colleges and universities during the period of close religious control. The causes of this were several, but the principal one was the diffuse secularization which gradually and progressively took hold of American higher education. As the college professor increasingly concentrated on imparting technical and compartmentalized information, the supervision of character development passed through a period of neglect. Presently, however, the development of student character found new custodians—the counsellor, the campus psychiatrist, the specialist in guidance. In some institutions, to be sure, the professor is still held responsible for inculcating morals and even religious convictions, but for the most part his character-developing function has become purely passive—the setting of a good example.

A second major trend since 1900 has been the rise of the doctrine of academic freedom. Younger members of the profession frequently assume that in appealing to this principle they are invoking an ancient and honored tradition in American higher education. Such is clearly not the case. Prior to the First World War the idea had little currency, and surely little force. The rise of the doctrine of academic freedom has done much to bolster a sense of security and dignity among college professors at a time when other forces have tried to restrict their freedom.

A third significant development since the turn of the century has been the sprouting of professional societies, and the tendency of professors to identify with their disciplines rather than their colleges. Here, as in other university developments, science has been in the vanguard. Another trend, in somewhat similar spirit, has been the rising importance of research and publication as marks of professional success and as the avenue to promotion and advancement. This is often the sole criterion on which employment in colleges and universities is granted or withheld. As a consequence, there has developed, particularly among younger members of the profession, an almost obsessive concern with early and persistent publication. This concern is supported by the entire pattern of doctorate training which is now the major pathway to admission into the profession of college teaching. Today the Ph.D. is aptly named the "union card" of the professor. Admittedly, a man can still become a professor without a Ph.D., but his opportunities are largely limited to the smaller and less illustrious colleges.

A more difficult trend to document or prove is the decline of the college professor's influence in public affairs. We should also note in this context that the political allegiance of the college professor has been, for a group of his education and class origins, far to the left of other professions. Over the past few decades, college professors generally have been Democrats rather than Republicans.

In the affairs of his own institution, the college teacher is rarely entrusted with the formation of top-level educational policy. That function is assumed by presidents and boards of trustees, who themselves are frequently ignorant about the immediate and vital problems of education. The result in many colleges has been resentment and feelings of humiliation among the faculty. It has raised the question of academic freedom and posed a sharp contrast between that ideal autonomy cherished by the professor and his actual subservience to administrative mandate.

A View of the Future

Future changes in the role of the college professor in American society will no doubt resolve at least one of the foregoing dilemmas, however unsatisfactorily. If present developments are continued, I cannot doubt that the pastoral or character-developing function which dominated the sectarian institutions of this country in the eighteenth and nineteenth centuries will be increasingly delegated to specialists. Bureaus of vocational and personal guidance seem likely to burgeon for a long while, and the professor will probably be called on less and less to concern himself with the individual character development of his students.

It is further expected that unless present trends are reversed a segment of the college teaching profession will cut themselves off from the main body of the profession and become a class dedicated principally to research and only incidentally to instruction. If this be so, the insistent demands for "creative research" from the general run of college professors is likely to subside, especially if, as projected, their number will almost double in the next decade.

Thus for most college professors teaching may well become the prime function. Ever more devoted to the work of instruction, and ever more bureaucratized in that work, they will steadily relinquished all hopes of scholarly attainment. Only rare individuals, placed in fortunate circumstances, will be able to achieve the ideal unity that combines character development, academic instruction, and research.

It will probably prove most difficult to reunite the teaching and research functions. Government and industrial research contracts, coupled with the growth of special research units within the university, threaten to disengage the teacher from original scholarship. This tendency, already marked in the natural sciences, is beginning to affect the social sciences; eventually it may even dominate the humanities. If the trend continues, it will seriously impair both the recruitment and the intellectual development of high-quality teachers. It will require planning, resourcefulness, and determination if the college professor is to unite creatively the two functions—teaching and research—as he once did.

Fortunately, the problem of how to combine academic instruction with character development should prove somewhat easier than that of how to combine instruction and research. The first problem was partly engendered by a peculiar psychology which has dominated American higher education for some decades but is now declining. This psychology, formally enunciated by John Watson, curiously neglected the more involved aspects of personality and learning. It presented man in general, and his education in particular, in a piecemeal and depersonalized form; it did not make much connection between academic education and personality. This tide of thought has now, I believe, spent itself. More educators today appreciate that the relations between teacher and student affect the latter's whole growth, both in intellect and in personality. It is now also quite widely recognized that intellectual learning, in turn, can have a marked influence on emotional fulfillment.

To reunite the professor's instructional and character-building functions, however, the very organization of teaching will have to be changed. At present most students see little of their professors and only then in large, impersonal classes. It is, alas, quite possible for a professor to teach in an American university without knowing personally a single one of his undergraduates. As long as such conditions remain, we will never reunite character development and academic training.

Five
Student Society and Student Culture

T. M. Newcomb

Student Peer-Group Influence

Birds of a feather flock together, and the kind of feathering that seems to be most essential for the human species is that of interests. According to this truism, people are most likely to interact and in all probability to develop close relationships when a shared interest in some aspect of their common environment brings them together.

Common interests include common problems, although of course only those that are not too private. The problems of the late adolescent in our society may not be harder to bear than those of other age groups, but many of them are the kind that invite college students to share them with each other. One such problem is frequently the struggle for independence. By its very nature this problem can be shared more with peers than with parents or teachers. In college, moreover, most students for the first time find themselves cut off from intimacies with adults; they probably see little of their parents, and their teachers neither invite intimacies nor welcome students into faculty society.

Such a combination of circumstances is hardly calculated to aid the student in his search for identity, precisely at the time when he is least certain about it. Small wonder, then, that students tend to be drawn together; their common problems and their relative isolation from nonstudents make them ready material for the formation of strong peer groups. Membership in a peer group is more likely to influence directly students' attitudes than their general skills, specific capacities, or basic personality traits.

There are at least four fairly well-established conditions that promote student peer groups' influence on their members' attitudes. No one of them is an essential condition; perhaps any single one of the conditions, under exactly the right circumstances, might prove effective in the absence of the others. When marked peer-group effects have been noted, however, it has been most common to find several or all of these conditions obtaining.

Size of Groups. By itself, membership in very large populations is not likely to bring about the strong interpersonal relationships that are so important an ingredient in peer-group effects on
attitudes. In fact small groups—entities where interpersonal relationships *can* be established—often transmit the attitudes for
which a larger population (like "the college") stands. Membership in the college population without the small groups' mediation
would probably not mean much.

Homogeneity. A second condition involves the relative simi-
larity of group members. Homogeneity of age, sex, social class, or
religious affiliation contributes to effective peer-group influence,
primarily because a homogeneity of *attitudes* tends to go along
with such similarities.

The group, in turn, that appears to agree in attitudes is all the
more likely to convince the individual that such attitudes are
"right." Closely related to this factor is the condition of *isolation*
—relative isolation from groups with other norms. Here we mean
physical isolation rather than a cutoff in real communication.

When we think of the role of peer groups in education, we note
that the condition of isolation produces a wry effect. Faculty
members frequently bemoan the directions in which the peer
group seems to be taking its members; we even wonder why student values are not more thoroughly permeated with our own.
Yet by contributing to students' isolation from ourselves we actually nourish the object of our complaint.

Importance to Individuals of Group-Supported Attitudes.
The final condition of peer-group effectiveness is obvious—the
importance to individual members of group-supported attitudes.
Other things being equal, the greater the importance attached
to attitudes for which the group stands, the greater will be the
group's solidarity. Whether the group itself engenders a high
premium on group attitudes, or whether the individual valued
group attitudes highly even before he became a member, the con-

nection between group solidarity and the importance attached to group attitudes will remain.

The Impact of Peer Groups. Among faculty members there is a strong assumption that the "quality of the college product" is more fully accounted for by characteristics that individual students initially bring to college than in any other single way. A great number of us, furthermore, assume that peer-group influence comes second in importance, leaving professorial tutelage in third-rank place.

When we assign these relative weights it does not mean that we are necessarily denigrating our own roles as educators. The characteristics of new students (intelligence level, for example) are indeed important, but not necessarily because they remain unaltered through college. On the contrary, the importance of some initial characteristics lies in their capacity to produce and accommodate *change*. In these instances, professors may provide the necessary mechanism for bringing about change.

And if, as seems to be the case, peer groups are also potent sources of change, our task as educators may be stated as follows: how can we ensure that student potential for change and peer groups' power to induce change will be most likely to serve our educational objectives?

As student bodies in most American colleges have become larger and less homogeneous, there has correspondingly arisen a kind of academic anonymity. The majority of students develop friendships with others whom they know as persons but not as students (in the scholastic sense). If peer groups include individuals who are sharing the excitement of academic-intellectual discovery, it is almost a matter of chance. Over the past few decades, individual students who know each other well, and who are important to each other outside the classroom, have become less and less likely to share excitement *within* the same classroom. There are exceptions, but they are all too infrequent; in general, the domain of peer-group influence overlaps but little with the domain of intellect.

Most college faculty members are no less capable of offering intellectual excitement today then they used to be. As we have already seen, however, they now operate mainly in social systems where whatever excitement they *do* offer is little shared by students outside the classrooms. As a result their academic impact is not compounded and magnified by student interraction.

Time was when colleges were typically small, their student bodies relatively homogeneous, and their general atmosphere that of a well-knit community. During the past few decades, however, many colleges have tended to lose these characteristics. The result has been that peer-group influences are as potent as ever, but increasingly divorced from intellectual concerns. It is no accident that the more conspicuous exceptions to this general trend toward student isolation from intellectual concerns are colleges that remain small, relatively homogeneous, and closely integrated communities. Small colleges can, almost without trying, provide the essential conditions for mobilizing peer-group influence around intellectual concerns. To do the same thing, larger colleges will have to take a good deal of thought.

If the teacher's influence is to be effective, it must be caught up in the norms of student groups, and the degree to which this occurs bears no necessary relationship to frequency of direct faculty contact with students. It can even operate at a distance, transmitted by some students to others—provided that colleges are willing to supply the necessary conditions.

What are these conditions? First, the existence of a formal membership group both moderate in size and characterized by relative homogeneity of interests—especially interests that are friendly to the educator's objectives. The formal group should be large enough to provide the individual with a range of choice in selecting companions, but not so large that individuals will be unlikely to recognize each other. The implication here is that larger colleges should be composed of smaller units—300 to 400 students being a reasonable guess as to optimal size.

Second, it is important to use the fact that students' living arrangements provide the major single source of daily contact. Peer-group influence is almost certain to be enhanced, for better or for worse, if there is a considerable overlap between membership in formal college units and in living units.

The third condition has to do with instruction and faculty contact. It calls, again, for overlap. This time, the requirement is that academic life overlaps *both* with formal college unit and with living unit. In the typical large university it is hardly more than a chance occurrence if a set of students, whose personal relationships are close, find themselves simultaneously excited by the same lecture, the same book, or the same seminar, with resulting reverberations in their peer-group life so that they reenforce and sustain one another's excitement. To base such an occurrence on *more* than pure chance, the curriculum, the housing of students and other facets of college life must be suitably arranged. When this is done, the mere frequency of student-faculty contacts will cease to be a matter for concern. Whether contact occurs in the classroom or in the coffee-bar—preferably both—there is one central question that must be asked: to what extent are students discovering that ideas suggested by faculty contact are worth further exploration with each other? If the discovery is being made, the teacher's influence can be strengthened and multiplied; if not, the multiple will all too often be zero.

John H. Bushnell

Student Culture at Vassar [1]

The campus at Vassar College is essentially a self-contained community, and it is not surprising to find that Vassar girls spend most
of their time with each other. The residence hall, by its very nature, contrives to place and keep its occupants in close association.
The great majority of students seem to thrive on a diet of gregari-
ousness, and the individual who seeks occasional respite from her
fellows must make a deliberate effort to isolate herself.

The sustained tempo of interaction among Vassar students places
a premium on being friendly, pleasant, and agreeable. Animosities
do occur, but critical remarks about peers are made in their absence and usually confined to one's own roommate or friendship
group.

Most important to the Vassar student, and hence crucial in her
college career, is the immediate group of girls with whom she
continually associates. The basic nucleus of a friendship unit usually is composed of roommates. Other girls may be appended to
the roommate group, and sometimes two or three roommate
clusters may form an unusually large social entity. The concept
of roommate, however, is so basically related to Vassar life that
students who prefer singles but have chosen to room near each
other will refer to a next-door friend as "my roommate."

Not all social groupings, of course, derive from dormitory life.
Extracurricular activities such as drama, athletics, or work on the
campus newspaper staff provide a meeting ground for students
with similar interests. The classroom, too, may bring compatible
students together, although this medium is perhaps the least fruitful in producing new friendships. But even when firm alliances
are made outside the dormitory, they are likely to be reflected
in roommate choices for the succeeding year.

Perhaps the most striking aspect of the friendship group is the

[1] This study was carried out while the author was staff anthropologist of
the Mary Conover Mellon Foundation at Vassar College.

ever- present and reliable support which the members provide for one another. Obviously some students are beset with more problems than others, particularly if there are sharp differences with parents, a floundering in class work, or an upset in a serious boyfriend relationship, but the course of the college career is never completely smooth for any Vassar girl. The strength of the immediate peer group is probably best demonstrated when a girl slumps into a severe and sometimes protracted depression. The loyalty and encouragement of roommates and other close friends is often the factor that enables the student to survive—to stay on as a student.

Attitudes held by the individual toward class work and higher education in general tend to be very similar to those of her friends. This alignment is reached by at least three different paths. First, there are those girls who transfer *en masse*, as it were, from the same school to the same college and carry with them a ready-made value system which is not usually subject to serious modification. Second, there is the freshman who arrived on her own. For her the impact of the new group in which she finds herself may be decisive, sharply coloring the four years to follow. And third, since assignment of roommates for the freshman year often has an element of chance in it, there are students who realize sooner or later that their preferences are at odds with the majority of their associates and who consequently gravitate toward new friends and roommates.

While many students are relatively content to be "B" and "C" level scholars, getting good grades is not, in itself, held to be an undesirable achievement. On the contrary, high marks are generally respected, and the girl who makes Phi Beta Kappa, particularly if she does so in her junior year, is frequently accorded general admiration. At a minimum, she gets credit for an academic performance beyond the reach of most of her peers.

The one reservation voiced by most students is that scholastic excellence should not be the sole virtue. If there is an ideal Vassar girl, it is the one who receives consistently high grades without devoting her entire time to the endeavor. In fact, the emphasis on combining good marks with a reasonably full social life is so strong that some students, who in reality have to work quite hard to maintain an impressive grade-point ratio, will devote considerable effort to presenting an appearance of easy competence and freedom from academic harassment.

With the possible exception of a few "bohemian" individualists, most students value moderation, friendliness, cooperation, and a smoothly moving collegiate experience. The premium placed on conflict-free, agreeable relations is reflected in the nearly universal specification that a sense of humor—in roommates, friends, or acquaintances—is a vital ingredient in the continued success and stability of a given group of contemporaries.

Because impulsive behavior or the loss of self-control are viewed as potentially dangerous, students avoid conflict with authority—not only with faculty but also with social regulations. The girl who has been punished by a campus court for a serious infraction of the rulebook may not hide the verdict, but neither will she take pride in a broken regulation.

Attitudes in two areas seem to be of special significance for the Vassar student. The first constellation centers about the assumption that in this country the existing social and economic order will prevail, perhaps with an occasional minor recession, for many years to come. Although students find it exceedingly difficult or impossible to visualize their lives twenty years from now, when their imaginations do project, they frequently see simply an older self immersed in a familiar, contemporary setting.

The established system is viewed, on the one hand, as a framework within which to plan and predict a future life (especially a husband's career) and, on the other hand, as firmly limiting one's plans about future work and style of life. Vassar girls, by and large, do not expect to achieve fame, make an enduring contribution to society, pioneer any frontiers, or otherwise create ripples in the placid order of things. Future husbands should mark out and work directly toward a niche in the business or professional world which provides adequate income and status, but a rise to the top is neither demanded nor expected.

The second important constellation of attitudes revolves about the Vassar student's concept of herself vis-a-vis the status and role of woman in modern American society. In the past the choice between marriage and career may have represented *the* decision for the young woman on campus; today it is virtually impossible to find a Vassar student who views the two as incompatible. Not to marry is almost inconceivable: even the strongly career-oriented girl fully expects that she, too, will some day become a wife and mother.

Not only is spinsterhood regarded as a personal tragedy but offspring are considered essential to the full life. The Vassar student believes that, if necessary, she would willingly adopt children to create a family. It is assumed that femininity is only fully justified and womanly potential only completely realized in the realm of marriage and family. This assumption tends, perhaps inevitably, to reduce student interest in intellectual, creative, and other allied pursuits.

ACCULTURATION AND ENCULTURATION

The analysis here of student life at Vassar College reaffirms the major findings of earlier campus studies. These, broadly stated, have suggested that the student peer group plays a decisive part in determining what happens to the individual during his or her college days. It would be strange, indeed, if Vassar did not reflect what appears to be a virtually universal phenomenon in American colleges and universities.

The student society has its distinct and viable culture. The equivalent is also true for the faculty (combined with deans and directors) to which the phrase "academic culture," Sutherland's terms for a common faculty way of life, applies. In the present concept of campus life, two societies, in effect, occupy the same territory, and cultural differences and consequent conflict are seen to bear importantly on the educational process.

Whenever two societies are in contact, there is also to be found the process known as *acculturation:* a constant exchange between the societies of cultural elements—be they languages, ideas, or artifacts—even where the societies exhibit a strong antagonism toward one another. In such situations, one of the two societies is usually the stronger, larger, or more technically advanced. Where this is the case, there tends to be a greater cultural flow from the dominant to the subordinate group than vice versa.

In the American college, the society of faculty and administrators can be viewed as the donor, since in student eyes it possesses authority and presumably prestige. Faculty society is obviously geared to the job of imparting information and serving as a model for emulation, at least in the intellectual sphere. There is also, however, a detectable counterflow from student society to the faculty and administration. Certainly this is so at Vassar and it is probably true on all campuses.

Like any society subject to acculturation, the student community can call upon techniques which ensure that its relation to the faculty is not solely one of passive recipient. Thus students can and do exert a selective control over the kind and amount of cultural matter actually transmitted across the faculty-student frontier: they may choose only those elements that seem easily adapted to the student culture and, conversely, they may reject ideas which might disrupt or unsettle. In areas where faculty "exports" do not appear to threaten, student acceptance of those exports will often be wholehearted and even uncritical. It is probably no coincidence that Vassar girls show a general preference for art, history, and languages—pursuits that seem highly compatible with student culture and peer-group values.

Another technique employed by student society in its relation to faculty influences is denoted by the term *syncretism:* acceptance of a cultural item without using it for the purpose the donor intended, as in the case of a student who avidly learns the subject matter of a course but does so merely to develop polished chatter at cocktail parties.

Rarely, if ever, do Vassar students overtly reject faculty demands; as noted, they are likely to be agreeable, cooperative, and obedient to the status quo. On the other hand, they seldom go out of their way to make contact with their professors, to speed up or intensify the acculturation process. More usually, students keep the faculty at a distance and turn to each other for counsel and support.

The very fact that student society *can* control the effects of its exposure to acculturative pressures suggests considerable unity, cohesion, and resilience in that society. This phenomenon is all the more impressive when we consider the power of faculty influence, the moral sanction behind that power, and the institutional devices which the faculty can bring to bear.

The strength of student culture is due, in part, to the fact that student values and norms are passed down—with some modification—from one student generation to another. This is the process of *enculturation*, the learning of one's *own* culture. At the college level, enculturation is a continuation of the socialization process formerly occurring within the family and play group; at college the process is mediated by friendship units, student cliques, and campus organizations. In contrast to *acculturation* on the campus (a process consciously organized in classroom and conference), the student's absorption of her own culture takes place largely at a primary group level in a manner which is more informal, less contrived and more immediate in its effect. Furthermore, student culture is easier to come by, since much of the content, for example, ground rules for peer behavior, the network of prevailing attitudes, values, and related symbols, can be absorbed effortlessly, almost by osmosis.

At Vassar, the student culture also derives strength from a widespread belief that the donor culture of the professor is, in fact, *not* the dominant culture nor in any important sense the better of the two. From this it follows that the offerings of faculty culture can hold only limited value. Such feelings are further fostered by the girls' own sense of self-satisfaction, by the conviction that they know their own problems best, and by an attitude of "we know where we want to go and how to get there."

This is not to say that Vassar students are, by and large, anti-academic. They place a definite value on familiarity with the intellectual approach, and many are willing at least to sample the apparent rewards of scholarly activity. Nevertheless, students tend to regard themselves rather than their professors as located in the mainstream of contemporary civilization. However much intellectual prowess is admired, academic proselytizing has its limitations, for the professor's life and work are seen as only marginally related to the larger world.

In this, as in most things, college students do not constitute an isolated society set in the middle of a vast and notably different national culture. On the contrary, the life style of a student culture like Vassar's, with its emphasis on moderation, collective harmony, and long-range security, receives direct and continuing support from the prevailing values of American society.

Everett C. Hughes, Howard S. Becker,
and Blanche Geer

Student Culture and Academic Effort

In the amount of effort put forth by teachers and students, in the
quality of their product, in the direction of their efforts toward
one kind of learning or another, our country may well exhibit a
larger variety in educational institutions than does any other country. Our schools also differ from one another in what one might
call rhythm and style of effort.

A man who teaches in the most gentlemanly of our state universities reports, without bitterness, that the students cannot be
made to work except for a mad burning of midnight oil during the
last ten days of term; only out-of-state "odd-balls" start work at
the opening of the term and do all of the assignments. It may be
that these gentlemanly students accomplish more than those of
another, much larger, and more folksy state university at which
the students are kept so busy at little daily-assigned chores that they
have no time to develop or pursue a program of study (not that
most of them had thought of such a thing). In the effort to get
some reasonable level of accomplishment and effort in his own
course, each instructor has resorted to the device of assigning a
quota of daily chores. The student gives each teacher his due,
claiming in return the right not to be held responsible several
months from now for debts for which he already has a receipt. The
rhythm is one of small, slight pulsations of effort.

At McGill University, the young ladies from the upper-middle
and upper slopes of Westmount seemed to have as their goal a
good, solid *Second-Class* achieved by competent, unstrained effort. *First-Class* would have indicated eager competitiveness
worthy only of those "pros" who were working for prizes and
graduate scholarships; *Third-Class* would have betrayed either
slackness or lack of ability to take things in one's stride.

How unlike those young ladies are the pious hard-working

students in a certain sectarian college who lack goals and style altogether, having no one to give them a model of either. How unlike also is the moderately bright, frightfully earnest young man who is rewarded with a teaching assistantship by a professor grateful to have at least one promising "major," and stays on for a dreary second-class M.A. Then, as an instructor at his home university or one of its satellites, he becomes that drone of American education, the premature pundit teaching too many subjects, who is driven by his wife, the administration, and the accrediting boards to get a Ph.D. by applying what are known as tests of significance (sic) to what are indeed *data*, since they were handed him by his academic master.

Although we have a good many tests of the levels of accomplishment of students in various schools and colleges, we have less knowledge than we should have of the way in which various levels of effort are set and maintained. We have assumed that the individual goals of students are more or less compatible with those of the college, and that the main thing required to raise levels of accomplishment in the college is simply to raise standards required of individuals for entrance and graduation. We have not systematically studied the way students form their own cultures. By the term, student culture, we mean a whole body of conceptions and images of problems and situations and of proper and justifiable solutions of them arrived at by the students; in part passed along from one generation of students to another, in part apparently rediscovered—or at least reenforced—by each succeeding generation as they pass through the same experiences. The students in the medical school we studied had a common goal— to become practicing physicians—and faced common problems: how to get through school without flunking out and how to prepare themselves to practice medicine. The resulting student culture is integral and homogeneous.

Ordinarily the students of a college or university will be less homogeneous as to goal and problems. That may make for a less distinctive and homogeneous student culture; it may be more difficult to discover just what it is in the case of institutions with heterogeneous student bodies. But it does not mean that there is not a student culture, or that the understanding of it is not essential to the making and carrying out of educational policy.

STUDENT CULTURE IN MEDICAL SCHOOL: AN ILLUSTRATIVE CASE [1]

Subcultures (of which student cultures are one example) develop best where a number of people are faced with common problems and interact both intensively and extensively in the effort to find solutions for them, where people who face the same contingencies and exigencies in everyday life have an opportunity to deal with these communally (Sumner, 1907; Cohen, 1955). Medical school is an ideal hot-house for such a plant.

Medical students live with a number of pressing and chronic problems, the most important stemming from the fact that they are continuously presented with an enormous and, in any practical sense, unlimited amount of material to learn. Although students and faculty agree that the criterion for choosing what to learn should be relevance for medical practice, there is enough disagreement and uncertainty among the faculty as to what is relevant so that the student is never presented with a clear directive to guide him in his own studies. Students worry together over this problem, in one or another of its many transformations, during their four years of school.

Similarly, medical school provides extremely propitious conditions—intensive interaction and isolation from outside influences

[1] This portion of the paper was originally read at the meetings of the American Sociological Society, August 28, 1957, Washington, D.C., and was later published in the *Harvard Educational Review*, Winter, 1958, 28, 70–80.

Our study of medical students was sponsored by Community Studies, Inc., of Kansas City, Missouri, and was further supported by grants from the Carnegie Corporation and the National Institutes of Health. Anselm Strauss has collaborated with us in both the field work and the preparation of the final report. The entire study is reported in Becker, H. S. *et al.*, *Boys in White*, Chicago: University of Chicago Press, 1961.

—for the development of common solutions to these problems. Students usually spend eight or more hours in school every weekday, working and studying together in the labs and on the wards, and are likely to spend many evenings and weekends together in similar activity as well. Much of their work is carried on in groups of four to twelve students, and these are arranged so differently from course to course that the students come to know many of their fellows with the intimacy that arises from close, continuous association at work. The students are insulated from contact with other people, both by reason of their crowded schedules and because they find it difficult to talk with people who are not suffering under the same pressures as they are. Even those students who have friends or brothers only a year or two ahead of them in school report that they get little help with their immediate problems from these people. Each class of approximately one hundred students goes through school as a unit, meeting the problems they face together.

When the freshmen arrive in medical school, although they come with the common intention of becoming physicians, they are not a group in any but the nominal sense that all are in the first year class. They begin to get to know some of their fellow students right away, but this takes place not in the class at large but within small groups. The small groups are of two types. First to form are friendship groups consisting of students similar in social status who have opportunities for leisure interaction because they live near or with each other. Fraternity members, for example, most of whom are unmarried, make friends in their own house, married students get to know other married students who live in the same neighborhood or trailer camp, and unmarried students who do not belong to a fraternity get together at the student center to eat and relax in their spare time. The second type of group forms in the anatomy laboratory. As the faculty assigns students in groups of four to a dissection tank, members of different friendship groups get to know each other under the intimate conditions that dissecton of the same cadaver imposes. The intersection of work and friendship groups makes it possible for each student to learn the attitudes current in other groups toward student problems, and, at the same time, carry back to his own friends solutions he and his lab partners have tried out in the course of their work together.

The spread of common understanding among the freshmen is also promoted by their isolation as a class, for, unlike most graduate students, all members of the class are taught together. As they begin to get a sense of themselves as a group, they think of the faculty as another group opposed to their own. To ask faculty advice is to break student ranks. Thus the students reach their own conclusions among themselves about what the study of medicine is and how it should be accomplished. Their notions are partly derived, it is true, from what the faculty says and does (not always the same thing), but they are also formed by the future they envision for themselves as physicians, and by their past experience in getting through school and college.

They agree that they ought to study the "basic medical facts." With so much to learn, these are the only facts they have time for, facts important for practice and certain to be on examinations —if the faculty is "reasonable." To this central proposition the students add a number of other understandings which they apply to their daily activities.

1. Basic facts are most economically learned from textbooks. Lectures that do not follow the text are a waste of student time, and a faculty member who strays from the text is a poor lecturer, probably with some scientific ax to grind in defense of his own research, a matter which does not concern medical students.

2. Demonstrations and lab work which repeat classical experiments are a waste of time; the results are most easily learned in the text and students cannot do them well enough to learn much anyway.

3. Theoretical material, concepts (except those which help to organize facts), and research findings not yet in clinical use are not *facts* and are not useful to medical students.

These expressions of medical student culture are summed up in the student phrase "give it to us straight," or the derogatory equivalent used by faculty, "spoon feeding." A student will say that he does not, in fact, want to be spoon fed, but at the same time he will point out that there is so much to learn he does not have time to think or worry about "minutiae" (details) and "all that academic crud" (nonfactual material). Once they have decided the question of what and how to study, the students settle down to hard work. They are no longer worried about how to select the important things to read; "you just go by the black type." In the same way, they learn to get through their lab work by various short cuts approved by student culture and not penalized in examinations by the faculty.

During the last two years of medical school—the clinical years —the student's work consists largely of taking medical histories from and performing physical examinations on patients. The aim here is to develop skill at these functions and to use the information so gained in learning how to diagnose and treat various diseases. Formal examinations continue to test his knowledge, but he is led to believe in various ways that the crucial decisions about his future in school—whether he passes or fails, for example— are based largely on the faculty's evaluation of his clinical work. In any event he feels it unlikely that, having got this far, he will be flunked out of school; few such cases are known to have occurred.

During the clinical years, the major problems requiring collective solution no longer lie in the realm of examinations. Instead, students focus their attention on how to meet continual pressure from a heavy load of clinical work and how to get the most benefit out of that work for a future career. At this point, students draw the following conclusions about their schoolwork:

(1) Patients whom it is really important to study thoroughly are those who have common diseases—whether simple or complicated —for which treatments are available that a general practitioner could utilize. (2) All those kinds of clinical work that they cannot imagine themselves doing in general practice are to be regarded as a waste of time. (3) Courses that do not give practice in techniques they consider important for the practitioner are to be disliked.

THE CONSEQUENCES OF STUDENT CULTURE

Student culture affects the larger social system in which it is embedded—the medical school—in two ways. On the one hand, it supplies the basis for a *modus vivendi* between students and their superiors; it provides a perspective from which students can build consistent patterns for the way in which they fit into school and hospital activities. In this respect student culture is an accommodation on the part of the students to the facts of school life.

On the other hand, student culture also provides the students with the social support that allows them, both in individual instances and as a group, to make an independent assessment of faculty statements and demands. So supported, they can reinterpret the faculty's scale of priorities and, to a large degree, make what they will of their education. In this sense, student culture is a mechanism creating the conditions for deviance from formally stated institutional rules. Not surprisingly, therefore, student culture becomes the cornerstone of many faculty difficulties with students, a fact of life to which teachers must, in their turn, make some accommodations.

Medical school represents an extreme case of the development and operation of student culture. We would not necessarily expect it to play so important a role in other educational institutions. But it exists in such places and probably performs there the two functions it performs at medical school—accommodating students to the difficulties of school life, and providing a basis for the re-direction of student effort, possibly in defiance of faculty stand-ards.

We all know that in many colleges and universities where the general level of aspiration and effort is miserably low, there are small nuclei of students of great intellectual verve. Such groups, in effect, create little subcultures of their own, contrary in many respects to that of the prevailing mass student culture. We need to study such groups, so as to learn more of the circumstances in which they arise and disappear, and so as to learn how they may be planted, cultivated, and emulated. There are many experi-ments of this kind going on. We suspect that those efforts to im-prove quality will succeed best that make the most use of knowl-edge of the propensities of groups of students for developing their own conceptions of their abilities, of setting their own group stand-ards and goals. Encouragement of individual "rate busting" will not succeed in more than a few cases (although all of us know of students who have wrung an education from an unwilling col-lege). Nor will a general raising of minimum standards, or a purg-ing of so-called extraneous matter and unworthy material, create and increase the number of nuclei of students of superior effort and accomplishment. We would lay our bets on efforts to create or encourage groups of special quality within the bosom of the con-glomerate institutions that go by the name of university or col-lege.

Many of our colleges are still making adjustments. Our prob-lem is to develop the means that will make it possible for experi-ments in excellence to be carried out in many of these weird and interesting going concerns; we waste our energies if we limit our-selves to thinking about the one ideal kind of institution with the one ideal kind of student. The problem is to develop, in real in-stitutions, combinations of functions and of kinds of students in which the number who will seek higher achievement will be made greater; this is, in turn and in part, a matter of getting some students—and their teachers—to create new images of themselves and their possibilities.

References

Cohen, A. K. *Delinquent boys: the culture of the gang.* Glencoe, Ill.: The Free Press, 1955.
Sumner, W. G. *Folkways.* Boston: Ginn and Company, 1907.

Six
The Role of the Student

Donald R. Brown

Academic Excellence: The Crucial Effects
of Environment and Personality

Education is not a disembodied phenomenon. It cannot be applied
to an individual as a bright finish is sprayed on a new automobile
at a certain point in its making. Complex and difficult to define,
it is, instead, a process which goes on continually as part of each
individual's total development. As men have come to realize how
interrelated an individual's intellectual development and his *total*
development are, they have become more interested in the way
personal traits and environment affect each other and together
produce academic achievement.

In selecting students, colleges may strive for some ideal combination of high scholastic performance and other personal attributes, such as athletic prowess or leadership qualities. The general aim of college selection, however, has always been to predict
academic achievement. Those colleges that do their selecting
largely by standardized aptitude and achievement tests have dis-
played growing ability to predict, and thus avoid, academic failure.
On the other hand, they have also shown a declining ability to predict the *relative* grade performances of those selected. It is impossible to make such distinctions clearly at colleges where high
College Board requirements restrict the range of talent admitted.

Nor, in any case, do academic tests themselves throw light on
student motivation. Grades may be obtained in quite different
ways—in the one instance by a brilliant, independent, versatile,
and flexible thinker; in another by a persistent, well-disciplined,
well-organized, and obedient student with a good memory.

In our study at Vassar [1] we asked individual faculty members
to name "superior" students in their classes and describe their per-

[1] This study of faculty-nominated ideal students was carried out while the
author was a staff member of the Mary Conover Mellon Foundation at
Vassar College.

sonal qualities. By their own statements, what the faculty meant by an *ideal* student was one who possessed marked intellectual power; who applied that power to intellectual subjects—and did so independently; and whose mind was incisive, analytical, and good at synthesis. A student's development, however, should not be one-sided, penalizing qualities of friendliness, helpfulness, co-operativeness, and other moral attributes.

To be considered ideal, of course, a student need not possess all these qualities. In the eyes of many teachers, an unusual amount of originality or flexibility, or skill at schoolwork will often compensate for other lacks. Furthermore, in matters of personality no less than in matters of intellect, the Vassar faculty honors *growth* as well as sheer attainment.

It appears, then, that the faculty admires intellectual ability but prefers to find it housed in a well-integrated, developing, pleasant, purposeful young person. They are not overly influenced by grade-performance alone. It must be admitted, however, that the Vassar faculty's values about students are by no means universal. National studies on the undergraduate origins of Ph.D. students indeed support the notion that scientific and humanistic scholars thrive in different types of college environments.

What happens when the sides are reversed and the students are asked to evaluate their teachers? Interestingly, colleges that produce many natural science Ph.D.'s possess faculties that seem warm and informal toward their students. Here, teachers are not embarrassed by open displays of emotion; and they often refer to colleagues by their first names when talking to students. Students do not describe them as "practical" or "efficient" in their dealings, nor do they feel it necessary to address them as "professor" or "doctor."

The faculties in these colleges demand high academic performance. They see through the pretenses and bluffs of some students, they push them to perform at capacity, and they give challenging exams. They also apply high standards to their faculty colleagues, emphasizing basic research. But in their teaching methods they are relatively nondirective, and they show some tolerance toward student mistakes in social life.

A different pattern emerges from colleges that are more productive in the social sciences and humanities. Students identify these institutions with a flexible curriculum, controversial and energetic teaching, and—not surprisingly—a first-rate social science faculty. Student cultures characterized by humanism, breadth of interests, and reflectiveness are conducive to humanistic interests and achievement, whereas both aggression and a high degree of social activity interfere with such achievement. Natural science achievement, for its part, is typical of student cultures high in scientism and aggression and is inhibited by those that stress social conformity.

Further light has been shed on the relationships among college achievement, personality, and early family life in a study of women who graduated from Vassar twenty-five years earlier.[2] From exhaustive research into the lives of these women before, during, and after college, five basic patterns of attitudes emerged.

Socially Active

Characteristically, these women led busy social lives as undergraduates and were closely attached to the peer group. Neither notoriously rebellious, nor primarily interested in the intellectual aspects of college, they were out for a "good time"—though not at the expense of a college degree. As a rule, they entered college from the better-known private schools where they had undistinguished records academically but gave evidence of "all roundness, independence, poise and spark."

They were strongly identified with their parents. The fathers were probably Ivy League graduates in law or business, seen by their daughters as busy, distant figures; their mothers were women

[2] This was an intensive, three-day study of fifty women who came to the college in groups of ten. It was a project of the Mary Conover Mellon Foundation. See Sanford, N. (Ed.). Personality development during the college years. *J. Social Issues*, 1956, 12, No. 4.

of poise, charm, intelligence and great energy, often graduates of the students' Alma Mater. Childhood days were remembered as vague worlds of stability and happiness.

Having left college they occupied themselves with Junior League activities until marriage. After marriage, a suburban life of child-rearing and some soul-searching seemed to make them liberal Protestants and left-of-center Republicans. At the time of the study these women were strongly authoritarian as compared with others in their group, and they lacked introspection, complexity, and the capacity for further growth. They did not find college intellectually challenging, nor did they gain high academic achievement.

Overachievers

These women had higher college performances than their tested ability would have indicated, yet they were not professionally minded and showed little evidence of being influenced by faculty values. Family history seemed to be the key to this overachievement—a college-educated mother with high aspirations, a greatly admired father who was a self-made businessman, a vaguely remembered happy home life. Close conformity with strict parental demands led, it seemed, to dutiful college careers where students worked hard, won academic awards, but acquired little serious appreciation of the intellectual life.

Their lives since college followed the conventional suburban form so caricatured in contemporary writing—routine upper-middle or lower-upper-class patterns, narrow in scope and opportunity, lacking much deep meaning, devoid of intellectual pursuits. Socially and politically, they were cautious, conservative. In religion they were traditionalist and Protestant. As a result, these women showed more signs of an approaching role crisis related to menopause and aging than did the other groups. All in all, this picture seemed to support the oft-heard complaint that grades can be achieved to some extent with only reasonable capacity, little intellectual curiosity, and a good deal of "proper" behavior.

Underachievers

Although their college performances were medium to low, these women often had a high capacity—witness their considerable intellectual growth while at college. This growth appeared to be for three reasons: either they came from politically liberal families, or they reacted strongly to the depression of the thirties during their college years, or their husbands, whom they began dating while in college, were liberal politically.

Although their main interest was marriage (a professional or businessman), and family (three to six children), many became active professionally during the early years of marriage, particularly in areas such as social work or nursery school teaching, where the interest was in people rather than ideas or professional status.

Backgrounds varied in this group. The women went to private but usually progressive and academically sound schools, and chose their colleges on recommendations from school officials and friends. Family life was happy and secure, with more than the usual amount of freedom and independence, and little threat of deprivation for nonconformity. Fathers were competent, "fun," loving, and part of the family picure. Mothers were warm, sociable, happy, and accepting—sources of identification.

Today these women hold conventional religious beliefs, although they were arrived at after much thought. Politically they are moderate, with leanings toward the Democrats or independents, and, in spite of family obligations and lack of servants, active in the community. Contrary to their earlier dedication to home and family, they are now looking forward to part-time employment.

High Achievers

These were women of capacity who did very well at college and went on to professional careers. They seldom married and even more rarely had children. Rather they attained advanced degrees and held responsible professional positions. Any problems of identity were solved through their high capacity, strong interests and actual achievements. Most often their parents were neither socially nor intellectually prominent, they came from public schools (unusual for the Vassar group) and they held scholarships. In childhood and adolescence they experienced conflicts arising from domineering and talented mothers, against whom they felt considerable repressed hostility and guilt, yet whose opinions they accepted. In fact, their childhood days, as a group, were not outstandingly happy, nor were they protected from such upsetting events as deaths or economic crises.

The intellectual development of these women may be described as early, intense, and continuing. From their earliest days they were decided on an intellectual career, and their colleges were chosen for academic prestige and because scholarship aid was available. These women were oriented toward liberal political and social philosophies, tended to vote Democrat, and were agnostic.

Identity Seekers

A miscellany of rather unhappy and confused people trying to break away from strong, domineering parents, or to adjust themselves to the college environment. Background ranged from extreme upper-class Victorian upbringing to lower-middle-class, small-town girls. And their identity-seeking ranged from open defiance to a maintenance of weak conformity awaiting an opportunity to break.

On the whole, these women were unable to achieve stable lives except after prolonged therapy or drastic changes in environment, or both. They came from unstable or oppressive families, and the sex-role conflict was sometimes so severe that normal heterosexual relations were seriously impaired. These students would have been the ones to profit most from currently existing therapeutic facilities on campus, but as it was, intellectual interests were largely forsaken in the intensity of the personal struggle.

These findings suggest that the selection of students should include the channeling of each to the type of college that can maximize his potential. It might even be necessary to create new types of environments if we want to be in a position to serve well as many students as possible.

Yet, although we must appreciate each student's individuality, we must also seek common factors that will allow educators to design the fewest possible types of institutional environments for the fullest intellectual development of the most students. Only with such knowledge of individual development, and a clear statement of the goals to be achieved, can education become less haphazard than it is now.

Carl Bereiter and Mervin B. Freedman

Fields of Study and the People in Them

Educators are concerned with helping individuals find fields of study that suit them. Thus far psychology has been of little help except in providing tests for describing people in various fields. Group for group, college students majoring in different subjects have been found to differ psychologically with respect to three main characteristics: intelligence, liberalism of attitudes, and psychological adjustment. In each instance, the ordering of groups seems to follow a consistent pattern.

Differences in Mental Ability

The average intelligence scores of major groups regularly fall into an order with the physical sciences, engineering, and mathematics at the top, followed by literature and the social sciences, and with the applied fields, agriculture, business, home economics, and education at the bottom. An obvious explanation for this ordering is that it reflects the varying difficulty of the subjects as they are usually taught at the undergraduate level. The order has, in fact, been found to match closely the reputations for difficulty that these fields enjoy among undergraduates.

For this reason, the average scores, although they may be of practical importance, have little theoretical significance. Any department could raise the average score of its students by raising entrance requirements or requiring a stiff course that would eliminate the dullards. It is one thing, however, to keep out the less competent students; it is quite another thing to attract those of superior intelligence.

In assessing the attractiveness of different fields of study it seems best to ignore less intelligent students who must, of necessity, be concentrated in the easier fields. When we consider only the college graduates who rank in the upper 60 per cent in general intelligence—students who would rank in the upper two-thirds of any group in the student body—what is most immediately striking is the even allocation of top talent among the various major disciplines. Fields, such as business and education, that look poor in terms of mean intelligence scores or overall distribution of scores come in for about the same share of the top students as do the more academic fields.

If we lump engineering with natural science, however, as is often done, it is evident that this field does attract a large portion of the more intelligent students—over a quarter of them. Moreover, this field is seen to attract a relatively larger portion of the top intelligence group than of the lower group, whereas the reverse is true of business and education.

There is, of course, nothing in data of this sort to prove that one field is intrinsically more appealing to the intellectually able than another. Such extrinsic factors as prestige and remunerativeness, as well as the intrinsic factor of difficulty, must also be considered, although the possibility of some fields being in a very general way more intellectually challenging than others should not be summarily dismissed without further investigation.

Differences in Attitude

During the past thirty years the attitudes of college students toward such public issues as war, Communism, labor unions, and religion have frequently been measured. With some consistency, students in certain fields of study have tended toward positions that are popularly regarded as liberal, whereas students in other fields have tended toward conservative positions.

More often than not, students in social science are found to be the most liberal group. With even greater consistency, students in engineering and agriculture appear among the least liberal. Literature, arts, and natural science groups are usually found between these extremes, with the natural science groups tending to be less liberal than the others. Students in education are difficult to pin down. Those in secondary education tend to reflect the attitudes of their prospective teaching fields, and those in elementary and physical education tend to be among the most conservative groups.

The most conservative groups are all in applied rather than purely academic fields. One factor that may help to account for this conservatism is that these fields tend to draw students from lower social-class levels than do the academic fields.

Looked at in another way, the attitudes of students in the applied fields differ from those of academic majors in the same way that attitudes of the public as a whole differ from those of college students. It seems quite reasonable to suppose that students who seek higher education mainly for some special vocational preparation should tend to resemble people in the work-a-day world more than do academicians.

Psychological Adjustment

Familiar academic stereotypes assign quite different personalities to such figures as the art student, the engineering student, the business student, and the history student. Attempts to investigate these types by mental tests have succeeded in establishing only that there exist what for the moment might be called differences in "adequacy of psychological adjustment."

The groups reporting the most fears, worries, conflicts, and the like are almost always in the literary or fine art fields, whereas applied majors, such as engineering, business, agriculture, and education, regularly show the fewest of these psychological problems. In the middle are natural science and social science students, the natural science students tending to show less disturbance than those in social science.

This order—humanities, social science, natural science, applied science—presents a hierarchy of increasingly concrete, down-to-earth content. Shall we hypothesize, then, that the more "neurotic" or complex and troubled people are drawn to intangibles or, conversely, that they are repelled by the mundane? There is evidence to support such a hypothesis. There are, however, some other aspects of the sequence of major fields also worth attending to.

To take another line of reasoning, it makes sense that a psychologically disturbed person should give some weight, in any major decision he makes, to alternatives promising relief from his disturbance. It has been found, for instance, that students who elect courses in abnormal psychology tend to be more abnormal than those who elect other kinds of psychology courses.

Fields concerned with human beings and their more human problems are certainly more directly relevant to an individual's own psychological problems. But this could be more a source of further disturbance than of alleviation. It might make more sense for the neurotic person to seek refuge from his problems in a field where they would not be brought to his attention so often. We need not delve here into all the psychological dynamics that might lead to one or the other course of action, but we should note one point that bears directly on the data.

The evidence on psychological adjustment of college students is based largely on scores on the Minnesota Multiphasic Personality Inventory and a few other tests of questionnaire type. Although these tests may have some power to unearth fairly deeply hidden disturbances, there is no denying that among reasonably normal subjects, like most students, those who are conscious of their difficulties will get worse scores than those who repress them. If so, it would make sense that those people whose adjustment depends more on repression of symptoms should tend toward impersonal fields—for example, engineering—where their repressions are in less danger of being shaken. The small differences in scores between major groups might, therefore, not really reflect differences in *amount* of disturbance at all.

Another complicating factor is that unconventional people are likely to give unconventional responses to diagnostic test items and thus obtain scores indicating the presence of psychopathology. Socially withdrawn students, likewise, may well give test responses that are scored as symptoms of psychological disturbance. Rather than consider these dimensions as indicators of degree of psychological adjustment, it seems to us more reasonable to consider them as indicators of *kind* of psychological adjustment. Thus among unconventional people we could expect to find some for whom unconventionality represented a healthy state of affairs and some for whom it was unhealthy. The same would be true for conventional people, people who are socially outgoing, and people who are socially withdrawn.

The personality differences noted here can all be grouped into two categories. On the one hand there are the differences related to signs of psychological disturbance, unconventionality, and awareness of psychological problems. These characteristics, which are hard to tell apart, all seem connected with the person's inner life—with his thoughts, emotions, and impulses—and how he deals with them. The fact that choosing a field of study is related to such individual facets indicates what we would of course expect, that a person's intellectual pursuits are integrated in some way with other aspects of his inner life.

The other important category of individual differences includes such things as sociability, confidence in social situations, and interest in people. It clearly centers around the person's social life. Since choice of field is also related to these kinds of attributes, we may suppose that the sort of intellectual activities a person pursues implies something about how he relates to other people, and vice versa.

The connection may be only superficial; some pursuits involve more contact with people than others, and a person's choice of field may be influenced by how much social contact he wants. Or the connection may be more profound. It might well be discovered that individuals have basic patterns of relating to things outside themselves, to people as well as to objects and ideas.

A better understanding of the way personality relates to intellectual interest would provide a sounder basis for selecting students. It would also help in counseling the individual student concerning his choice of field. We should remember, however, that guiding a student toward a field that best fits his *present* characteristics tends to preserve the status quo both in the individual and in the field he enters. Ideally, the student ought to pursue the curriculum that would produce in him the most beneficial growth, even if it meant taking a course in which he did badly and had a very trying time; but in the face of academic and social pressures to get good grades, the demands of employers that people study whatever they plan to work at, and the general "materialistic" view of education as preparation rather than as development, it is understandable that students, with the blessings of their counselors, play it safe.

David C. Beardslee and Donald D. O'Dowd

The Career Has Its Shadow

Rapid change, both in higher education and in American occupational structure during the first half of this century, has greatly affected the relation between college and career. This is dramatically illustrated by the evolving recruitment patterns of business and industry. Many observers report that until the 1930's it was common for business firms to look with suspicion on the college graduate, preferring to hire and promote men with more limited educational attainments. It is now becoming difficult for a man *without* college training, regardless of his intellectual capacities, to rise in the structure of established business concerns. Similar changes have also taken place in the professions. Engineers without college credentials have all but disappeared.

It is quite clear that college has become the gateway to professional and higher managerial status. This situation is exerting a powerful influence on the orientation of millions of young people approaching college age. Their parents, teachers, guidance counselors, and the mass media are constantly impressing upon them that a college education is indispensable for achieving a respectable and satisfying status in American life.

We cannot wonder that students show great concern about careers when we remember the social pressures behind that concern—the vital link between occupation and status, and between occupation and upwards mobility; and the simple fact that college training promises a better job. Moreover, until he finds the place where he fits in the world of work, the young man often has not discovered the kind of person he is. Since each career also implies a certain style of life, desirable or undesirable, it is not surprising that the student feels under considerable pressure to select an occupation early and to cling to it.

This is certainly unfortunate at the college level where many young men and women are being prepared for generalist roles requiring a maximum of self-confidence, flexibility, and originality. Ideally, a liberal arts education should provide a basis on which students whose personal integration is still weak can develop a sense of competence, mastery, and direction that will allow them to choose wisely and not prematurely among occupational alternatives.

This process of forming character through higher education is just as vital for women as for men. Women graduates should feel free either to enter careers immediately, or to undertake family responsibilities with the confident belief that they can claim a place at a later time in the occupational world because of their personal talents.

The images or stereotypes of occupations that merge in the talk of college students are not always very close to the descriptions of occupations in guidance literature! They frequently do, however, bear definite resemblance to the findings of occupational sociology and psychology. These stereotypes reveal a variety of connotations about careers, each of which is associated with a certain kind of personality, a certain status, and a certain style. On the other hand, little information is volunteered by students about the kind of day-to-day work that would be expected in an occupation.

Stereotypes of Occupations

From the foregoing it can be seen that occupational stereotypes provide information about how a career places a person in the community, and what kind of person would commit himself to it. Of particular importance is the marked amount of agreement among students about these non-work features of several major careers.

Once a person has expressed preference for some occupation, he is assigned by others the traits—personal and social—associated with that occupation. For college opinion not only governs what one believes of the people out there in the active world, it also affects how one student reacts to another student who is now in the throes of selecting his future personal attributes. Small wonder that choosing a career involves some anxiety for college students.

Our own research into these matters was designed to gain more knowledge of the images students attach to the career world. We tried to determine rather precisely how students perceive a number of high-level occupations. The investigation was expected to shed light on the ideal personality traits to which students aspire; and we also wanted to know why liberal arts students overconcentrated their choices on the *professional* occupations.

During the spring of 1958 questionnaires were administered to a random sample of freshmen and seniors at Wesleyan University. In the winter and spring of 1959 questionnaires were distributed at three other colleges; a small, highly selective men's liberal arts college, a highly selective women's liberal arts college, and a state university college of arts and sciences, all located in the northeastern part of the country. Random samples from the freshman and senior classes were questioned at each of these colleges. The following vignettes summarize the statistical profiles that emerged from the analysis.

Doctor. The doctor is a culture hero for college students. He anchors the desirable end of a surprising number of scales. Medicine is rated by students as a calling richly rewarded by high social status, wealth, and success.

The doctor is favored with high opportunity for advancement, and he derives great personal satisfaction from his work. Compared to men in most other occupations he can count on an unusually pretty wife and a happy home life. The doctor is very much a realist. He approaches the world responsibly and with perseverance; he is outstandingly calm, confident, and self-sufficient; and his great stability, caution, and rationality are balanced by his adaptability.

The doctor is clearly oriented to people. Although this attitude may be partially a professional concern, still he is thoughtful and unselfish, giving of himself to others. The doctor's cheerfulness and optimism fit well with his unfailing "human directedness." His high intelligence appears to be more closely related to his strong, active, masterful qualities than to participation in the highest intellectual culture. No undesirable traits are attributed to the doctor; all students recognize the remarkable personal and social attractiveness of his role.

Lawyer. The image of the lawyer has many characteristics also attributed to the doctor, but the doctor is usually rated more favorably on traits that they have in common. The lawyer possesses high social status, success, and wealth. He has considerable opportunity to advance in his job, and he is outstandingly powerful in public affairs.

The lawyer is viewed as an outgoing, sociable person who likes to be with people and is at ease in the company of others. The lawyer shares with the doctor realistic, persevering, forceful, strong, and active qualities. He is a person who is effective in the world of objects, events, and people.

These characteristics are qualified, however, by a high degree of hardness and self-assertiveness. There is more than a hint of the selfish and manipulative in the lawyer, attributes wholly lacking in the doctor image. The lawyer is perceived as having high intelligence and good taste. He rates a pretty wife, but his home life is not seen as particularly happy.

The lawyer image combines most of the rewards promised by the medical profession and possesses many of the same desirable personal properties, while providing somewhat more scope for less service-oriented, less unselfish ambitions. Of particular prominence is the stress placed on sociability and access to public power.

College Professor. A dominant feature of this image is the great stress on intellectual competence accompanied by sensitivity to artistic or aesthetic experience. The professor is seen as an individualist with colorful, interesting, exciting qualities coupled with a degree of rashness, changeability, emotional difficulties, and lack of adaptability. It is quite likely that he is interesting *because* of his emotional, unpredictable nature.

In spite of these characteristics and a high score on radicalism, he is granted considerable power in public affairs. Students deem the professor a valuable man, and they see in his role a source of great personal satisfaction. On the debit side, the professor is described as not well-to-do and lacking in opportunity for advancement. He does not equal the independent professionals in either social or worldly competence. Whereas the doctor and lawyer are stable and dependable, he is changeable and unpredictable.

Intellectual qualities are the greatest asset of the college professor. Probably the most striking impression emerging from this profile is its lack of masculinity. It is predominantly a volatile feminine picture with the emphasis on intellect, sensitivity, and impulsiveness.

Scientist. Two strong impressions are conveyed by this profile. First, the scientist is characterized by high intelligence dissociated from artistic concerns and sensitivities. This cool intelligence is linked with strong individualism in personal and political realms. Second, there is a clear lack of interest in people on the part of the scientist. A good deal of self-control is implied by the description of the scientist as self-sufficient, rational, persevering, and emotionally stable. He has power in public affairs, but he is rated only moderately responsible and quite radical. This suggests that uncertainty about the motives and trustworthiness of the scientist, an uncertainty noted in younger people by other investigators, lingers on in college students.

The personal life of the scientist is thought to be quite shallow, his wife is not pretty, his home life is not very happy. But he is rewarded by great personal satisfaction, considerable success, and reasonable opportunity for advancement. Furthermore, he enjoys moderate wealth and social status.

In summary, the scientist is a cool, self-controlled individual. He is competent in organizing the world of things, but disdainful of the world of people. Materially better rewarded than the college professor, the scientist contrasts strikingly with him in aesthetic sensibilities and social skills.

Engineer. Engineering is a less colorful profession for liberal arts students. The engineer is rated generally intelligent but not nearly so strong in this regard as the scientist. On the other hand, he is considerably more socially adept than the scientist, though no social lion.

The engineer is quite successful and reasonably wealthy, but he gains less satisfaction from his work than the scientist derives from pure research. He is also more conservative, and more likely to be a conformist. Except for these important differences, the engineer is almost identical with the scientist.

School Teacher. In every classification of careers according to social status, the school teacher is located in the second or third tier among the professions. Yet school teaching accounts for the occupational preferences and choices of a substantial percentage of college graduates.

The school-teacher image is dominated by the depressed economic state of the profession. The teacher scores conspicuously low in wealth, social status, and opportunity for advancement. He has little power in public affairs, and he cannot even command an attractive wife although he can count on a happy home life—just the opposite of the lawyer's situation.

The teacher is considered intelligent, sensitive, and, like the professor, interested in art although to a lesser degree. Furthermore, he is attentive to people and unselfish in his relations with them. In this regard he has a dedication to service somewhat like the doctor's. Finally, the teacher is supposed to lack confidence and hard, assertive properties.

Business Executive. The avoidance of business occupations by freshmen liberal arts students is at first glance surprising when the image is studied. The business executive is extremely high in social status, wealth, and success. He has power in public affairs, ample opportunity to advance himself, and even a very pretty wife. He is classified as very conservative, but when his conservatism is paired with his good taste, a picture of quiet elegance emerges.

He possesses the sociability noted in the lawyer, accompanied

by a confident, assertive, masculine manner. He is also rated strong
and active, responsible and persevering. But the business executive
lacks both the high intelligence and the hard, rational properties
that make the lawyer a most formidable figure. The executive is
even less service-oriented than the lawyer; he is in fact a selfish individual.

Finally, the businessman is believed to possess a component of
excitability and emotional instability, a condition related to the
popular belief about executives and ulcers.

The business executive has weaknesses and personal problems
that offset to some degree his wealth and status. The road to this
role is not as clear or as predictable for most college students as
the way to high-status occupations through the professional
schools.

Accountant. This occupation represents a lower-status business activity, perhaps comparable in some ways to the status of
school teaching among the professions.

The image that surrounds the field is remarkably negative. If
the doctor is the occupational hero, the accountant is the "anti-
hero" of the occupational world. He is low in status, not well-to-
do, and unsuccessful. He has little power in public affairs, not
much opportunity for advancement, and his job is the lowest of all
the occupations studied in providing personal satisfaction.

A conformist, he has a minimum of social skills, limited intelligence, and inadequate personal and aesthetic sensibilities. He is
rated as passive, weak, soft, shallow, cold, submissive, unsure of
himself, and evasive in meeting life. His positive characteristics of
caution, stability, conservatism, and calmness rest on a shaky emotional interior. This combination is probably linked to his professional specialization, his sway over a limited field.

Students have a rather specific model in mind when they produce this wretched portrait. He is apparently something of a
Victorian bookkeeper, chained to a desk and ledger, from which
he has no inclination to depart for traffic with the world or contact
with man. Given this description, liberal arts students may even

seem to doubt whether the accountant is living flesh and blood.

Artist. On a number of scales the artist stands at the end opposite to that of the doctor. The artist's noble sensitivity to matters of aesthetic importance is associated with a variety of traits reflecting violent emotions and impulsive expression. He is, for example, intuitive, rash, changeable, excitable, attention demanding, and at the same time, deep, interesting, and colorful.

His outstanding individualism and radicalism accompany a group of traits indicating irresponsibility and unwillingness to contribute to society in a disciplined way. The artist is uninterested in people, and evidently unsuccessful with them. His moods tend to be dark, depressed, and pessimistic.

The only reward that he can expect for his work is a high sense of satisfaction. Neither wealth, nor status, nor any other marks of the rich, full life are associated with the artist. Given the foregoing description but not told that it applied to "the artist," one might easily connect it with a teenager in the throes of adolescent problems.

OCCUPATIONAL ASPIRATIONS AND LEARNING

In a penetrating study of college students' values and beliefs, Gillespie and Allport (1955) write, "The best way to generalize (the American student's) goals seems to be in terms of the search for a rich, full life." They note further that the contemporary college student is not concerned with the political and social problems that surround him. He is not even concerned with philosophical or religious issues. In a most profound sense he is involved with himself and his future.

One of the keys to this future is the occupational role that fulfills the promise of a college education. This place in the occupational system is seen by most students not as a chance to achieve great heights in work, but as an opportunity to find comfort, variety, interesting experiences, and pleasant acquaintances. For students, the occupation even specifies the personal qualities of its present and future members, providing a ready-made personality for those who cannot establish a secure identity from their own experience.

It is likely that widespread agreement among students about the qualities of mind and personality associated with careers limits the *variety* of human types any high-level field can attract. In trying to encourage students to direct their talents toward fields for which they are especially suited we should recognize that they often will already be inclining toward other careers. To promote greater freedom of occupational choice and more efficient social utilization of abilities, we must do two things.

First, occupations promising scope to talented people must be presented on more equal terms. In this reeducation process, educators have an important part to play, as have those organizations concerned with maintaining standards in the major occupations. Such efforts, however, will probably be limited in their effect, since the image of a career grows out of major cultural trends and receives constant reinforcement from peers, parents, teachers, and mass media.

But there is a second way by which the problem may be approached. The interest that students show in careers reflects for many a lack of self-confidence. If, therefore, we can nurture in students those attributes that will strengthen their claim to an independent identity, we may be able to lessen their dependence on packaged occupational personalities. This in turn will increase students' readiness to take a new kind of initiative, to create a place in the world of careers for their own individual talents. In all probability a self-confident youth would stir to the challenge of social and political problems—matters needing dedicated attention—in a way quite beyond the resources of insecure, self-centered young people.

A prime responsibility of education is to see that the educated man's *character* enables him to use the fruits of his academic experience. Accepting the concern of students with their own development and their place in the future, it may be possible to use this very concern to engage their energies. Students attach great importance to the growth of aspects of their personalities. If their education is organized so as to develop their personal powers, they will grasp its significance and gain a degree of personal autonomy. For example, it is becoming increasingly clear that in every field of endeavor requiring a college education, new skills and concepts must constantly be learned by an alert adult. An education that succeeds in giving adults confidence and flexibility in the face of new learning situations will involve them and equip them for excellence in whatever they are called on to do.

Reference

Gillespie, J. M., and Allport, G. W., *Youth's Outlook on the Future*, New York: Doubleday, 1955.

John Summerskill

Dropouts from College

American colleges lose, on the average, about half their students in the four years following matriculation. Some 40 per cent of college students graduate on schedule; 20 per cent more graduate after delay at some college or other. These have been the facts for several decades in American higher education.

FACTORS ASSOCIATED WITH DROPOUTS

Age at Matriculation. Age per se does not affect attrition, although older undergraduates may encounter more obstacles to graduation.

Sex. The most recent nationwide survey found attrition rates of 61 per cent for college men and 59 per cent for college women, a difference that is not significant. Compared with men, more women withdraw for nonacademic reasons, primarily for marriage.

Socioeconomic Factors. College counseling experience suggests that a student's economic and social background affects his adjustment to a given college and is, therefore, a factor in attrition. Research findings on this hypothesis are equivocal.

Home-Town Location and Size. A student's home-town location and size may be factors in attrition. For example, in three studies higher attrition rates have been found among students from rural homes than among students from cities or towns. One survey found that "out-of-state" students are likely to be "underachievers"; another found that students from cities with populations over 100,000 are likely to be "overachievers."

It is questionable whether location and size of home communities are *in themselves* factors that determine a student's chances of graduating from college. The quality of secondary schools, however, does vary between different cities and towns. Home towns also differ culturally—in the number and range of cultural facilities. Students growing up in these differing environments enter colleges that differ along the same dimensions.

Secondary School Preparation. Secondary school grades are generally recognized as the best existing prediction of college grades. Many students, however, drop from college with quite satisfactory grades, so in negative form the question remains: Are grades in secondary school significantly related to college attrition?

The answer is yes. The writer found that in ten of eleven studies specifically concerned with this question, college dropouts had lower average grades in secondary school than did graduates. This is not to deny, however, the influence of other secondary school factors. There is, for example, some evidence that students from larger high schools have significantly better chances of graduating from college.

Scholastic Aptitude. Not surprisingly, the indications are that colleges can reduce attrition by rejecting applicants whose scores on scholastic aptitude tests fall below the minimums set by the college. But this fact is not especially valuable to the many colleges now in a position to admit only students with the highest aptitude scores from an astonishingly large pool of applicants. Such colleges are besieged by many more students meeting the official test requirements than they can possibly accept.

Here, then, we must search beyond the student's measured intellectual potential to find how well he will receive college instruction. And we need to know much more than we do about his capacity for real scholarship, with its demands on curiosity, initiative, and intellectual energy.

Academic Performance at College. Generations of students would testify that college grades are a key determinant of college dropouts. There have been at least 35 studies on college grades and attrition, and it is clear that an interesting relationship between them does exist.

1. In a series of twenty-three studies the percentage of academic failures among those who dropped out ranged from 3 to 78 per cent, an immense spread reflecting differences in the policies and standards of colleges and in the composition of student bodies.

2. One out of three dropouts occurred for academic reasons.

3. Academic failure was typically cited as the leading single cause of dropouts, or as one of two or three main causes—depending on the college studied.

4. Poor or failing grades at the beginning of a college career indicated a likelihood that the student would later drop out.

Despite the academic factor, however, the majority of students leave college for nonacademic reasons. Furthermore, even those dropouts that college records ascribe to "academic failure" undoubtedly include many cases in which the underlying problems are psychological, parental, social, or financial. In such cases "academic failure" may serve the student as a *device* for leaving school when the problems seem insoluble within college walls.

In general, then, student dropouts arise largely from failure to meet psychological, sociological, or economic demands rather than the strictly academic demands of college life.

Motivation. This is not to deny that motives for dropping out are very much connected with college living itself. In most existing studies, the largest proportion of dropouts are attributed to "lack of interest in college," "lack of interest in studies," "marriage" or "marriage plans," "transfer," "entered military service," "accepted job," and so forth. Basically, the trouble is that we just don't know what kinds of motive *do* indicate future college success. In fact, we don't even know how to discern student motives with much accuracy.

Change and Conflict in Motivation. A good third of college dropouts have demonstrated clear academic capability but leave school to pursue other interests and goals. According to many studies, most dropouts state, upon leaving, their intention to complete their undergraduate education eventually. The majority do not, however.

There are two dimensions to the dropout problem that are not immediately apparent in the classroom. First, the student is still highly responsive to psychological and sociological forces, changing pressures that originate outside the immediate college environment. Second, although colleges are principally concerned with rational matters, students are human beings who act according to emotion and desire.

In the wider circle of influences on the college student, parents occupy key positions. True, they are constantly advised by PTA speakers, school counselors, and the like not to influence actively their children's motives concerning college and career. Accordingly, it is not uncommon for parents to tell the college counselor how carefully they have refrained from influencing young Johnny's decisions. But such abstinence is superficial: the lives of many college students are molded in important ways by feelings of dependence, ambition, fear, guilt, and rebellion, feelings which stem from family aspirations, sanctions, or disapproval.

Adjustment. Surveys indicate that dropouts who *report* feelings of dissatisfaction, in personality matters or their social situation, are a minority.

According to clinical observation, however, the percentage of dropouts with some degree of emotional difficulty is much higher than the foregoing statement might suggest. Among the psychological characteristics that have been attributed to unsuccessful students are immaturity, rebellion and nonconformity, worry and anxiety, social inadequacy, nonadaptability, lack of independence and responsibility.

Extra-Curricular Activities. Interestingly, research evidence does *not* support the common notion that dropouts are frequently caused by overparticipation in extracurricular activities. Similarly, fraternity or sorority membership is not generally a hindrance to graduation.

Illness and Injury. Dropouts due to illness and injury constitute a small but significant fraction of the total dropout population. In eighteen studies reviewed, the percentage of dropouts citing medical reasons was, on the average, 8 per cent. The range was from 1 to 24 per cent. Information from Cornell University indicates that more than 90 per cent of the student body there seek medical attention during the four-year college stay. Forty-two per cent are hospitalized at least briefly.

Financial Difficulty. This is an important cause of college attrition.

1. As a reason for leaving college, personal financial difficulties were ranked third in importance by the men and women surveyed nationally.

2. In sixteen of twenty-one studies reviewed by this author, finances were rated as one of the three most important factors in attrition.

3. Parents of nongraduating students enjoy an appreciably smaller average income than do parents whose young remain in school.

4. Self-support and part-time work seem to have little to do with success or failure at college.

All in all, there are no conclusive figures showing us exactly how far student dropouts in the nation as a whole are due to financial trouble. We can safely say, however, that the financial factor in dropouts ranks next only to study problems and the question of motivation.

Seven
The College Community

Christopher S. Jencks and David Riesman

Patterns of Residential Education: Reflections from a Case Study of Harvard [1]

In the fall of 1930 Harvard opened the first two of seven "en-riched" dormitories, each complete with common rooms, a library, and resident tutors who were to share the dining hall with under-graduates. Thereby was inaugurated the experimental "Harvard house system." Twenty-nine years later, the University opened an eighth residential house, while soliciting money for two more. This decision to invest a substantial amount of new capital in dormitories gave public notice that the house experiment is now a "success," and that the Harvard administration believes money spent on these buildings will do as much to improve undergraduate education as money spent on faculty salaries, library books, and other essentials.

It is true that measured by utopian standards the houses have not been a complete success. They have not reconciled work and leisure in the college, nor have they created a community in which ideas belong primarily to people rather than to the classroom or the library. Measured by more modest criteria, however, the houses have done more to preserve intellectual and humane qual-ities in the academic community than most educational ventures, and they suggest further experiments either at Harvard or else-where. Although the houses are unique institutions, they suggest some of the problems and possibilities in that immensely com-plicated undertaking—the creation of an intellectual community.

During the whole development of the house system there has been a tension between the ideal of solidarity, friendship, and se-curity, and the ideal of diversity, conflict, and adventure. Neither of these ideals can endure alone. Students must be stretched, but

[1] This chapter represents general inferences for college education, drawn from a fuller, more detailed analysis of the Harvard house system by the authors.

not to the breaking point. They must become involved in conflicts, but they must have enough security to believe that they may emerge victorious, for otherwise they become rigid with fright and learn nothing, or only by rote. Only in a university such as Harvard, where the presence of a graduate school, research, and academic departments guarantees the intellectual currency, can we afford to urge that the college should be made more sheltering and homelike. In small provincial colleges the houses and the utopias they suggest are irrelevant or even dangerous. These communities are likely to be so supportive and homogeneous that there is neither incentive nor room for original or imaginative thought. Harvard and other colleges which have been through the academic revolution can worry because their students and faculty get verbal indigestion from reading the massive "assignments" and often read for pleasure and curiosity only during vacation. But for most colleges such "postacademic" concerns are still over the horizon. These colleges are still faced with students who do not read at all, and with faculty who suffer not from the esoteric malnutrition of journals but from the intellectual pellagra that comes of reading only textbooks and best sellers.

Yet even in colleges where the students' intellectual potential is still latent, and where the academic revolution has not yet transformed the faculty into scholars, there are powerful national pressures which may make the houses relevant. The number of talented college applicants is growing faster than the number of spaces in the elite colleges, so that an increasing number of colleges get a share of the intelligent younger generation. Much depends, however, on how these students, often forced to attend second-choice colleges, react to the less prestigious institutions they are made to discover. On the one hand, the whole country is doubtless becoming more sophisticated, possessing many decentralized centers of light and learning; on the other hand, there is an enormous number of American colleges which are intellectually vacuous and where a bright but not exceptionally energetic student will have trouble finding an education on his own. This may even be an increasing trend as the competition for faculty among the leading institutions leaves the less privileged institutions, seeking accreditation or eager to retain it, with a mass of sadistic and otherwise incompetent teachers whose sole virtue is that they have managed to get a Ph.D. or want to obtain one locally.[1]

Let us add that we must be cautious about using such terms as "bright" or "intellectual" students in any absolute sense, although colleges, like other factory-like institutions, find it convenient to grade and label their products. Given a certain minimum of intelligence and energy, and an ideal college setting, most students transcend the limitations of their families and secondary schools to discover intellectual interests. But even the very best colleges are far from ideal in this sense, far from reaching all their students, or even the great majority, no matter how much work they get out of degree-hungry and honors-hungry undergraduates.

Most of the places that do come close to this ideal are small. In all these settings, even the urban ones, some kind of physical community would seem essential for the creation of an intense intellectual style. This does not necessarily mean the architectural splendor of a Harvard house. Although physically unified buildings, facing onto "their" courtyard or quadrangle, encourage their residents to identify with the community, we doubt that this is as important as many less-expensive aspects of the physical and social architecture. It is proximity, not unity, which is essential. This means proximity not only of the bachelors who—with a few married tutors—inhabit the Harvard houses, but also of married students and professors, who at Harvard often live in the suburbs. Unless the academic relations of classroom and the professor's office are extended to the social and personal relations of dining room and living room, we doubt that the faculty can play an important role in shaping the community which educates the stu-

[1] For rather different conclusions about the same subject, see B. Berelson, *Graduate Education in the United States.* New York: McGraw-Hill, 1960.

dents. Something can be done, as at Harvard, by providing free lunches for faculty who eat with the students, but this is only a limited answer so long as home base is miles away.

It goes without saying that nostalgic and often snobbish values are frequently used to defend residential colleges as against commuter colleges; there is no magic about living together, and ingenuity and imagination can overcome some of the disadvantages of a commuter college. Certainly, as the critics of "bedroom communities" constantly urge, the place where students and faculty sleep is less important than where they do their waking business. And, as the commuter center (Dudley House) at Harvard illustrates, much can be done when residential patterns are anarchic, and the community provides only limited curricular and extracurricular facilities. If the community also requires every member to contract for a certain number of meals as a condition of membership, it assures that every student and faculty member will automatically have some opportunity to accept or reject his fellows. Students are embarrassed at *planning* to meet people they hardly know, especially if sex is not present to legitimize such breaches in the ideology of casualness. Sharing meals provides an acceptable opportunity for renewing and deepening casual acquaintances, which are likely to wither in a college that is only a collection of classrooms.

Spontaneous meetings can also be increased by providing coffee breaks between meals in the common rooms. "Morning coffee" gives even the busiest professor an excuse and opportunity to make nonbusiness acquaintances if he wants. As we have already implied, with such arrangements even a commuter college could create the human relationships required if scholars and students are to have a sense of intellectual identity which transcends their departments and courses—or the kind of intellectual curiosity which looks beyond advancing the discipline.[2]

Whatever the variations in living arrangements, we suspect that

[2] At Monteith College, a small Student Center in a run-down building has in fact provided some of these ties for a minority of the students.

the size of the community is a critical factor in its shape. Unfortunately, we know no formula for determining optimal community size. In the first place, some individuals can cope with larger communities than can others; and undergraduate transfers in both directions between "small" and "large" colleges indicate that students themselves often cannot always tell in what environments they will prosper, or change, as they progress through college. In the second place, no community, intellectual or otherwise, encompasses the entire social life of the student, and optimal size will vary according to the alternative resources and diversions. A Harvard student invests only part of his energy in knowing and enjoying his fellow house members, for he has other interests as well. With such limited capital, his house must remain relatively small or it will become a dormitory in which the student maintains a small clique of friends while looking at the other residents from the defensive perspective of an outsider. In contrast to Harvard, a small liberal arts college can count on almost all a student's curricular and extracurricular activities to bring him into contact with other members of "his" community. Thus, unless the small college must compete with the student's home, job, or local community for his energy, it can perhaps afford to be larger than a house. Indeed, if a liberal arts college is to provide the special subcultures which make life endurable for many students, and make it interesting for the rest, it must be larger than a Harvard house, for unlike a house such colleges cannot count on a cosmopolitan university setting to counterbalance the parochialism and dogmas which thrive in all small communities.

The size of the community depends not only on the environment, but on the temperament of the recruits. If the students are slow to meet one another, as at Harvard, the community cannot contain as many as Harvard's 4500 people and develop solidarity in three short years. In a somewhat more sociable community such as Yale, 400 students in a college might prove manageable. Experience does show that the 20 to 40 members of a club are too few, and equally certainly, the 1250 members of the Harvard freshman class, or the 4500 members of the college (5700 when Radcliffe is added), are too many. One possible index of optimal size is that the residential unit should be small enough so that everyone can know everyone else's name. Indeed, students should know enough about everyone in a house so that they know which students they might want to know better, and in this context it is important to realize the danger of making a house even slightly too big. For if a student feels he cannot know everyone, he reduces his efforts to know even a majority, so that, for example, few Harvard freshmen know 400 classmates, although some sophomores may learn the names of all their fellow house members. On the other hand, once numbers are below the critical size at which the residents "massify" their image of one another into some defensive stereotype, further reduction of the population also means reducing the human resources available to the energetic student. In a house so small that everyone knows more than the name of every fellow student, privacy may become attenuated. Fraternity may replace community, with every brother so committed to the others that he fears antagonisms or the development of important "divisive" differences.

The question of size also depends on how initially different the students are from one another. If, as at Oxford and Cambridge, there are yawning chasms between social classes, and between preprofessional students in various fields, the community must be quite small if it is to bridge the gaps by driving students together at meals, say, or, in extracurricular activities.

Another factor affecting size is the span of time the student has to identify with his community and meet his fellows. The Harvard house is a three-year community, since undergraduates spend their first year in freshman dormitories; if the house were a four-year venture capitalizing on the enormous energy and adaptability of freshmen, it might be able to encompass more people than it now does.

As in all problems of social architecture, the problem of size depends also on structure. Any intellectual community, therefore, probably ought also to be an administrative community. Like the Harvard house, it should have its president and dean, and should do as much as possible to reduce to human scale the impersonal and often awkward and harried officialdom who otherwise may make the student in a large university feel like an otusider. The community should also administer its own recruiting process: Harvard's houses retain a notable sense of self-perpetuation by exerting at least the power of negative selection.

But an educational community needs more than a political-administrative system to survive. It must also have its own culture and ideology, and for this it should be able to look to the faculty. At Harvard the problem is difficult. The house faculty consists largely of graduate students, occasionally supplemented by professors. To graduate students who are only in rare cases graduates of Harvard College, and to a faculty that often regards the houses as a refuge of outworn gentlemanly values, the houses naturally appear as alien, if entrenched, ground. Since perhaps 70 per cent of the faculty remains unconnected with the houses, they largely forfeit their opportunity to reach the undepartmentalized among the students. The latter, while sufficiently touched by Harvard to regard classrooms and scholarship as praiseworthy, are reluctant to commit themselves to these ends permanently. If these students are to be brought into intimate affective contact with the curriculum, it might make sense for the faculty to follow the lead of the administration in decentralizing itself and moving a great deal more teaching to the houses than presently occurs there. Decentralizing the curriculum in this way would also give both students and faculty some sense of manageable mutual responsibility. No faculty member, however conscientious, can do justice to 7500 "responsibilities" (4500 Harvard undergraduates, 1000 Radcliffe students, and 2000 graduate students). So he delievers lectures, and then waits in an office to which only the delinquent or the brash usually come.

A serious objection to decentralizing the curriculum is that the student would lose the intellectual resources of that majority of the faculty associated with houses other than his own. Insofar as the student knows what he wants and knows how to get it from the faculty, this objection is valid.

But the student who is not apprenticed to a particular discipline cannot so easily tell which professors and courses he needs. His problem is not to get what he wants but to figure out what he wants. Under the present system he usually fills requirements and then wanders aimlessly, hoping to find a man who will speak to his particular dilemmas, and often winding up in the lecture hall of some pundit who has grown famous for addressing his parents' generation. If students had only to decide among the offerings of that tenth of the faculty associated with "their" house, they would be choosing among men whom they would very likely know at least casually after a year or two of residence, and about whom they would be able to gather considerable information from friends. This might actually give them a wider range of real choice than they now have. And for the specialist who found the house offerings inadequate there would always be the graduate departmental program, in which many Harvard upperclassmen already enroll. Likewise, for the scholar who really thought he had something of general interest to say, there would always be the open lecture series—perhaps incorporated by some houses into their curricula if that seemed appropriate.

What we have sketched here as a residential utopia already exists in some measure in one or another of the houses. Thus two of the houses have recently "affiliated" with Radcliffe dormitories, making possible joint tutorials in one case, and joint artistic and musical activities in another, and in both cases helping to break down the characteristic American dichotomy between the intellectual and the social. It seems conceivable, indeed, that an even closer, more localized relationship between students and faculty might well influence the latter toward less intense professional concern. This would not necessarily mean less specialization, but the specialization might revolve around concerns shared by students and teachers as well as concerns shared by teachers with other teachers. The "post-industrial" era into which our society is moving has found that productivity is not necessarily lowered by making the morale and well-being of the workers an additional "factor of production." Similarly, we think that a college of the "postacademic" era could introduce broad intellectual standards in addition to the older departmental criteria of academic achievement without risking superficiality or stagnation. To some extent this postacademic world already exists in various institutes, a few free-wheeling industrial laboratories, and some interdisciplinary research centers, which emphasize problem-solving rather than development of "the field." So long as every teacher gets his degree in a graduate department and retains his affiliation with it, we doubt that there is any serious danger of watering down knowledge either in "applied" research or in "applied" teaching. Just as applied research should give the customer what he needs rather than what he wants, so the kind of teaching we have in mind would not be what one master scathingly brands the "baby knows best" approach to education. For one thing, the undergraduates are themselves less and less like babies, but increasingly precocious, demanding, and capable of responding to intellectual intensity. For another, as all we have said has made clear, the houses are never going to become the sole base for the Harvard faculty, with its ramified contacts in its own fields of scholarly endeavor and its increasingly worldly connections in government, industry, and the mass media.

Despite all the guidelines that the houses suggest, the difficulties of creating an intellectual community are enormous. In the first place, students do not want to be patronized by their elders for their youth and inexperience, and they hasten into adulthood at breakneck speed. An intellectual community must attempt to resist such momentum, to provide a moratorium in which the young may reconsider what they are about to become. For many, however, such shilly-shallying seems insufferable, and at Harvard nearly a quarter of the students withdraw for a year or two to discover "real life." (Most of them later return.) Nor is the faculty itself ready to resist American activism. Academicians distrust the dilettante and the ruminative person. Professors justify their own curiosity by harnessing it to the "pushing back of the frontiers of knowledge," and they try to bring students to this professional level of research as rapidly as possible, often seeing little point in a play of ideas which has subjective rather than publishable consequences. Like their students, professors want professional identities and would rather describe themselves as chemists or anthropologists or musicologists than as mere professors, or—still worse —intellectuals.

Nor is there any model for the kinds of relationships that the intellectual community must encourage. In terms of educational ideas, the last dozen years have been a time of consolidation rather than advance in the major universities, with older experiments becoming partially assimilated and incorporated. Most educational debates have become so platitudinous and tired that intelligent professors yearn for the end of ideology and prefer not to debate such issues as general education, progressivism, or the relation between an intellectual and a residential community. In universities where men are harried by multitudinous demands and where real and relaxing intimacy sometimes seems difficult to find, proposing that men share not only friendship but also ideas may merely add one more "impossible" demand to their burdens. And in a world where togetherness based on superficial similarities makes rugged individualism nostalgically attractive, an appeal for solidarity on any basis seems untimely. Most of all, to a culture in which ideas are seen as either tools or possessions, the possibility of finding students and teachers who will use them as the basis for constructing a more livable community seems remote. Nevertheless we are convinced that closing the gap between the professionally academic and the amateur intellectual will become an increasing problem for higher education as the values of the academic professions spread throughout the university world.

Since World War II the great universities have made many changes designed to increase productivity, both among students and among staff. Increasingly careful selection of undergraduates has meant that more and more students are digesting unprecedented amounts of printed matter. (Reading lists have become the tail-fins of the faculty.) Students are making themselves at home in the academic atmosphere of libraries, laboratories, and seminars. Such achievements inspire envy among less selective or less cohesive institutions, but they provide inadequate ground for complacency among the successful. Just as Americans must eventually come to realize that a viable world order requires more than raising underdeveloped countries closer to the plateau of industrial affluence, so too educators can now begin to see that an adequate educational system demands more than the victory of university departments and academic professionalism over the collegiate fun culture.

Harold Taylor

Freedom and Authority on the Campus

The progressive or liberal view is that people become better when freed from authority, when they make their own choices and think for themselves, when they act out of personal judgment. The liberal and progressive movements of this century have called for the liberation of the individual from the authority of the state, the church, the family, from moral coercion and cultural orthodoxy. The general theory which holds together these applications of the liberal position is the idea that the true human community is a group of individuals bound together by common interests and an ethic of mutual respect.

As the liberal sees it, therefore, authority is a set of general agreements which the members of the community are willing to abide by; these agreements change from time to time as circumstances change, the community develops, and different experiences are shared in common.

When the ideas of progressive philosophy are translated into educational practice, the school and the college are organized as institutional models for a liberal society. The teacher is not an authority who tells his students what they should know, what they should think, or what they should do. He is a friend who is helping students to become educated by the experiences he is able to bring to them. He wishes no intellectual or personal authority over the minds and attitudes of his students; he does not direct their ideas toward established conclusions but acts in ways designed to help them to form their own judgments. Students in the progressive college may choose the courses they will study, take part in forming educational policy, form their own self-government for student and college affairs.

In the same way, the principal of the progressive school or the president of the progressive college is not an administrator running faculty and students, but a chairman of the whole, serving at the will of the governing board, the faculty, and the students —a democratic leader who orchestrates the variety of interests, judgments, opinions, and decisions of all those connected with the educational institution, including students, faculty, parents, the board of control, members of the community, and alumni.

Interactions of Students and Educators

By contrast with the foregoing, American colleges have historically taken a great deal of responsibility and authority for students, with explicit rules which must be observed if the student is to remain in college, and with the authority of the dean and the president used to enforce college-made rules. In earlier years the college served in place of the family as the arbiter of conduct. This has been particularly true of the colleges for women, where rules have been strict and rigorously applied.

Over the years, however, the concept of college authority administered by the dean to those in his charge has shifted away from the punitive toward permissive policies. Students sometimes have a part in forming policy, for it is assumed that learning to handle personal-social problems is one phase of the process of maturing in the young adult.

THE EXPERIMENTAL APPROACH

Among the experimental colleges that grew out of the new movement in education during the 1920's and 1930's, a new concept of social structure and the relation of freedom to authority was developed. This concept rested on the idea that, by planning a certain kind of social community, educators could create ideal conditions for individual fulfillment. Through planning, the democratic virtues of tolerance, understanding, generosity, cooperation and respect for freedom could be taught as values *implicit in the social structure.*

As an experimental college, Sarah Lawrence has tried in a number of ways since its beginning thirty-two years ago to build such a community. The principle underlying Sarah Lawrence practice at the founding was that students should be liberated from all restrictions of college authority and should be given powers of self-government for which they took full responsibility. The students were asked to make the rules themselves through a system of representative government and to administer the rules through a student discipline committee without faculty control or supervision. The students were also responsible for making up their own social groups, both in forming student organizations and societies and in choosing friends with whom they wished to live in the dormitories. There were no sororities or honorary societies, and no prizes, awards, grades, or any other symbols of prestige except those won through the respect of others for service to the community.

Throughout the 1930's and 1940's, this degree of freedom was vigorously used, and the student prerogatives were jealously guarded against any suggestion by the faculty or administration that they should be changed or modified. Students expressed their views strongly on most subjects, organized student meetings to take political action, kept their literary magazine, student newspaper, and student organizations almost completely to themselves, and seldom requested help from the faculty or administration in student affairs. The Student Council and the Student Discipline Committee made the rules and dealt with infractions; council and committee members shared actively in making college policy through a Joint Committee of students and faculty, and through the Student Curriculum Committee.

Beginning about 1950, however, the older assumptions on which the college system rested were shown to be in need of revision. It could no longer be assumed that liberation into freedom was the exhilarating experience that it had been for earlier generations of Sarah Lawrence students. Whereas in earlier years it had been possible to count on the strong motivation and initiative of students to conduct their own affairs, to form new organizations, to invent new projects either in social welfare or in intellectual fields, it now became clear that for many students, the responsibility for self-government was often a burden to bear rather than a right to be maintained. For others, the Sarah Lawrence system of community government was one to which they had already become accustomed in high school, and it lacked the degree of freshness as far as their experience as students was concerned. Many able students who would have been first-rate student officers refused to accept nomination in student elections. They felt they did not wish to take the time away from their college work. They also felt that they had had all the experience they could profitably absorb in the field of student affairs by their involvement in such matters in high school.

Nor was there a high degree of vitality in the concept of student freedom itself, since it was already theirs and it was not necessary to fight to keep it. From 1950 on, interest in political action declined to the point that even a student meeting on McCarthyism could not attract an audience which included the students who organized the meeting. Students tended to devote themselves to their own studies, to their own friends. They were apathetic about events or occasions planned for the whole college. They made less effort than before to identify themselves with the rest of the student body or with the college as an institution. They preferred to work within a smaller framework in which only the teachers with whom they studied and the small number of friends who meant most to them were significant parts of their college life.

Beginning about this same time, morale in the dormitories also showed evidence of decline. Infractions of student rules were more frequent than before and the mechanisms by which the students could correct the situation were little used. Some house presidents responsible for the conduct of individuals within their houses often failed to report glaring infractions; others who did report were punitive in their attitude and caused dissension in the houses when they exercised their authority. At the same time, attempts on the part of the college administration to provide more guidance were opposed by the students.

In accounting for these new attitudes, we might point to the pressures against political unorthodoxy that characterized America in the 1950's; to special pressures directed against Sarah Lawrence by congressional committees and patriotic groups; and to the helplessness that young people felt when they thought about an international situation dominated by the Cold War. These forces certainly played a part, but there were other factors too. One of these was the possibility that a system of complete self-determination did not necessarily liberate the student. Undergraduates who were given complete freedom to make their own decisions often did not wish to do so, and not wishing to do so, they did not achieve a real, inner freedom.

THE NEW GENERATION

On analysis, several other reasons could be found for the shift in student attitude. The 1950 generations of college students were born from 1935 to 1940. During their first six years they were living in a society recovering from a depression; they then entered the war years with a growing period of prosperity for their families, and a postwar period in which the world closed in more and more upon the United States, while the United States increased in prosperity and power. The combination of tension from the world situation and the growth in national prosperity produced an attitude of caution and conservatism in the country which was bound to be reflected in the attitude of families and of children to their lives.

At the same time, the growth of a new attitude to child rearing meant that most parents in bringing up this generation have made a genuine effort to understand their children and not to impose parental authority in ways which might inhibit the young child. As a result, it is extremely difficult for the child to rebel, since he is understood rather than repressed. This has its consequences in giving him nothing but feather pillows to fight, and in developing an attitude of self-understanding before there is a great deal of self to understand.

Most sixteen-year-olds are sufficiently sophisticated not only to know the limits of power possessed by their parents if it were to be put to the test, but are also prepared to live an independent emotional life by depriving the parents of a return of affection, by appearing a minimum amount of time at home, by surface conformity to demands, or by simply leaving home altogether. With the removal of the concept of parental authority, the balance of power in family life has shifted to the young. Having staked everything on a warm and affectionate relationship with the child, the parent cannot later resort to older methods of authority with its expectation of respect and obedience.

In this situation, the strongest force that parents exert for compliance with family wishes is usually to induce a feeling of guilt on the part of the child for causing distress to the parents whose requests are disregarded, a guilt which may from time to time have its own aggressive manifestations in a confused rebellion and a sense of frustration. A new syndrome thus emerges in which there is no longer a clear-cut authority-freedom issue for the adolescent, but instead there are ambivalent feelings of obligation, responsibility, and guilt. Whatever satisfaction there may be in open rebellion is stifled at the source. The adolescent is unable to rebel, since before overt rebellion occurs, his parents will no doubt demonstrate their "understanding" of his wish to rebel by assuring him that it is perfectly natural. The tension of opposites, so often a part in the healthy emotional situation of the adolescent disappears in a warm bath of parental affection. The parent therefore has no control over the child, whereas the child often has not yet had sufficient experience to exert control over himself.

This underlies and creates a new and different attitude on the part of college students to the authority of their parents. It also creates a different attitude to the authority of their college. Such a shift in attitude has been foreshadowed by a change in the social structure of the high school and preparatory school. Much more is arranged for the students, although at the same time, students are given more responsibility for sharing in educational and social policy making. Added to this is the provision of entertainment by football games, television, radio, mass magazines, and community projects. The young person's attitude toward entertainment in general becomes that of a spectator, and he no longer takes up with the same enthusiasm his opportunities for self-expression, either in student planning or in social affairs.

SOME RESEARCH AT SARAH LAWRENCE

During the years from 1948 to 1952, a group of Sarah Lawrence faculty members under the chairmanship of Dr. Lois Murphy conducted a research project designed to discover something about the process of change and growth in college students.[1] The social life of the campus, the relationship of students to each other and to the college, their morale, their personal concerns, their attitude to the educational system as it was then operating were all part of the research interests of those who carried out the study.

In what follows, I have taken from the Sarah Lawrence research some material which might throw light on the question of how the concept of student freedom worked in practice.

My own experience in working with the students had led me to believe that during the early 1950's the transfer of responsibility to the students for running their own affairs was producing apathy rather than the creative results we had been accustomed to expect. If faculty members, on principle, remained aloof from working with the students in organizing student affairs, very little happened. Students were more often than not frustrated and discouraged. They said that they had few ideas of their own, and that even if they did, they would not know how to carry them out in the face of the apathy of other students. They spoke continually of the need for faculty guidance. By taking attitudes which, in educational terms, were intended to make the students

[1] Some of the results of the research have been published under the title *Achievement in the college years*, edited by Lois Murphy and Esther Raushenbush. Harper and Brothers, 1960.

independent of adult authority, we seemed in fact to have made them more dependent.

Student Morale

First let us comment on some aspects of student morale, since the factor of morale is directly related to the question of how students respond to the absence of institutional authority. Do they enjoy what they are doing? If you simply give them a free hand, do they have the personal resources and the maturity to make a satisfying life for themselves out of their own materials?

One major assumption underlying the Sarah Lawrence program and curriculum is that learning in depth occurs only when the student moves with some zest toward the material to be learned and feels sympathy for the aims of the course and of its teacher. The students choose the courses they wish to study, there are no examinations or competitive grades, and subjects are not formally divided. From freshman year on, most of the work is independent study. This is not to say that the college assumes that students should study only those things which interest and stimulate them, but to say that the student must engage himself willingly in the tasks of learning before the discipline and rigor of learning can be realized in action.

The morale of the students is thus a particularly important ingredient of education at a school like Sarah Lawrence.

When we asked the students to say whether or not they were happy at Sarah Lawrence, two-thirds of the students said that they were very happy. Nearly all the rest said they were fairly happy, with 2 per cent who said that they were not. Eighty-eight per cent said that they would choose to come to Sarah Lawrence if they had it to do over again, and about half the students found life at the college better than they had anticipated. Twelve per cent found their experience at the college disappointing in one way or another.

We wanted to know as much as we could about the factors that contributed to low or high morale, and found that when asked to list their most satisfying experiences, the top of the list by a large margin had to do with the students' intellectual experience—a particular course, a teacher, or the satisfaction of working well with a teacher or in a course. Forty-three per cent of the students mentioned this. A third of the students mentioned the satisfaction of general intellectual achievement, and specifically such satisfactions as learning to read well, to take in new ideas, the chance to work independently and in small classes. We had expected to find a fairly large number of answers which would put a high value on the amount of personal freedom granted to the students, and on the richness of the cultural life available on the campus. This did not turn out to be the case. Only 3 per cent mentioned as of particular importance the amount of personal freedom granted; 7 per cent mentioned activities outside their courses as being their most important experiences at the college. Since the degree of personal freedom is as great as is possible, consonant with the ordinary social proprieties, we can only conclude that the students, very shortly after their arrival at the college, take that freedom for granted.

We also asked the students what they worried about when they *were* worried, by presenting a list of 48 "worries" with the request to check "the ones which have been of some concern to you during the past year." The list was fairly comprehensive and was based on knowledge of the students; for example, items had to do with concern about money, conflict with the family, not being popular.

Without comparable statistics on the responses of students on other campuses, it would not be possible to say whether the social organization of the Sarah Lawrence campus, which has tried to eliminate competition, social snobbery, or false prestige values has accomplished more in this direction than the conventional system. But it is significant in a free system that only a very few students in the total number had worries connected with not being popular or not achieving student prestige. Nor does the lack of rules seem to be as important as we had been led to believe by student comment, since only 1 per cent of the students mentioned this in their replies.

The Role of the Faculty

The normal concerns of the college student—difficulties in concentration, feelings of inadequacy, lack of self-identity, worries about personal relationships—seem not to have developed to extremes of anxiety through the openness of the Sarah Lawrence system. At Sarah Lawrence we have counted on a direct relationship between students and teachers to meet some of these concerns. Each student has a faculty adviser, known as a don, with whom the student usually confers once each week, and who is responsible for the general welfare of the student. Other teachers with whom the students are working in their courses also give help and advice when asked.

We were interested in knowing how far the students counted on the advice and help of faculty members, and to whom the students went with their personal concerns. In their answers to our questionnaire, nearly four fifths of the students listed "a friend" as the person to whom they talked. Over half mentioned their mothers, about two fifths mentioned their dons; almost as many mentioned a male friend or their fathers.

If we count those who talk with a faculty member other than their don, there are well over half the students who turn to faculty members for guidance; about as many as turn to their mothers, while around 80 per cent talked to other students. This confirms the notion that most of the talk about personal problems goes on between students, and that the relationships among students in the residences are the greatest single factor in their general attitude toward the college and toward themselves.

In further discussions with the students it became clear that they were against the idea of residential counselors or faculty members. Certainly they wanted the presence of faculty members around the campus, at student meetings, or as informal visitors to the dormitories, but not as representatives of college authority. The student house presidents were in fact in the role of residential counselors, and it became clear through further analysis and discussion that the quality of life within a given residence depended most of all on the qualifications of the house president for holding office. Student suggestions about this problem resulted in marked changes in the nominations and election procedures, and changes in the methods by which student choices for residence in a given house were screened and allocated.

To me this was one of the most revealing parts of the study. The combination of the research results and further discussion with a variety of students showed that the big reasons for student apathy or frustration—the world situation, public pressures, McCarthy, and so on—were less important than the spirit and personal relationships of the students among themselves. When we saw that a group of thirty students who lived together could develop negative, nagging, and emotionally unhealthy attitudes simply from three or four of their number who were working out their problems at the expense of the rest, the need for more organization of residence life became obvious.

It also became obvious that in the selection of a student body to function in a free community, it was of first importance to consider the personal attributes of the appliants every bit as seriously as their academic qualifications. Intellectually ambitious students with a drive toward personal gratification could, if present in sufficient numbers in a given residence, produce sufficient tension and difficulty within their own environment to prevent the healthy development of the students around them and to block their own growth. This is true not merely for experimental and progressive colleges, but for those which are at present moving quickly toward the establishment of what are called high academic standards, by which is usually meant a population of students who got good grades in high school.

The "Social" Life

At the time of our research, the campus was usually deserted on weekends, and the Student Entertainment Committee found that when it went to the trouble of arranging a party or planning a concert, or in general making the weekend at the college an interesting and stimulating one, very few students stayed. From the questionnaire we found that nearly 60 per cent of the student body left campus on about 60 per cent of the weekends. Since they did this of their own volition, and had the means of planning events for themselves if they wished to stay, we asked whether they were satisfied with this arrangement. We found that 67 per cent thought there was something wrong with the way weekends were arranged at the college. Thirty-seven per cent said they would have stayed had there been something interesting to do.

The criticism of the college's social life most often heard was that it did not exist on weekends. Yet when given a full opportunity to make it exist, the students were unable to plan anything for themselves which they found interesting enough to engage in. After seeing the results of the 1952 study, the college itself took the initiative in planning such events as intercollegiate conferences, tennis tournaments, student concerts, student theater performances on weekends, and discovered that in answer to the same questions in 1953, only 45 per cent of the students as against the previous 67 per cent found the social life inadequate.

Although the students themselves were unable to solve this problem, we did discover something about the way in which the students spent the time they had for recreation, social life, and entertainment. When presented with a list of eighteen sparetime activities, the students put "engage in bull sessions" first (72 per cent), followed by "listen to records" (71 per cent), "go to concerts, plays, etc." (66 per cent), read newspapers (65 per cent), read unassigned books (64 per cent), write letters (59 per cent), listen to the radio (52 per cent), do household chores (49 per cent), go to the movies (45 per cent). Only 19 per cent indicated that they watched television.[2]

The preferences for private activities with small groups of friends meant to us that the regular attitude which college students are assumed to possess—the wish for incessant togetherness, to live the intercollegiate sporting life, to be "social"—did not exist in any degree on the Sarah Lawrence campus. Although the students missed the regulation college events and would have liked more of them, they found substitutes in activities which on the whole seem preferable to the things which might have been substituted. They wished their social life to take place around common intellectual interests rather than on the basis of conventional dating practices. I would conclude that our students had the great advantage of possessing private interests and having occasional periods of loneliness.

The Practice of Self-Government

We asked some direct questions about student government and the use of student freedom in rule making and rule keeping. We found that nearly one quarter of the student body did not think that the Student Council represented them. More than half the freshmen and 23 per cent of the seniors did not know what the council did. On the matter of keeping rules, the answers suggested that there had been about as much rule breaking as we thought there had been, and that the students felt that the faculty should take more responsibility for the organization of the student community.

The Student and the Curriculum

Another phenomenon of the 1950's had been the amount of criticism by the students of the free curriculum and unconventional methods at Sarah Lawrence, a kind of criticism which had not seemed to exist at the college during the 1930's and 1940's.

[2] There were only two television sets on the campus at that time.

Students began to ask questions at student meetings about why Sarah Lawrence offered no lecture and survey courses in Western civilization of the kind in effect at other colleges, why there was not more systematic coverage of departmental subject matter, why there could not be examinations and grades so that a student would know her performance compared with that of others.

We therefore asked for student views of the Sarah Lawrence educational methods and found that approximately 85 to 90 per cent of the students supported the discussion method, although many of them called for more positive direction by the teacher. From the standpoint of this essay, indeed, the most important finding was that 52 per cent of the freshmen and 76 per cent of the seniors asked for more direction.

Social and Political Attitudes

One other fact about the student attitude of the 1950's has caused much public comment—their lack of involvement in social issues or political action. The irony in the Sarah Lawrence situation was that the college has always been looked on as a place where radical thinking is fostered and where freedom of thought nourishes political radicalism—when in fact, the students are generally conservative in their politics, and, as our research showed, are not influenced in a given political direction by their Sarah Lawrence education. The study of political attitudes on the basis of the questionnaire was made during the height of the McCarthy time when the college was attacked over a period of two and a half years by a variety of organizations and individuals. The effect of the complete freedom of political action given to the Sarah Lawrence students was that they favored strongly the defense of academic freedom by the college, but did very little on their own initiative either in arranging meetings to discuss political issues or in taking specific action. On the basis of the questionnaire research and other findings it is evident that in the early 1950's, Sarah Lawrence students in general, (like students in other colleges) were conservative, that they tended to accept their society as they found it, that their college education did not affect their political affiliation in any marked degree.

It is not the function of a college to make an effort to change students' political affiliation. It is its function to teach students to become aware of social and political issues, to enable them to reach independent judgments on the merits of such issues, and to understand and participate as citizens in the functioning of the American system of government. We know enough about the way the Sarah Lawrence students conduct their own community affairs to say that the initiative in raising political and social issues was not coming from them, and that unless the issues were raised in the context of classroom and course discussions, or in student meetings sponsored jointly by faculty and students, it is unlikely that they would have been raised at all.

CONCLUSION: TRANSACTIONAL RELATIONSHIPS AND INTELLECTUAL GROWTH

The shift in attitude of Sarah Lawrence students toward their own freedom is certainly real, when the comparison is made between the early 1950's and the 1930's and 1940's. If students are given responsibility and authority for an autonomous student community, without a direct and working connection with the two other essential community components—the faculty and the administration—the system grinds to a stop and ceases to function as a true community.

Our research findings, however, do support the fundamental principle of progressive theory: that true intellectual growth feeds on environmental factors of all kinds—emotional, social, and physical. The growth in ethical sensibility occurs as an effect of the total college atmosphere, but the seed of idealism is sown in the environment by teachers and educators; it is not magically produced by the student community through the operation of a free social system.

It is fallacious to assume, as the older progressive theory held, that absence of institutional authority and the award of freedom to the young in a radically democratic system will develop an understanding of democracy. On the contrary, we have found that in many cases it actually tended to foster authoritarian attitudes. The fallacy lies in assuming that because students have student rights and an equal *status* with faculty and administration, they should perform the same *role*. If this fallacy is acted upon in educational planning, students may insist on the right to make decisions on all questions, regardless of competence, experience, or knowledge, and regardless of the rights and judgment of faculty and administration. It may also result in so much student bickering over legalisms and procedure that no student enjoys any part of real self-government.

The teacher does not contribute to student freedom by withdrawal from a going relationship with the student subculture, nor by the older, nondirective, permissive approach to students. On the other hand, the alternative to laissez-faire or permissive attitudes is not a revival of institutional authority to control the students, any more than the answer to student requests for an examination system, grades, survey courses, and a conventional academic apparatus is to give it to them.

The faculty-student relationship must be conceived as transactional rather than mutually autonomous. The danger to be avoided on the one hand is a kind of orthodox liberal piety which by good fellowship smothers a community with so much tolerance and understanding that everyone becomes a neutered, polite, and conformist liberal. The danger on the other hand is that if there are no clear-cut aims, rules, and procedures with sanctions and authority of some kind against violations, there is endless discussion, ambiguity, confusion, and emotional fatigue from devoting too much energy to discussion and not enough to getting on with the program.

Students need all the freedom we can give them. But they need equally to learn by example whom and what they can respect.

George G. Stern

Environments for Learning

The influence of the emotions and personality on learning is generally approached from the point of view of the individual learner —his motives, inhibitions, aspirations, and fears—for the ultimate purpose of helping him to become more receptive to education. But there are other factors, independent of the learner, that are associated with the emotional atmosphere surrounding the learning experience itself, and these also are of considerable significance for education.

In the 1930's experimental comparisons of the effects of democratic and autocratic atmospheres on group performance drew attention for the first time to the sociopsychological aspects of environments in which learning takes place. These studies were the forerunners of nondirective innovations in psychotherapy and of permissiveness in pediatrics. The implications of these several lines of development were that the key to learning must lie in the establishment of more democratic, nondirective, and permissive classroom environments.

The evidence from subsequent studies of the relative effects of student- versus instructor-centered teaching techniques proved ambiguous, however. Current research suggests that group atmosphere and pupil personality are interactive; the success of the learning experience may depend on the optimal combination of teaching technique and student need, rather than on a hypothetically ideal procedure of universal application.

THE AUTHORITARIAN PERSONALITY AND GENERAL EDUCATION

The recent literature on classroom atmosphere provides an interesting example of an ecological relationship between certain kinds of student personalities and certain kinds of academic environments. Subcultural personality types have been isolated in student populations, and each type is known to respond in its own way to what appears superficially to be a common educational setting.

Authoritarian Personalities

These personality types, identified by their pervasive nativistic-fundamentalist ideological commitments, tend to underachieve in the social sciences and humanities and strongly to dislike both of these areas. Their occupational choices lie in business, law, medicine, or engineering, and they view higher education as having no other purpose than that of specific vocational preparation.

The typical authoritarian student prefers studying alone in the same neat and orderly place throughout the year. He associates study in groups with bull sessions in which nothing definite is settled. He rejects theoretical discussions in class for the same reason, and prefers a straightforward exposition by the instructor to any other classroom activity. The authoritarian has rigid time schedules for studying, reading, and review, and relies heavily on formal study aids, the suggestions of his teachers, on outlining and notetaking, and on rote memorization of significant facts. When the reading materials are difficult, he goes to the instructor or to better students for help.

Authoritarians enrolled in an outstanding general education program complained of the lack of professional courses and the looseness of a pedagogical approach that tolerated smoking in the classrooms, did not require attendance, and expected students to answer their own questions. They viewed the program as diffuse and lacking in specificity, and showed poorer grades, more emotional disturbance, and a higher frequency of withdrawal than the rest of their classmates.

Antiauthoritarian Personalities

These personalities have been identified on the basis of an ideological orientation stressing internationalism and relativism. They excel in the social sciences and the humanities, and most of them plan a professional career in one or the other of these areas.

Antiauthoritarians say they prefer cooperative study because they like to hear other points of view, enjoy discussions, and like being with people. Class discussions of side issues are similarly enjoyed, and these students take notes of stimulating or challenging ideas which they intend explaining later. They do not care where they study as long as it is quiet. Readings challenge them and they seek out additional materials to improve their understanding. Preparation for final examinations involves an attempt to arrive at some sense of the course as a totality.

Although outstanding as students, with broad cultural and intellectual interests, the antiauthoritarians are likely to be regarded with mixed feelings by instructors as a result of their challenging argumentative manner, marked independence, and social and intellectual impulsiveness.

The Authoritarian Personality in a Special Environment

A social science instructor who had been assigned without his knowledge to sections composed exclusively of each of these types of students observed that the authoritarian students lacked curiosity and initiative. He found it very difficult to get them involved in a class discussion, although direct questions indicated that they were well informed on the text, and he was constantly tempted to lecture to them. The antiauthoritarians impressed him at first with their critical attitude. They asked many questions about his teaching procedures, wanting to know why various things were done. He subsequently decided that their criticism and controversy was friendly, and he came to enjoy the fact that they took nothing for granted.

Authoritarians did not like this particular course and tended to do poorly in it. Antiauthoritarians on the other hand enjoyed it and got the highest grades. This was true also for students of either type assigned randomly to other instructors in mixed sections. But the authoritarians in the experimental section did just as well on the final common objective examination as did the anti-authoritarians. The authoritarians' high level of achievement does not seem attributable to the general superiority of the instructor since his antiauthoritarian section did no better than other antiauthoritarians distributed among nonexperimental discussion groups.

The instructor emphasized that his primary objective was to stimulate the free exchange of ideas, superabundant among the antiauthoritarians but initially nonexistent for the authoritarians. His efforts to get the authoritarians to respond included: (1) continued pressure in the form of direct questions, (2) a refusal to lecture or to provide direct answers, (3) encouragement and acceptance of any response from the students, and (4) insistent adoption of absurdly extreme positions, for example:

Week 3: Major discussions were about women in politics. I took the position initially that women were useless except for maternity purposes. I refused to call on any woman, accepted and agreed with all male opinions and added to the slurs on the females until every girl in the class was ready to tear the plaster off the wall. From this impasse, we moved on. . . .

Week 5: I took the position that voting was useless. . . .

Week 7: I favored "slavery," that is, putting the mob in any civilization into its place—"so you intelligent folks can operate a *good* democracy."

The slavery issue apparently marked the turning point. He observed that the authoritarians began "to fight back against the brutally dogmatic totalitarian rantings of the professor. I tried to seduce them to totalitarianism, and they indignantly, but politely, told me I was wrong." The following session the authoritarians finally broke down and began asking one interpretative question after another about the course, behaving for the first time in a manner similar to that which had characterized the antiauthoritarians in the opening days of the term.

The significance of this study does not lie in the use of the discussion method, but rather in the techniques used to achieve an effective level of discussion among students who had been unable to participate. For the antiauthoritarians the experiment described here was superfluous; they showed no gains, and succeeded mainly in demonstrating a competence they had already enjoyed prior to taking the course. The authoritarians on the other hand had been both deficient and resistant, but proved clearly responsive to the specialized techniques to which they had been exposed in their own isolated classroom environment.

STUDENT ECOLOGY

We may conclude, then, that the same educational ends can be achieved by very different types of students if the environment is appropriately modified for each type. The study of personalities in relation to their environment, however, requires a broader foundation than the special case of authoritarian students and the discussion method.

A more general framework for relating personality types to types of institutional environments is available in a theoretical system devised by H. A. Murray. This is a scheme for classifying all psychological tendencies that appear to give unity and direction to personality. He called these tendencies *needs*, but the terms *drive* and *motive* have a similar connotation; they refer to the objectives that a person characteristically pursues for himself.

The external counterpart of the personality need is called an environmental *press*. There are three levels of meaning associated with this concept. Subjectively, the term stands for the private world of the individual—the unique view each person has of the events around him. There also is a level at which the person's private world merges with that of others like him. People who share a common ideology—whether theological, political, or professional—also tend to share common interpretations of the events in which they participate. These interpretations may be quite different, however, from those of a more detached observer. The inferences we make as observers constitute a third form of press, in terms of which we may classify differences among environments.

To make accurate inferences about needs and press, we must know about a range of events—characteristic events—which typify the actions of individuals on the one hand and environmental occurrences on the other. As an example of a need, consider the case of someone who likes to play practical jokes. By itself this preference might mean many things, but if we also learn that this person likes to shock people by saying things that distress them, pick arguments with authority figures, and tease people he deems conceited, we may begin to suspect that a strong tendency toward aggression and hostility underlies these otherwise discrete activities.

Press are inferred in an analogous way. For example, when we learn that there are regular drills for fire and civil defense at an institution, any of several interpretations might suggest themselves. But if we are also told that there are no contact sports, that there are frequent and thorough medical examinations, and that students are sent to the infirmary at the first sign of any kind of illness, we may assume that much pressure is being exerted here to concern students with potential dangers to their physical well-being.

When American colleges are classified on the basis of need-press concepts—utilizing psychological scales (Activities Index, College Characteristics Index) devised especially for this purpose—the vast majority are found to emphasize some degree of social and emotional conformity. There is, to be sure, some variety in these patterns of constraint, varying between tradition-directed and other-directed sources of social control. The major source of diversity among these institutions lies elsewhere, however, in the caliber of their intellectual press.

The most extreme in this regard are the schools that have been known to exert considerable influence over their students in the long run. These are the small but elite private liberal arts colleges, which appear to be distinguished by the high level and breadth of their intellectual press and by an emphasis on personal freedom and informality. Within this class there are two main kinds of variation: (1) substantive specialization with regard to the arts, science, or service, and (2) role specialization as reflected in differences of emphasis on the development of student appreciation (criticism) versus innovation (creativity).

Another type of school revealed by the needs-press analysis appears to be the remaining stronghold of the Fitzgerald tradition— fountains of knowledge where students gather to drink. These are, typically, large state universities but there are also some large private institutions included among them. These schools place a double emphasis on the technical and professional orientation of their undergraduate curricula: to their supposedly anti-intellectual clientele, academic vocationalism is presented as a sign of hardheaded virtue; to themselves it is defended as a necessary and practicable antidote to obdurate student values. In any event, everyone does have fun, outside of class.

The students' own appraisals of these schools is unmistakable in meaning; they concede that they are just a bunch of Cheerful Charlies, playing together, helping one another with their lessons, sharing one another's problems. But there is an undertone of necessity in this togetherness since, apart from themselves, the students see no other strong figures in their environment. The faculty are not only conspicuous by their absence from the students' press, but there is also an undertone of criticism directed at the lack of course organization and the uninspired teaching. In other words, these students have an image of academic excellence, an image which they judge to be missing from their own institution.

This implicit image may be the reflection of a more widely shared ideal concerning American education. But we have already seen that different students require different treatment in order to arrive at the same end. One of the many tasks ahead for educators is to determine the consequences of practices now based on preference rather than on purpose. An environment must be suited to the species if optimal growth is to take place.

But what is an optimal environment for learning—one that satisfies, or one that stimulates? Pearls come from aggravated oysters, but milk comes from contented cows. Which metaphor should we use for education? Each seems to have its place, according to the kind of student and the aims of an educational program. The answer is that the characteristics of the student and the objectives of the program must both be employed as guides in the design of the most effective environments for learning.

Eight
The Effects of Higher Education

Harold Webster, Mervin Freedman, and Paul Heist

Personality Change in College Students

People change in divers ways during college. First, a student
simply acquires more information on different topics and becomes
more skilled at performing certain tasks. Secondly, there are
changes in interests and attitudes toward the self and the world.
And then, in some cases, there are fundamental personality
changes, accompanied by the emergence of new values.

The change most generally expected of college students is the
acquisition of skills and information. Among all the kinds of
change that occur, this one is most widely sanctioned as a legitimate educational goal, partly because it is thought essential for
later activities, but also because it is believed to be achieved individually by hard work. The value of individual effort that
produces tangible results is generally acknowledged in our culture; and colleges have been eager to prove themselves by emphasizing the importance of their own tangible rewards, the most
immediate of which are grades and diplomas.

The "grade-point-average" is regarded by many teachers—perhaps a large majority today—as an inadequate measure of educational growth. There are a number of reasons for this belief. First,
most instructors directly restrict the meaning of assigned grades
by informing students that grades will be based only upon specific
kinds of material, usually assigned reading or set problems. Second, when faculty are asked to identify students for whom the
college has been most successful in its aims, those named are not
always A-students. Third, grades achieved in college are usually
obscurely related to functioning or performance after graduation.
Fourth, college grades are only moderately related to recogniz-
able factors in the student's past. Fifth, interviews show that the
motives impelling students to achieve high grades are often indistinguishable from the desire simply to please and to obey parents
(or similar authorities) who happen to value high grades. Sixth,

students and teachers alike often suggest that high grades are only formal requirements—requirements for graduate school, prerequisites for later professional status, and the like—and it is inferred that grades cannot at the same time be measures of general educational status or development. Seventh, just as the achievement of high grades is insufficient evidence that education is taking place, failure to obtain high grades may not indicate that education has *not* taken place; certainly this is found to be true with persons who later reveal themselves as creative or highly productive. Eighth, other measures of personal growth and development are now known. Finally, nearly everyone knows a few students in whom the need to achieve high grades seems to interfere with his real education.

Nevertheless, despite their obvious limitations, grades are not likely to be abolished. Indeed they are undoubtedly becoming more, rather than less, difficult to eliminate. Increasing numbers of young people are attending college, and grades based largely on achievement examinations form part of the traditional bureaucratic machinery for "processing" these students. And because of the kind of curriculum in most colleges, grades have to be used as indicators of educational progress, however inadequately they serve that function. Then again, emphasis on formal requirements for admission into various professions, or into graduate school, is increasing rather than decreasing, and assigned grades are one of these requirements.

Changes in Mental Ability

There are large individual differences in the time of life at which a maximum, or ceiling, of measured mental ability is reached. Some individuals will fail to gain beyond age 18; many will continue to gain after age 21.

A number of studies have demonstrated that more intelligent persons not only increase in measured ability at a faster rate than individuals of lesser ability but also stand further from their point of maximum ability—further both in time and in amount of ability. The corollary of this is that at any given age, persons of higher ability in these samples could expect in the future a greater total increase in ability than could persons of lower ability.

The erroneous idea that gifted persons mature early has undoubtedly arisen from comparisons of their behavior with others of the same age. Such comparisons provide evidence of superior performance by the gifted, but they cannot give information about the *growth* or maturing of ability within one individual. Historic accounts of youthful, precocious geniuses may seem to contradict our theory, but too often we fail to take into account their later work. The theory is certainly valid for such men as Beethoven, Freud, and Picasso, whose later productions reflect increased maturity.

It is commonly believed that any student's intellect can be trained by the simple expedient of working him very hard. As a result many of the ablest freshmen enrolled at the "better" liberal arts colleges today complain that they do not have time to think. And in the more "typical" liberal arts colleges students assert that a lot of sheer memorizing of minute details is required, and that the work is neither new nor challenging.

In many colleges the low-ability student has difficulty keeping his head above water. We have interviewed students who spend almost all their waking moments memorizing material in order barely to remain in college. Yet there is little doubt that any student can benefit from education beyond secondary school, providing he is not expected to compete directly with those who far exceed him in ability.

Even though the more intelligent freshman is likely to be less mature than older students, he is well able, because of his high ability, to profit from great freedom in his studies. For this reason honors programs are probably to his advantage. At the same time, he may need *more* guidance, guidance tailored to his needs, since the total change in his personality during college is likely to be greater than average.

As we come to know more about the educational process it will be found that, owing to the complexity of personality, there are more and more students who are exceptional in some way. Study and apprciation of such diversity among students is more profitable than inventing reasons for ignoring their differences. The individual colleges could make a start here by trying to understand both differences in ability and differences in the rate at which abilities mature.

Changes in Values and Attitudes

Research on attitudes and values made before the end of World War II showed that, generally speaking, college students changed toward greater liberalism and greater sophistication in their political, social, and religious outlooks. There was also evidence that during the college years their interests widened.

Religious crises, or disillusionments, with consequent shifts in values are still fairly common among college students today. In most institutions, freshmen are confronted for the first time with a wide range of professed religious beliefs and disbeliefs, and with a variety of seemingly disparate moral practices. They naturally compare the values of peers and faculty with those of parents, sometimes without much deliberation, but often with some misgivings.

Take religion, for example. In a study carried out at the Center for the Study of Higher Education, University of California, Berkeley, National Merit scholars attending a wide variety of colleges were asked about their need to believe in a religion. The proportions of affirmative replies for 395 men and 175 women, attending a wide variety of institutions, varied from year to year as follow:

	Men	Women
At time of entrance	88%	91%
By end of freshman year	70%	76%
By end of sophomore year	61%	74%
By end of junior year	51%	69%

Responses to this and other questions about religion make it clear that a sizable minority of highly able students change their religious attitudes during three years of college. Not only is the need for religious faith felt less and less, especially among men, but the belief that colleges should teach religious values dwindles.

The study of National Merit Scholars also supports past findings that students become more "liberal" during college. When asked how they would vote if they were old enough, 30 per cent of these able young persons checked "Republican," about 17 per cent "Democrat," and about 50 per cent "Independent." After two years the humanities majors reduced their Republican vote considerably—for men the change was mostly to Democratic; for women, to Independent. Many mathematics majors who previously checked Republican also shifted to the Independent category.

It seems safe to conclude that today's students, like those of the 1930's and 1940's, become more "liberal" in the sense of being more sophisticated and independent in their thinking, and placing greater value on individual freedom and well-being. Liberalism in religion, and tolerance of ethnic differences, would appear to have much the same meaning today as in the recent past.

Perhaps the major feature of recent and contemporary studies, as distinguished from the earlier studies discussed previously, is that they have been directed to more generalized tendencies in the personality, tendencies conceived as underlying and integrating particular attitudes and values. In an interesting study by Heath (1958), differential progress in college was reported for three types of students. Over 2000 interviews, plus many group discussions, were recorded in a longitudinal study of a representative sample of 36 men during their years at Princeton. The subjects were classified on an impulse-control dimension, and also according to their degree of involvement with work and with people. Students varied in impulse-control from moody, spontaneous "plungers" (N = 8), to the achievement-oriented "hustlers"

($N = 9$), and stable, noncommitted subjects ($N = 19$). It is interesting that the last group were relatively numerous; they showed more movement than the other groups during college, however, in the direction of genuine increased involvement with work and people. Heath observes that the three types responded best to different educational treatments.

At Vassar College,[1] measures of the expression of impulses and of certain aspects of ego functioning and development were devised. In this research it was planned to emphasize such personality characteristics as intellectual functioning and achievement, authoritarianism, (and its opposites), masculinity-feminity, and psychological health. It was possible to obtain measures of these characteristics—in some cases through carrying out a special program of test development. Brief descriptions of some of the "tests" follow.

Social Maturity. Low scorers are authoritarian, compulsive, rigid, punitive, submissive to power, conventional, cynical, antiintellectual, and emotionally suppressed. High scorers are relatively free of these characteristics. The scale provides a measure of authoritarianism that is less ideological than the original F scale (Adorno *et al.*, 1950).

Impulse Expression. High scorers, in contrast to low scorers, have a greater readiness to express impulses, or to seek gratification of them, in overt action or in conscious feeling and attitude. High scorers are relatively dominant, aggressive, autonomous, exhibitionistic, and express interests in sex, excitement, and change.

Developmental Status. This scale is made up of attitude items that distinguish younger from older students. In a sense such items reflect development from the freshman to the senior year—hence the name. High scorers (seniors) in comparison with low scorers (freshmen) are flexible and uncompulsive, disinclined to pass judgment on people but critical of the institutional authority of family,

[1] For an account of a program of research at Vassar College, carried out under the auspices of the Mary Conover Mellon Foundation, see Sanford, 1956.

state, or religion; high scorers are also nonconforming, free of cynicism, realistic, and mature in interests.

Masculine Role. High scorers are active persons with interests and attitudes characteristic of men in our culture; low scorers are, on the contrary, more passive, acquiescent, and conventionally feminine.

On all of these measures, seniors score higher than freshmen. At the same time some rather striking institutional differences between two leading liberal arts colleges have been observed.[2] Obtained means for Bennington College freshmen on Social Maturity, Developmental Status, and Impulse Expression are greater than the corresponding means for Vassar *seniors;* yet the means at Bennington increase between freshman and senior year. In both schools the older students are more developed, more mature, and more free to express impulses than the younger students; yet the differences between colleges are also impressive. Bennington seniors are the highest of any group on Masculine Role. It seems reasonable, therefore, to infer that the other high scores of Bennington students are not achieved at the cost of a retrogression to a more conventional or passively feminine role.

These results support the view that differing public images attract different students to the two colleges, and that the differences persist despite developmental processes which lead students in both schools in the same direction—which is one of less conservatism, increased tolerance for individual differences, and more freedom to express impulses.

When the same students are examined at different times during their college careers, the results are essentially the same as those just described. Test-retest difference scores are significant, and they increase in magnitude with time spent in college. When plotted, using time as the abscissa, the gains usually form a convex

[2] The data for Bennington students were provided through the courtesy of Dr. Howard Smith, formerly of Bennington College, now with Rohrer, Hibler, and Replogle, Toronto, and President William C. Fels of Bennington College.

decelerating curve, showing that greater changes occur during the earlier part of college careers.

Included in the regular test batteries used at Vassar were the well-known Ethnocentrism, or E scale, and the F scale for measuring authoritarianism, or antidemocratic trends (Adorno *et al.*, 1950). Without exception there were always large decreases in mean scores on these characteristics between freshman and senior years. The personality syndrome now known as authoritarianism constitutes a particular failure of maturity about which a large amount of convincing research of a quantitative type is available. Persons with high F scores have been described as anti-intellectual by a number of investigators. If, as it appears, many college freshmen are anti-intellectual, the study of authoritarianism in college students should be of value in educational research. The fact that many high scorers at Vassar were changeable, to the extent that *large* decreases occurred in their F scores during college whereas others did not change at all, merits further study. It appears from interviews that in a few authoritarians the earlier fixations are so severe as to prevent a significant decrease in F scores during college.

Vassar students were also studied by means of the Minnesota Multiphasic Personality Inventory (Hathaway and McKinley, 1951), a test designed to measure the type and degree of psychopathology in the personality. Seniors subscribed more frequently than freshmen to statements indicating psychological or physical disturbances and instability. These differences were small, although they were statistically significant for large groups. They were taken as evidence of the seniors' greater openness to experience.

Three of the Vassar scales, Social Maturity, Impulse Expression, and Developmental Status, have also been administered at a variety of other women's colleges, for example, a Negro college in the South, a Catholic college in Canada, and an Eastern women's college that differed somewhat from Vassar. In all cases the kinds of trends found were similar to those found at Vassar. There are impressive intercollege differences, but whatever the initial freshmen means may be, the students subsequently gain in scores during college.

The theoretical implication of these findings is that systematic personality changes take place during the college years, at least in college women, and that the developmental changes during this period of late adolescence entail certain regularities in the way problems and conflicts are met and resolved.

Limitations on Personality Change

Most new students are enthusiastic about college experience, but very few have developed those psychological characteristics that will permit them to become seriously committed to intellectual and aesthetic problems. For few students have the kind of autonomy (or social alienation perhaps) to defer vocational or marital plans in favor of other pursuits. Few, consequently, become interested in learning for its own sake. Despite the tendency to grow more liberal, most students soon forego both experimentation with different roles and the questioning of basic values. They make such sacrifices in order to arrive at a comfortable, fairly definite blueprint of the future as early as they can.

This pervasive caution may be due in part to the absence of conflict during the precollege years. When we studied the background of Vassar students, we found that, contrary to generally accepted theory, adolescence had not been a time of strife or rebelliousness for the majority. In fact, the most common "crises" during secondary school had been worries about acceptance by peers.

In America, college is regarded as an ally of the parents in the prolongation of adolescence. And the college years are a time in life when there happens to be a maximum concern with—and perhaps in recent years a maximum respect for—cultural standards and values. In our affluent society the majority of college students regard social issues or movements as irrelevant to more immediate problems; social reform is considered secondary to such concerns as career, marriage, and personal development. The result is the prevalence of a basically conservative attitude.

During late adolescence, as during the college years themselves, student interests normally diversify and intensify. Yet a great many people pass through college without experiencing much change in basic values, or without becoming greatly involved in problems that interest teachers. The vast enterprise that is American higher education today cherishes traditional values, including a premium on vocational training, rewards for hard work, and social adjustment. These concerns have prevailed, and they have exacted their price: the attrition of real interest in intellectual and aesthetic matters.

References

Adorno, T. W., Frenkel-Brunswik, Else, Levinson, D. J., and Sanford, N. *The authoritarian personality*. New York: Harper and Brothers, 1950.

Heath, S. R., Jr. Personality and student development. In *New dimensions of learning in a free society*. Pittsburgh: University of Pittsburgh Press, 1958, pp. 225–245.

Hathaway, S. R., and McKinley, J. C. Manual for the Minnesota Multiphasic Personality Inventory (Rev. ed.). New York: Psychological Corp., 1951.

Sanford, N. (Ed.). Personality development during the college years. *J. Social Issues*, 1956, **12**, No. 4.

Mervin B. Freedman

What Happens After College: Studies of Alumni

In the long run the best evaluation of a college education is likely to result from studies of alumni. What are college graduates like five, ten, twenty, and thirty years after graduation? How have they been influenced by college experiences?

Few studies have been made in this important area. Most of the empirical ones center on various gross sociological factors, such as the income of college graduates, the age at which they marry, or the number of children they have. There are also several studies, chiefly ones utilizing questionnaires, that assess such factors as the aesthetic values of college graduates, their interests and opinions, and their attitudes toward various aspects of their college careers. Rare indeed are studies of the same people in college and again as alumni.

In *They Went to College*, by C. Robert Pace (1941), samples of the men and women who entered the University of Minnesota in 1924, 1925, 1928, and 1929 were surveyed by means of a fifty-two-page questionnaire given in 1937. About half the subjects were graduates, the others having withdrawn prior to graduation.

The general findings are consistent with those of Philip Jacob's more recent *Changing Values in College* (1957). The lives of alumni were centered in the "private" sphere, with the family, work, and recreation as the predominant interests. The alumni voted, but otherwise tended to be rather politically passive. Nor did intellectual and aesthetic pursuits loom large in their lives. This finding led Pace to suggest that "colleges may not be producing the cultural values they so frequently claim."

The chief differences between graduates and the people who dropped out of college were in the vocational realm: the income of the graduates was somewhat higher and their reported job satisfaction somewhat greater. Otherwise, differences were inconsequential.

A second book with the same title, *They Went to College*, by Ernest Havemann and Patricia Salter West (1952), reported on questionnaire returns from 9064 respondents representing 1037 colleges. According to the authors' findings, satisfaction with a college experience in general was almost universal. Ninety-eight per cent of the respondents would choose to go to college again, and 84 per cent would choose the same college.

This satisfaction did not hold, however, for the general type of curriculum or course pursued in college. In fact, this area was the focus of greatest dissatisfaction with the college experience. In the matter of general versus more specific kinds of education, 44 per cent were satisfied with what they had had, 35 per cent wished they had received a more specific kind of training, and 21 per cent would have preferred a more general educational experience.

Graduates in the humanities were distinguished by their relatively low incomes, and the situation was "even worse for social science graduates." In the professions, those who had had a more general type of undergraduate education tended to be "the more active and interested citizens." The college graduates most dissatisfied with general education were those in business.

Students with high grades were more likely to enter professions, and in a given profession to earn more money, than were students with lower grades. Grades tended to be related to financial success in all fields except business. The degree of satisfaction with the college experience, although related to grades, was little related to type and extent of extracurricular activity. Alumni who had obtained higher grades as students were more content than others with their college, their major, and their extent of specialization.

CHARACTERISTICS OF COLLEGE ALUMNI

Income

Most studies demonstrate a direct relationship between amount of schooling and amount of income. College graduates predominate in the higher-paying occupations and earn more money job for job than people who have no college education or who have left college prior to graduation. (As we would expect, when educational level and occupation are equated for the two sexes, the incomes of women are lower than those of men.)

In recent years, however, several studies have discerned a decline in the purely economic rewards of a college education. As college education becomes accessible to more and more people, its particular value as an avenue to large financial gain diminishes. And as the incomes of groups with less education rise as a result of union activity and social legislation, the gap between college-educated people and others narrows. Allied to this tendency is an indication that upward social mobility, which has been an important product or by-product of American education, is somewhat on the decline—at least at the highest levels.

Values, Attitudes, and Opinions

There is evidence that the values, attitudes, and opinions with which one leaves college are likely to persist into later life with but little modification. Consequently the college years take on enormous importance; one cannot think of them as simply one period among others in which substantial modification also takes place. For many students, apparently, any changes that may occur in values, attitudes, and opinions end with graduation.

The origins of changes in values, attitudes, and opinions during the college years are obscure. It could be that such changes reflect more the social forces impinging on the college and its students than the effect of deliberate educational policy. But even if this be the case, the college years are characterized by a degree of openness to change that is not later duplicated. One is reminded of the remark of William James: "Outside of their own business, the ideas gained by men before they are 25 are practically the only ideas they shall have in their lives."

THE MELLON FOUNDATION INTERVIEW STUDIES OF
VASSAR COLLEGE ALUMNAE [1]

The Mellon Foundation staff interviewed fifty Vassar College alumnae of the classes 1929 to 1935, and forty alumnae of the classes 1954, 1955, and 1956. Since these women were volunteers who responded to invitations to be studied and interviewed, they cannot be assumed to be representative of their fellow alumnae in each class. It is likely, however, that the great majority of patterns of life and modes of thought characterizing Vassar College alumnae in general may be found among the women who were interviewed, although we cannot tell exactly how predominant these patterns are.

It appears that many of these alumnae had enjoyed a sense of accomplishment after graduation—either in additional schooling or at work—that they did not experience as undergraduates. To some extent this may have been a function of lessened competition. At Vassar College they were competing academically with many other intelligent and studious girls. After graduation, the competition was probably much less keen. Many of the married alumnae reported a similar kind of experience when they took part in community activities such as the League of Women Voters. For the most part they found themselves able to handle with dispatch the demands made upon them.

We cannot help wondering whether many of these women would not have benefited by experiencing the same sense of accomplishment *during* their undergraduate years rather than afterward. If their college life had been so enriched, their achievements—both before and after graduation—might have been greater. Not that stern competition is solely to blame for the lack of a sense of accomplishment during the school years. Academic procedures themselves may often reenforce feelings of guilt instead of fostering feelings of competence and adequacy in students.

[1] For an account of the program of research in which these studies had a place see Sanford, 1956.

This is particularly likely to happen with college *women* who are usually anxious to please and do the right thing.

The Middle-Aged Educated Woman

In a society characterized by early marriage and labor-saving devices in the home, a housewife is likely to have some twenty or thirty years of relative freedom after her children have become at least partly self-sufficient. The point at which the housewife rather suddenly acquires this freedom can be a time of emotional stress. Take, for example, the study made of fifty Vassar alumnae who graduated between 1929 and 1935. The study showed that some women who had previously seemed quite stable emotionally later experienced some kind of personality difficulty. These women had ordered their lives around various forms of external definition: school and college, marriage, then children. These were the things that everyone did, and they kept the young wife very busy—for a while.

Then quite suddenly the youngest child entered adolescence, and the housewife no longer felt very much needed—certainly not in the physical or material way that she had been previously. For perhaps the first time in her life, she found herself thrown back on her own resources. Bereft of external guideposts to provide continuity and order, she faced a psychological crisis that had better been dealt with at an earlier age.

At an earlier age, however, few alumnae had thought much about what life would be like in fifteen or twenty years. Of course the situation was somewhat different for those alumnae with major professional or career commitments. These women were ready to remain in the home when the children were small, but they intended to resume their careers as soon as family commitments made this possible. The majority of alumnae, however, who had no strong involvements outside home and family were little concerned for the long-range future. Busy with their daily and monthly rounds of activities, they appeared to feel that the future would take care of itself.

Difference in Educational Patterns between Younger and Older Alumnae

When Vassar alumnae of 1954 to 1956 are contrasted with those of 1929 to 1935, what seems most striking is the absence of clear-cut educational patterns among the younger group. A generation ago, strong commitment on the part of a woman to intellectual pursuits or to a professional career carried with it a more or less explicit assumption that marriage might thereby be precluded. Nowadays, almost all Vassar students expect to marry. On the other hand, fewer students today are preoccupied with social activities to the exclusion of intellectual interests, and a higher proportion of the gifted ones are stimulated to achievement that accords with their abilities. To this extent, the blurring of the more distinctive patterns of a generation ago may be regarded as an intellectual step forward.

But this clouding of boundaries has another side. In the 1920's and 1930's there was a "high-achievement" group of Vassar students for whom intellectual life was all; today such students are less evident. Gone, or almost gone, is the kind of girl who skipped lunch so that she could have more time to spend in the library; who went through four years of college without a date and hardly felt that she was missing anything because her studies were so fascinating.

Even the most dedicated of current students are likely to lead balanced lives and to have their share of recreation and social life. Just as the increasing homogeneity of our society has delimited ethnic and regional differences, so it may be observed that the current educational patterns within student society are less sharply distinguished.

The Problem of Continued Growth

Most young alumnae who were interviewed had married and were getting along quite well. They reported few difficulties or strains and their test scores showed that, compared with their state as seniors, they were relatively stable emotionally and free of anxiety. But the picture has one flaw. There is some indication that for many women, personality growth stops after graduation. During the college years themselves, by contrast, considerable growth takes place. (See the preceding chapter.) Changes in mental ability and functioning, in attitudes and opinions, and in other qualities of personality—for example, authoritarianism and impulse expression—occur in this period. We may say that seniors, are more developed and more complex than freshmen. They are less bland and more flexible, more aware of themselves and more open to new experiences. Certainly this seems to be true at women's liberal arts colleges. In this sense we might say that college seniors are now *ready* to be educated. The resistance to new experiences characteristic of so many freshmen has been dissolved, or at least eroded.

But what happens after graduation? Do we see in alumnae some integration of the personality at a higher level of complexity than we find in seniors? Our test findings at Vassar reveal no important changes in personality among the majority of alumnae during three or four years after graduation, except that alumnae are more stable and less neurotic than they were as seniors. In a minority of cases, on the other hand, considerable change in personality does seem to have occurred. We still need, however, to develop tests designed specifically to measure postcollege change. Such tests might expose modifications that are not now apparent.

Perhaps what stands out more than anything else in the Mellon Foundation's studies of alumnae is the *complex* relationship between college years and later life. By comparison, it is relatively easy to compare graduates of different colleges or different age groups, or to compare college graduates as a whole with individuals who never went to college. In such cases clear differences can be discovered between the groups being compared. This is not so when we try relating college experience to later life, however. One student who graduated with honors goes on to do well in graduate school. Her classmate, who also graduated with honors, is a failure academically in graduate school. Family-oriented "underachievers" may be alert and alive intellectually twenty years after graduation, whereas family-oriented "overachievers," the better students in a formal scholastic sense, have stagnated intellectually. And so on for other educational types.

In short, when we consider ends in education, we must go beyond the college years themselves; we must view all of life as potentially a developing process. And so, when we ask about "ideal" student characteristics, and how they can best be fostered, we should also ask this: will those characteristics persist into later years, can they persist, how can they persist? What college experiences enter into the making of the "ideal" adult or citizen?

References

Havemann, E., and West, Patricia S. *They went to college.* New York: Harcourt, Brace, 1952.

Jacob, P. E. *Changing values in college.* New York: Harper and Brothers, 1957.

Pace, C. R. *They went to college.* Minneapolis: University of Minnesota Press, 1941.

Sanford, N. (Ed.) Personality development during the college years. *J. Social Issues,* 1956, **12**, No. 4.

Nine
The College in Society

Christian Bay

Toward a Social Theory of Intellectual Development

INSTITUTIONS AND RATIONALITY

Striving or effort of any kind presupposes some kind of problem or difficulty. This is a fundamental principle of individual development as well as of social and cultural history.

Growth and maturation in the child can take place only when mere repetition no longer serves him well. The child's accustomed responses may become inadequate either because changes in his developing physiology bring changes in the nature of his drives, or because his parents or peers come to expect more mature behavior as he grows older; both things keep happening, of course, in the life of every child. To the extent that he can cope with these problems and frustrations, he not only grows but matures; whenever they overwhelm him, neurotic developments ensue.

Every child faces "social" problems of at least two kinds: how to be accepted by or win approval of parents or peers, and how to understand why they behave as they do and thus to anticipate their future reactions. The former problem is resolved by palatable opinions; the latter by the development of beliefs that are realistic and that improve the child's capacity to understand and predict. For the adult, too, to hold and express a given opinion may serve primarily the purpose of facilitating his immediate social acceptance, or the purpose of cognitive enlightenment of his universe. Some opinions, however, may serve a third kind of purpose: they are self-defensive; they allow the individual a psychological escape from reminders of problems and past events with which he could not cope and which now persist unconsciously as sources of much anxiety.

Discovery of the motivational basis of an opinion makes it possible to understand how it can be influenced. A rationality-motivated belief can presumably be influenced by new knowledge; a conformity-motivated belief can be influenced by opinion leaders within the group to which the person belongs or aspires to belong; whereas a belief that serves self-defensive functions is a hardy perennial that may be subjected to change only in the course of psychoanalysis or some other sequence of profound experience. It should be added that many of our beliefs and attitudes serve more than one of these kinds of motives; this circumstance sometimes means that we are pulled in opposite directions at the same time, and respond with conflicting impulses, indecisive acts, and vague language.

In a limited sense each type of motivation or tension is a *rational* basis for the appropriate opinion, in that the opinion does serve some immediate function for the personality. However, if a time perspective is added, the question of rationality comes into a different light. Self-defensive opinions may for the moment help keep anxieties in check, but they are self-defeating in the long run in that they also help prevent the individual from seeing and grappling with the sources of his anxiety. Conforming opinions make for temporary external adjustment but keep the individual from gaining a broader understanding of himself and of society, an understanding that could help him anticipate his own future needs and society's changing requirements. Only what have been called rationality-motivated opinions indicate a type of response to problems that is constructive in terms of the individual's long-range needs, to say nothing of the fortunes of the society in which he has a stake as a citizen. The term "rational," consequently, will henceforth be used with reference to task-oriented efforts only, and never to self-oriented or self-defense-oriented efforts.

Relatively simple traditional societies may require very little rational effort on the part of their members. Complex modern societies, on the other hand, require a great deal of rational intelligence of many of their members, and this is the ultimate reason for the existence of colleges and universities. It does not follow, unfortunately, that the colleges actually deliver the intellectual power they are assigned to produce. In fact, most of them fall far short of producing even a moderate proportion of graduates who have been educated to utilize their own minds effectively for meaningful purposes of their own choice.

Our discussion will focus on the present and the future rather than the past; and we proceed on the bold assumption of our time that the university is duty-bound to open its gates to all persons who can and who want to become educated, regardless of whether or not they can pay for what they get. "America needs all its brain power," is one familiar rationale for this; our preference is for another: "Individuals need to grow as much as they can; this is what America is for."

Our theoretical point of departure is in the following fundamental hypothesis: all organizations, however rational in design, tend to become transformed as they endure and become institutionalized. The dynamics of this process needs study, with particular reference to the college; and this kind of study needs some clarification of concepts. In the next section I shall attempt to define some key concepts in the study of what may be called the erosion of rationality in the processes of higher education. Utilizing these concepts, I shall in the third section very sketchily review various factors in the college community and in the larger society that seem to militate against the development of rational, independent, intellectually bent individuals. In a fourth and final section I shall seek to account for the fact that some students nevertheless do become well educated, and to support the view that many more students—theoretically all—could, with incentives possible under different social circumstances, gain a fuller use of their rational faculties.

SOME KEY CONCEPTS

"Intellectual development," though of course a crucial concept, nevertheless will be given a somewhat open-ended definition here. The reference is to man's rational faculties, the extent to which the person becomes able to question conventional and habitual beliefs and to develop a truly autonomous individual outlook on the basic issues of life and of society. "Intellectual" will mean roughly the same as "rational" in the sense developed in the foregoing; more precisely the reference of "intellectual" is to a rationality for the whole person and for his whole life span.

A person is an *intellectual*, one might say, to the extent that his mind produces and utilizes the insight—into himself, into others, into the nature of society—that is required for coping with and anticipating the problems of living a full life and facing death with serenity. The long-range rationality associated with "intellectual" is also a broad-gauge rationality, moreover, in the sense that the intellectual recognizes his stake in an enlightened society and in enlightened citizenship on his own part. It is this propensity of the developed intellect that makes a rich and continuing supply of intellectuals not only an advantage but a necessity for a civilization if it is to survive in a complex and rapidly changing world.

The student's social surroundings should for present purposes of analysis be viewed as a variety of *social systems*. A social system is conceived as being composed, not of individuals, but "of the actions of individuals, the principal units of which are roles and the constellations of roles" (Parsons and Shils (1953), p. 197). Like Chinese boxes, large social systems contain a succession of subsystems. And, what is more important, many social systems overlap, so that most individuals in a complex society belong to a variety of social systems. Sometimes overlapping systems are in harmony, but sometimes they are in conflict, and the man in the middle is torn.

Every new rational venture—for example, a new college, or department, or type of course—creates a new social system. The difficulty of keeping a new venture rational should be apparent already from the fact that each individual who takes on a role in the new system continues at the same time to play many of his familiar roles in other systems, of which his habitual or deliberate kinds of behavior are component parts.

New social systems frequently are the result of deliberately planned human efforts; if so, they are *organizations* as well as social systems. By "organized" is simply meant: deliberately arranged with some purposes in mind. Generally speaking, organizations are established to solve problems, that is, to expand the rational at the expense of the institutional components of social interaction.

However, as already stated as a fundamental hypothesis, no organization works entirely according to its rational design. Even the procedures for making decisions are invariably molded in directions that deviate from those on the organizational chart. Partly, this may be because no planners, however well informed and wise, are capable of making rules that fit all future situations. Partly, also, because social systems develop a momentum of their own, so far insufficiently explored by students of behavior; the merging and meshing of new institutions with old lead to unanticipated types of stresses and opportunities, which are influenced also by varying personalities of individuals in key roles at crucial moments. Partly, again, leadership groups in any social organization may be in a position to utilize their prerogatives of leadership to bolster their own power at the expense of other groups or potential groups within the organization. Every stable organization, to conclude, has presumably developed some informal compromise between deliberate plans with purposes in mind, unanticipated stresses and incentives, and general tendencies toward entrenchment of leadership, of privilege, and of institutional stability. This informal structure is often referred to as the "informal organization."

Most American colleges are stable formal organizations, within which a variety of informal organizations or social systems operate. It is always legitimate to ask to what extent the informal institutions tend to defeat the purposes that the organization should serve. But if we want to pursue this inquiry, we need to focus on what the college experience means to the student. How does he see his role as student, and how does he feel about it?

Suppose we define "role" as "a set of evaluative standards applied to an incumbent of a particular position," as Gross, Mason, and McEachern have done (1958). This concept begs the question: applied by *whom?* As these authors have shown, the same role can be defined very differently by the incumbent(s) and by various relevant others, and these discrepancies can be studied.

Yet, no matter how much of an agreement may be established about the requirements of a given role, different incumbents may approach it with very different degrees of independence, "willingness to play the game," loyalty to the various reference groups, personal involvement in objectives, and so on. Moreover, the same person's attitude to his role may undergo considerable changes during a given time interval, and such changes may be due primarily to factors in his own private life or personality development, and not necessarily be responsive mainly to changes in the social environments of his role.

For a supplementary concept that helps to connect "role expectation" and "role definition" with the whole range of motives that account for the individual's attitude to a given role, I shall here use the term *incentive*. This term will refer to the relative prospects of motive satisfaction by way of a given role or a given effort, as these prospects are seen from the individual's point of view at a given time, when compared to roles or efforts which he sees as available alternatives.

Incentives are in a sense embedded in the social system, where they correspond to motives in the individual; as the individual perceives the various elements in his situation, those elements that he values or disvalues, and thinks or feels that he can do something about, are for him incentives. The fact that no organization ever keeps functioning entirely in terms of its rational design and initial purposes can probably best be accounted for, generally speaking, in terms of the difficulty of designing a self-perpetuating system of overriding incentives; that is, of incentives prone to keep activating motives that remain stronger than all possibly less appropriate motives combined, in all persons influentially involved in the organization.

Let us now define three types of incentives of significance to the role of student.

By *social incentives* is meant the relative attractiveness of prospects of social acceptance, of being admitted to membership in desired groups, and of being respected, liked, admired, or loved by relevant persons. By *academic incentives* is meant the value the student attaches to making a good academic record, in terms of conscientious fulfillment of course requirements, and, above all, the achievement of good grades. This is something very different from *intellectual incentives*, which here refers to the intrinsic satisfaction the student perceives in striving to broaden his understanding and sharpen his power of reflection. Combinations are of course frequent, but this makes it not less but more important to distinguish the three concepts.

SOME SOCIAL DETERMINANTS OF STUDENT INCENTIVES

Each student who enters college is motivated by a variety of *social* incentives; the immediately obvious reference group, or group in which he aspires to be accepted, is normally that of his peers or that of a section, at least, of the student community. Because all students on each campus will have many interests in common, a social system of all students will develop, along with a *student culture* influenced by and in turn contributing to the various norms and expectations that make up the variety of student subcultures.

For the average entering student his new social role must appear a very complex one. There are, first of all, the role expectations developed by his peers in the student culture; in the vast majority of the colleges these norms are primarily nonintellectual as well as nonacademic, and sometimes anti-intellectual though rarely anti-academic. One reason for this nonintellectualism may be that students with social skills almost inevitably acquire more influence in the shaping of peer-group culture than do those with intellectual skills, who by and large participate less persistently in social activities or at any rate tend to strive less for student leadership (at least when it comes to purely social leadership or leadership in organizations without independence and political influence). Furthermore, those who become social leaders will tend to be recruited in part from those with a self-assurance and relative lack of concern for academic achievement associated with a relatively wealthy upper-middle-class family background, and in part from the star athletes.

In many colleges the system of fraternities and sororities serves to magnify even further the dominating influence of the less intellectually bent students in the continuous development of the student culture; very frequently these socially adept nonintellectuals dominate the formal organs of student governments as well, and with the university administration's blessings, more often than not. From a public relations point of view, these are the best students: never radical or even militantly liberal; outwardly submissive to authority and as obedient to the deans as they are to their own fathers. And they find the conventional limits to academic freedom fully in order; their interest is not in questioning any fundamental assumptions, either in politics or in other fields of inquiry. They are in college to achieve credits and formal qualifications, and also to have a good time.

Yet, *some* academic incentives are likely to confront even the otherwise carefree good-time Charlie; and in the better universities they may well be the overriding incentives for the majority of students. Every college—possibly excepting the "open-door colleges" [see Clark (1960)]—can make their students work hard by toughening academic requirements, and this is of course the way up in the status hierarchy of colleges and universities.

It may be allowed that efforts to do well in courses will benefit most students more, with respect to their intellectual development, than efforts merely to be liked by their peers. Yet the hunt for grades need not be very much of an improvement over the hunt for peer-group popularity. Neither the social nor the academic status seeker is primarily concerned with developing his rational powers; both shun bold reflections and cling to what seems safe and sound.

If academic incentives in this narrow sense tend to overshadow intellectual incentives for most students, this is largely because the system of teaching so frequently is tuned to the desires of the academic strivers rather than to those of the intellectuals in the class. This is so for many reasons. One is that academically oriented instructions are easier to communicate to students, who usually want to know specifically what is expected of them in each course; it is hard to be specific about how to meditate and become wiser. Another is that the proliferation of courses and the fragmentation of the student's time, and the process by which he is given a daily spoonfeeding of reading assignments and lectures, all militate against opportunities for quiet reflection. Still another circumstance is the fact that the teacher's time is fragmented, too, by the variety of courses he teaches; it is easier to throw the narrowly academic course requirements at one's students than it is to try to develop the frame of mind for embarking on a joint intellectual adventure. Also, the teacher has to give grades, and it is far simpler to assess narrowly academic achievement than to evaluate intellectual effort or reflective achievement.

A further circumstance that strengthens the academic at the expense of the intellectual incentives is the tendency for many teachers in uninspiring environments to lose whatever intellectual interests they may once have had, so that for them, too, the classroom experience may tend to become a primarily social experience with students, regulated only by the essential academic duties of teaching performance that are stipulated in the college employment contract. The problem of "dead-wooditis" is not limited to second-rate colleges, of course. And among the younger teachers, less susceptible to this disease, the desire for financial security through academic tenure may well forestall the development of a strong interest in teaching. In the better colleges and universities, these teachers are given to understand that their prospects of promotion depend almost entirely on the quantity or quality of their published research and other academic works. Most young professors are in effect told to publish or perish, and they by and large choose to publish at the expense of time and effort invested in teaching, in preference to becoming first-rate teachers who will perish for lack of published output, or at any rate will be relegated to less prestigeful and lower-paying colleges. Tenure is normally granted only when the instructor is too old to take a renewed interest in his students and to improve his teaching. Moreover, the race to publish tends to be a lifelong one, with both future salary raises and academic prestige, and sometimes even one's self-esteem, dependent on—as one college faculty employment form is alleged to have phrased the question—one's "current rate of publication."

Another circumstance of pervasive significance is that the horizons of most schools of education appear to have been limited by the far greater ease with which research can be done on academic than on intellectual achievement. The large literature on prediction of college achievement has invariably focused on narrowly academic achievement. So has the vast literature on experiments in teaching techniques and classroom arrangements (see Chapter 4). The reason much of this literature is so uninspiring is that one so often gets the feeling that what is studied is not particularly important. We study grades because they offer a convenient measure, even though the crucial task of the educator, most of us would agree under close questioning, is to help develop the minds of the students, rather than equip them with masses of facts and the kinds of skills that make for good grades in the majority of college courses.

One of the crucial needs, I believe, if academic incentives are to allow more room for intellectual ones, in the role perspective of the average college student, is a greater inventiveness in the study of educational processes. It is obviously easier to count A's and B's than to make estimates of intellectual alertness and vigor; but this is not a good reason for continuing to count A's and B's to the exclusion of more meaningful inquiries. It is difficult but not impossible to develop a variety of indices of such variables as reflectiveness, intellectual curiosity, depth of intention in interpersonal and political attitudes, universalism of moral judgment, psychological insight, and so on—qualities which in an intellectual college community would be promoted in preference to agility in memorizing.

There is yet another and possibly even more pervasive source of pressures that militate against allowing intellectual incentives much scope in the educational experience in most colleges. I refer to the nature of the larger society of which the college is a small part, and in particular to the tenuous relationship in this society between intellectual quality and social mobility. To what extent and in what ways may *intellectual* effort seem *useful* for the long-range career purposes of most students? To a very limited extent, I suspect. From the perspective of certain academic career aspirations, intellectual incentives are likely to become prevailing in a fair proportion among the hopefuls. But in most fields there are few if any incentives for the average student to exert his mind for any purposes other than mastering the isolated fragments of human knowledge to which he is exposed. His mind becomes tailored to the anticipated needs of the type of job to which he aspires, not to the needs of his own person and to the fuller individuality that he might have developed.

A relatively low esteem for the intellect and for intellectual excellence prevails in contemporary American society; although "ability" in all jobs is admired, a display of articulate reflectiveness is widely considered "high brow," or something peculiar to a special breed of impractical people who are not to be imitated. The somewhat derisive term "egghead" tells more than volumes of analysis could about the orientation of the contemporary mass culture toward the more reflective and sophisticated minds.

From the vantage point of many a student who hopes for future success in our kind of society, to develop skill in "selling his personality" may appear far more important than to develop any personality worth selling, or indeed worth having, in terms of his own long-range personal needs. A manipulative congeniality may appear more useful to the student than a contemplative genius, if he has acquired or held on to the conventionally supported goals of a suburban ranch home and the like. Students with this attitude toward learning, whether they are conscious of the attitude or not, may acquire no more profit from college than a verbal glibness and the shallow smugness of half-learning; by a trained incapacity to serious reflection, they may become genuine bores and be doomed to bored lives.

It would be beyond the scope of this chapter to pursue an inquiry into the probable determinants of and the long-range prospects for anti-intellectualism in the American society as a whole. It seems clear enough that political changes could bring about a better college. Let us instead ask: given substantially the present political and economic system, what can be done most effectively to improve the American college? The principal answer is, I believe, in the small experimental college within the larger college. We cannot build the intellectual university community, much less the intellectual society, all at once. Ideas must become truly important to a few professors and students before they can excite most members of a college community; and a good beginning is made if we by way of organizational experimentation can learn how to create small groups within the college in which a vigorous exchange of intellectual stimuli is pursued. This is not the occasion for describing the characteristics of proposed experimental ventures [see Sanford (1960)]. The point I wish to stress is that piecemeal innovations are possible within the present system of higher education, innovations which conceivably can lead to wider changes of educational processes even in the absence of any previous improvement of the intellectual climate of the larger social system. For the rest, I have tried in this section to contribute to explaining why the current turnout of truly educated minds from the colleges as they function today is so distressingly low.

THE ENDURING INTELLECT

For all that has been said about social circumstances inside and outside the college, which at the present time appear to forestall intellectual learning and development, the fact remains that some students nevertheless do develop into full-grown intellectuals.

Harry Stack Sullivan frequently spoke of a basic tendency toward health, both mental and physical: man has somewhere in himself a will to recuperate; the organism is not indifferent to the alternatives of illness or health. Educators need a similar assumption: embedded in every man and woman is a will to grow, mentally as well as physically; the personality is not indifferent to the alternatives of unfolding or stymieing the rational faculties. The intellect is like a fragile plant. It requires the right kind of surroundings and nourishment, of soil and air and water; within the limits set by the surrounding social circumstances, the intellect will grow to whatever stature each individual is capable of achieving.

The social limits to intellectual growth appear from the individual's perspective primarily as anxieties; in addition, there is the kind of limit that is imposed by keeping information or knowledge or stimulation away from the individual. Since the colleges in the Western democracies give students physical access to almost all varieties of books, the failure of most students to take advantage of this opportunity to broaden their rationality must be explained largely in terms of the limits set by their various kinds of anxiety.

Some anxieties are deeply rooted and subconscious; they drive the individual to acquire and hold on to beliefs and attitudes that serve self-defensive needs. These anxieties usually revolve around fundamentals such as guilt and shame and doubts about one's own worth as a human being, and they frequently emanate from feelings of rejection by one's parents during infancy or early childhood. Other anxieties are preconscious or conscious and revolve around one's social relationships; some take the shape of worries about being accepted in the appropriate peer groups or by the appropriate reference groups, whereas others are concerned with the unknown future and are manifested as worries about adequate performance or rewards in future social roles.

All varieties of personal and social anxiety presumably have one thing in common: while they may or may not stimulate mental effort, they invariably forestall a fully rational, fully task-oriented approach to human and social problems. It may be said that our anxieties keep our gaze focused on the ground immediately or in a straight line ahead of us most of the time so that we fail to study the wider horizons, even though the wider vision might have eased our walk and certainly would have helped us decide more independently where to go. Like rats in the psychologist's maze, most of us are driven through our social labyrinths by our needs and anxieties; physically we walk erect but mentally we are too unsure of ourselves and our steps to stand upright and gain an overview of society and a perspective on life.

Higher education exists, I assume, to give us this opportunity, both for our sake as individuals and for society's sake, on the assumption that a fuller view of reality produces a more responsible and a wiser, more foresightful citizenry. Students will take advantage of this opportunity to the extent that they can; but the social odds against any spectacular unfolding of the fragile intellect are large, given the present type of college community and our present social order.

Genuine curiosity belongs to the child, and to the child in man. In most lives the capacity to be curious keeps declining; every time a young person is induced to accept an answer for self-defensive reasons or on the ground that a belief is socially expected, his capacity to be curious is cut. On the other hand, every time a person is permitted to make an intellectual discovery on his own, to see a new connection, or make sense of a new idea, for example, his curiosity is nourished and expanded. This is how it happens that intellectual development tends to become either stymied at an early age or self-generating in a lifelong process. It becomes stymied in college or earlier if the student remains a prisoner of his immediate or anticipatory social anxieties; a person who has no intellectual curiosity at twenty is unlikely to develop it later, though there are exceptions to this rule.

The intellect becomes liberated in college or earlier to the extent that the student has been helped to achieve a fair degree of mastery of his personal and social anxieties, and has developed the courage to define for himself what kind of life *he* wants to live. The chances are that he will want, if he in a real sense is able to choose for himself, a life of long-term humanitarian solidarity with his fellow men, in preference to a psychologically lonelier life in quest of more narrowly self-centered, short-term goals.

References

Clark, Burton R. *The Open Door College: A Case Study.* New York: McGraw-Hill, 1960.

Gross, N., Mason, W. S., and McEachern, A. W. *Explorations in role Analysis.* New York: John Wiley and Sons, 1958.

Parsons, T., and Shils, E. A. *Toward a General Theory of Action.* Cambridge, Mass.: Harvard University Press, 1953.

Sanford, N. Theories of higher education and the experimental college. In Harris, S. E. (Ed.), *Higher Education in the United States: the Economic Problems.* Cambridge, Mass.: Harvard University Press, 1960.

Frank Pinner

The Crisis of the State Universities: Analysis and Remedies

The careers of the newer American colleges and universities resemble those of religious denominations. In their early, sectarian state they appeal to special clienteles, often local or regional in character, recruited from narrow social layers, and largely agreed on fundamentals. As they proceed toward churchly universality, however, they shed some of their old clienteles and aspire to new ones; they seek to enlarge their geographical domain by erasing its boundaries; and the undisputed verities of the past give way to a multiplicity of aims and convictions. Perhaps this is the growth pattern of all successful institutions in a highly mobile society.

"DISSENSUAL" KNOWLEDGE AND THE UNIVERSITY'S PUBLICS

We who teach in the large new universities of America experience daily the strains and stresses of such transformations. These arise not merely from the growth in staffs and enrollments, the addition of teaching programs in areas previously neglected or deliberately omitted, and the development of physical facilities, but they also reflect many changes in policy.

There is, for instance, the steady and insistent effort to stimulate "research," which administrators and professors alike regard as the open sesame to the world of universal scholarship. Many of the newer institutions, seemingly ashamed of their former provincialism and bent on escaping its remnants, eagerly embrace programs that will bring the faculty into closer contact with national and international affairs. Government-sponsored or foundation-sponsored programs of technical assistance to underdeveloped nations typically are conducted by recently emerged large universities rather than those with older and more cosmopolitan traditions.

Some will see such involvement with national policy as nothing more than a shift from local provincialism to that of the nation-state. At the very least, the province itself has become larger. And the enlargement of the university's geographical reference does imply some broadening of its intellectual scope.

But this very urge toward universalism makes for ambiguities and tensions. Although it reaches toward far-flung horizons, the newly emerged university cannot and dares not forsake its familiar surroundings of town and countryside. It is bound to these by its own alumni and other benefactors, by its older faculty, by the origins and the expectations of its students, and by those of the surrounding community. In playing to two rather disparate publics, the local public of its immediate surroundings and the cosmopolitan audience of the republic of letters, it risks raising suspicions in both.

The alienation of the university from one or both of these publics tends to become a particularly acute problem for state universities. More than other institutions of higher learning, they depend on the good will of local people. Since public funds are the most important sources of their income, they must find ways to stimulate the generosity of lawmakers. They must not merely maintain good relations with legislators; they must also nurse, within the state, their own social constituencies, groups of people who believe in the benefits of higher education and who are capable of exerting pressure toward its expansion.

Administrators of state universities, in appealing to the legislature and to supporters in town and country, tend to make two points: their university performs services important to the people of the state, and their university is among the "greatest" or "most distinguished" in the country. The two arguments do not necessarily reflect congruent sets of facts; what is conceived to be "service" to the state is not likely to be closely related to the criteria of "distinction" in the academic world at large.

Thus the state legislator or the small-town businessman may feel that the main services of a university are undergraduate training and consultancy for public and private bodies; but the current mood of the larger academic community bestows "distinction" on schools with large programs of graduate—not necessarily undergraduate—instruction, and of "basic"—not immediately utilitarian—research.

The separation of the state university from its local publics has not occurred in spite of the improvement of its faculty, but because of it. Where once there was a community, there are now two or more separate groups. Where once there was implicit understanding of common purposes there are now many purposes.

Administrators are caught between their loyalty to the older members of the faculty and their esteem for the new men they have fought so hard to win. Unable to take sides they must, for they are human, rationalize their situation. They must make themselves the bearers of myths which might restore to the university the unity of a tribal society.

One of these myths is the consoling belief that knowledge can be pursued in many ways, and that each new set of facts is a building block destined to find its place in the structure of truth. We call this belief "consoling" because it so conveniently relieves its holders of the most arduous task facing academic administrators: to define criteria for encouraging some academic endeavors while discouraging others. Because it yields no guide lines for policy, I would call this belief a myth. The dilemmas of our state universities bring into sharp relief some basic problems in the growth and management of human knowledge. As teachers and researchers, we must become articulate about our grounds for preferring certain kinds of knowledge to others, for only thus can we expect university administrations to act with appropriate discrimination in allocating resources.

What criteria, then, can we propose? Which knowledge is it most urgent to pursue, to teach, to explore? I believe that the university must give preference to the knowledge that is least likely to be sponsored and supported by any other institution of society, the knowledge that only anxieties and fears prevent man from pursuing, the knowledge that is most needed *because of* these widespread apprehensions. This is "dissensual" knowledge.

I term "consensual" all those disciplines about which the public at large tends to have no reservation, either about the competence of the scholars and the truth of their findings or about the values which inform their work. Correspondingly, I term "dissensual" all disciplines whose value or procedures are widely questioned among the public, either explicitly or implicitly.

Few people in the community will express doubts about the research findings and teachings of a chemist, nor will they ever question his motives and wonder about the values underlying his work. But the findings and teachings of philosophers and economists do not elicit similarly general confidence. The public tends to wonder about the worth of these scholars' work; it tends to look for hidden motives and it easily discounts their teachings and even their data, either by directly opposing or by conveniently forgetting and ignoring them.

This has nothing to do with the public's understanding of these disciplines. The man in the street knows no more about chemistry and the life work of chemists than he knows about economics and its practitioners. His reactions are not based on direct experience, but on the status the consensual disciplines have achieved in the community.

The logical deductions of a philosopher are just as secure, and the empirical findings of a sociologist often just as convincing, as are theories and findings of scholars in the consensual disciplines. It could be argued that disciplines in which aesthetic judgments play a role, for example, music, are perhaps on less secure ground since these are "matters of taste." I doubt that this is so, but I agree that this part of my argument is more difficult to sustain. Personally, I am convinced that standards of beauty are as ascertainable as standards of truth in scientific endeavors. In either case, the exact formulation of such standards is by no means easy; and the fact that we have thus far made greater advances in formulating standards of truth than standards of beauty testifies to the direction of our interests more than to the feasibility of either task.

There was a time, not very far in the past, when the medical man was looked upon with as much suspicion as is the psychotherapist today; and the findings of the early chemist (or alchemist) were held up to as much ridicule as those of the social scientist today. Even in the recent past, advances in agriculture were made the butt of ridicule by farmers who saw agronomic innovations as a challenge to their accustomed way of life.

To be sure, the disciplines which are now consensual have undergone a great expansion in knowledge and have gained greatly in precision an security of propositions. But much of this gain was made because the public came to perceive the utility of these disciplines and was willing to support them by the grant of money and status. Growth of knowledge and growth of public acceptance are closely interrelated, and neither of the two can for long proceed without the other.

Much of the recent expansion of the newer state universities has taken place in the dissensual disciplines. The liberal arts, the social sciences, and education have seen great increases in the strength of their faculties and in student enrollments. Nor is this all. The frame of mind of the men who have recently joined our faculty tends to favor those areas of inquiry which are still largely dissensual. Also they are less likely than were their predecessors to compromise with community sentiment. They hold values and are led to findings which typically are not shared by the community.

Economists know, for instance, that productivity is not necessarily a function of competition and that, indeed, productivity in our country has increased at an accelerated rate at the very time when insecurity in business and jobs was greatly reduced. No matter how well founded such findings of the economists might be, they do not really reach the public. Rather, at every public meeting of businessmen, orators will sing the praises of business and job competition as the surest stimulants to productivity. Unaware of the questionable nature of such beliefs, the public expects the university professor to confirm them, rather than to challenge them.

The implications are clear: the weaker the faculty, the less its concern for the inviolability of thought, the more likely it will be to make concessions to the conventional wisdom and to say what the community wishes to hear. Bring to the university people with better training, more deeply committed to their discipline, more enamored of the truth as they have come to know it, and a breach is bound to arise between the proponent of objective knowledge and the public committed to the conventional wisdom.

THE MAIN BASES OF CONFLICT

The resistance of the public to the proponent of unconventional beliefs is automatic. It can be active or passive, and I have seen both types among my own students. Active resistance takes the form of overt rejection; the less acceptable teachings are discounted as being impractical, "long-haired," or heretical. Passive resistance takes the form of systematic but unconscious misunderstanding, or selective perception, and gross distortion of the teacher's message.

Active resistance is somewhat easier to deal with than passive, because it exists on the conscious level and is therefore a possible topic for debate. Unfortunately, it is comparatively rare. In the great majority of instances, resistance is passive, that is, inarticulate, unrealized, amorphous. Passive resistance, at the same time, is most likely to sever all possible community ties between teacher and students, for it makes communication impossible. Similar observations can be made, no doubt, about the relations between the able teacher of a dissensual discipline and the larger outside public of the university, but they are not so apparent and not so easily detected.

Resistance to unaccustomed knowledge and doctrine is generally not surprising, but when it occurs in universities as frequently and consistently as, in my judgment, it occurs in ours, we have reason to be perturbed. Our students do not expect to learn in the profound and the only meaningful sense of the word learning. They do not expect that their understandings of the world will change, that their beliefs will be altered, that old interests will be replaced by new ones, that on the day of their graduation they will be—as human beings—quite different from the freshmen who entered the university four years ago. They attend the university not as the truly religious person attends to worship, for the sake of an experience which will transform him; but rather as does the average Sunday churchgoer, for the sake of social conformity and from habit.

The gap does not arise from the differences in intellectual preparation and maturity which is ordinarily expected between students and teachers. All important ideas can be taught on many levels of complexity; and I have seen people of great profundity in their fields of knowledge genuinely excited by the task of teaching highly sophisticated ideas in a manner which will make them accessible to students with minimal preparation.

The gap arises, rather, from a difference in foci of interest. The good academician focuses on changes in the structure of knowledge, and he does so in both of his capacities, as a scholar and as a teacher. Our students and our wider publics are interested only in accretion.

Our students are the products of a mobile society; their very presence in the universities attests this. Yet as a rule they appear to be intellectually and emotionally more rigid than are students in less mobile societies. Oddly, the presence of barriers in the mind reflects the relative absence of barriers in society. Where education is still regarded as the privilege of gentlemen, students of plebeian lineage show a grasping and combative eagerness to acquire knowledge, refinement of taste, and new interpretations of human experience. To them, education is a step in the fight for social equality, and they enter it with a will to change. Such attitudes are still common in some of our Eastern universities where many of the students come from minority backgrounds. But our Midwestern students, although frequently from homes of moderate means and meager education, exhibit no such eagerness. They happily take it for granted, as does our society, that there are no social hurdles to learning. Our students, in entering the university, cannot feel that they are overcoming ancient restrictions and embarking on a new way of life. For them education spells advancement rather than change, improvement rather than transition. The fixedness of their points of view is thus a counterpart to our equalitarian ethos.

Yet we know such attitudes to be ill adapted. Great transformations are under way in our society, and there are so signs of respite. It is imperative that our students, once they leave the campus, be flexible enough in mind and personality to cope with unexpected and perhaps still inconceivable problems. A few simple precepts, such as those contained in conventional wisdom, can scarcely be of any help to the engineers of a still clouded future, however broadly or narrowly the term "engineer" might be construed.

We have thus two seemingly incompatible conditions of education: a changing world which calls for a leadership of insight and originality; and students who, in view of the relative ease with which they can cross social boundaries, are under no compulsion to play new roles and to cast off old habits of mind and heart.

In an effort to cope with this difficulty many universities now have programs of general education designed to give the student the background that was lacking at his arrival on campus. We bring to the campus great artists, lecturers, foreign films, and a variety of other "events." These efforts have usually fallen far short of expectations, and not for lack of good will or hard work. In our own classes, teachers often find no difference between students who have been exposed to the general education course in our specialty and those who have not. Even if the teaching in general courses were dismally poor (which by no means is the rule), this would hardly explain such minimal results. The number of students who attend concerts, theatrical performances, and discussion meetings is disturbingly small. Again, even if these performances were consistently mediocre (which by no means they are) this would not explain such perennial truancy. Our students have no use for these things. Neither our own lack of talent nor theirs inhibits our students' understanding. We must accept it as a hard social fact that much of human thought and culture is, in the form in which we present it to them, unrelated to their experience and hence unintelligible.

We have our own share in the academic tragi-comedy of misunderstandings. Like their students, American professors are the creatures of a fluid social milieu. Since status is achieved rather than conferred, we feel forever impelled to prove to ourselves and to others that we deserve the trust and responsibility placed upon us.

Such proof is difficult, for we are producers of intangibles, and thus status anxiety is our most frequent occupational disease. Nor can we find comfort in aristocratic pride. Most of us do not issue from a nobility of rank or wealth, nor even from a patriciate of letters. We come from every social layer in every region of the United States and of the world.

Thus we are both similar to our students and different from them. Like them, most of us are recent arrivals, and like them, we came to the university because the hurdles were not too high. We are, perhaps, of more diverse and more mingled extractions than they are. But the main difference is this: we have experienced change within ourselves, and they have not. We are not too sure of our position in the world; they are too sure of theirs. Their status striving has the determined push of careerism; our status anxiety is a gnawing worry lest we fail to live up to the expectations which we ourselves and others attach to our position.

Such feelings do not make for good teaching or learning. A snobbish professor alienates the student as he inculcates the unattainability of knowledge and good taste. His earthy colleague, by exhibiting an excess of common sense, affirms that there is not very much to be learned or communicated. The student, sharing the American public's ambiguous attitudes toward men of letters and sensing moreover his professor's disquiet, vacillates between formal subservience and excessive informality. This does not help the professor, who becomes even more defensive; and it does not help communication, which becomes even less articulate.

TOWARD THE ACADEMIC COMMUNITY

To me education means openness to change. It means that we help the student shed the conventional wisdom and enable him to make rational choices by the use of information, insight, and sensitivity. It means, first of all, that we generate the willingness to change. We communicate excitement about the worlds of knowledge and of the arts, so that our students will want to expose themselves to unaccustomed experiences. To the extent that they do, they will gain the respect of the faculty, and they will learn to appreciate their teachers. Thus education is the same thing as the creation of the academic community.

For the teacher, education is forever an act of self-revelation. The good teacher does not simply attempt to fill minds with information as one fills barrels of wine; it is not a physical process. Rather, he exhibits himself as a demonstration case, showing his students how at least one member of his profession tackles a problem, how he feels about it, how he judges his own work, how he doubts and battles about its social value and the truth of his findings, how he is often tempted to cheat himself and others by saying more than can be responsibly asserted. Science, the humanities, and the arts are human and fallible activities and must be understood as such.

For the student, too, education is self-revelation. He must be able to expose himself to the teacher and to other students so that he may be helped better to realize his own potential. All discussion that is not to some extent self-revelation is, in fact, anti-intellectual. The student of mathematics has not learned anything about his discipline unless he is able to exhibit the process whereby he arrives at a solution. The most elaborate repertoire of mathematical formulae and operating rules will never add up to the first beginnings of mathematics.

In the dissensual disciplines, self-revelation is even more important; almost invariably questions of value are mingled with questions of theory and fact, and if the student does not learn to be articulate about his values, if he takes them for granted, he has not begun to penetrate into his field of study. Self-revelation is the surest path to self-awareness; and without the latter, change is impossible and education an empty ritual.

The academic community must be an assembly of men and women humble enough and yet secure enough to exhibit to one another their doubts, their weaknesses, and at times their wretchedness. This is the price of knowledge and of truth. Set the teacher up on a pedestal and ascribe to him all the conventional virtues, and you will reduce his scope to that of a dog trainer. Limit the student's range of experience by imposing disciplines other than those emerging from the search for truth and understanding, and you will make him into a parrot. But foster understanding and the free but organized search for new forms of thinking and living, and you will be educating people.

Ten
Conclusions and Proposals for Change

Nevitt Sanford

Conclusions and Proposals for Change

THE DEVELOPMENT OF THE INDIVIDUAL

We appreciate the goal of optimal individual development best when we think of our own children and what we want for them; other people's children can have their talents discovered, processed, and put to work in the interest of purposes they do not necessarily share.

All the resources of society should be utilized for the development of children and youth. This, I should say, is mainly what a society is for. If suitable agencies and institutions do not exist they will have to be created.

It appears that the kind of institution that is needed will have to be very much like a kind of college. Even if we were to set up youth reservations, or work camps, or overseas projects, or kinds of facilities or organizations for which no models yet exist, it would be necessary to offer instruction and exercises of a more or less intellectual nature. If colleges did not exist they would have to be invented.

Development after the age of about two, after the acquisition of language, is in considerable part a cognitive—one might even say "intellectual"—matter. This involves in a crucial way the use of symbols—words, images, thoughts. Development is largely a matter of expanding the range of things that can be appreciated —images, concepts, ideas—and the range of responses—largely involving the use of symbols—that can be made. Books, with their gift of boundless vicariousness, are a great benefit to parents or teachers who would develop personalities. It is through utilizing the symbols of his culture, in the life of the imaginations, that the individual may most appropriately, and most joyfully, express his deepest impulses and feelings. It is through solving problems with the use of his intelligence—typically in the manipulation of symbols—and through being held to the requirement of seeking and being guided by the truth that the individual develops, through exercise, the abilities that enable him to control himself and relate to the demands of reality. And it is largely through confrontation by a wide range of value systems and ethical dilemmas that conscience becomes enlightened and therefore stabilized.

The human individual functions as a unit, and his diverse features develop in interaction one with another. Intelligence, feeling, emotion, and action are inseparable aspects, not separate parts, of behavior.

We know this from our own experience. *Our* productive work is a very passionate affair; creative endeavor leaves us limp with emotional exhaustion, and the hot pursuit of truth keeps us jumping with excitement. And for *us* to learn anything new, to have our minds changed, we have first to be practically shattered as personalities and then put together again. Why then should students be regarded as cool and well-oiled machines for storing and retrieving information? There is something to be said for teaching machines, for they may spare the teacher some machine-like work, but there is nothing to be said for a learning machine.

It is frequently said that the proper concern of higher education is with the intellect only. But the notion that the intellect is somehow disembodied, or separated from the rest of the personality is not only unintelligent in that it favors no legitimate educational aim, it is actually perverse in its implications, in that it encourages the assumption that if one takes it upon himself to be a student he cannot at the same time be a human being.

Let us take an example of the interaction of the intellectual and the emotional. At a southern college I was told that the students were on the whole very bright but afraid to think. This was meant quite literally. They were afraid that thinking would lead to their alienation from their culture, and there was recognition of the fact that if we are afraid to think about some things, then for all practical purposes we are afraid to think about almost anything. We need not, in considering this state of affairs, limit ourselves to

students in southern schools. I have encountered the same phenomenon in seniors at Stanford University. Very probably in all
our leading colleges there are young men or young women who
have a very clear conception of what life for them will be after
they have graduated; they are quite certain that this life is going
to be rewarding and that it will be theirs as long as they do nothing
to upset the applecart. As long as they are willing to participate in
the style of life that can be anticipated, not allow themselves to
be critical of it, or to kick over the traces, they have it made, as
they say. We can almost see the wheels turning as these students
ask themselves: should they or should they not allow themselves
to be influenced by this teacher with these ideas, or to commit
themselves to this or that ideal of the college. They act as if they
knew that giving in on one point, or opening themselves to influence by one teacher, would threaten the whole structure of
beliefs and values according to which they live and propose to go
on living. This is clearly the situation of a student who comes
from a family that is upholding traditional southern prejudices,
but let us remember that it is also true of some students at the best
colleges in this country. These students are the nonthinkers, and
the great educational task is to free them of their fear-born parochialism.

This task is not just a matter of finding some deep-lying psychological motive and using this to make students want so much
to think that they will do so despite its fearsome consequences.
There is also the possibility that these structures can be pene-
trated by strictly academic or intellectual means.

At another southern college some of the faculty and I were
talking about authoritarianism and how it might be reduced by
educational means. I suggested that if we succeed in teaching
people to think in quantitative terms, to think in terms of variability, probability and the like, thus making it impossible for
them to think in terms of rigid categories, we will reduce scores
on our authoritarianism scales. This led one of the teachers to say
to me later that she had now a fresh appreciation of the possibili-

ties in lecturing. She explained that she lectured in psychological statistics and had had the usual feeling that many of the students were not understanding it, and that most of the others could take it or leave it alone. But one day after a class in which she had been lecturing on probability she encountered one of her students in a corner, crying. This young woman was willing to talk to a sympathetic listener, and it turned out that she was crying because, as she said, she didn't know what to think any longer. She felt that her whole belief system was crumbling. She realized, we may well suppose, that if she went along with this teacher and thought about quantitative distinctions among things, or about human variability, or in terms of what was probably true and probably untrue she would have to give up those rigid categories which up until now she had used in facing the world.

This is saying, I think, that an intellectual change can ramify throughout the whole personality and initiate changes in fundamental structures. If it is really true that a person with an authoritarian personality structure has difficulty in learning certain aspects of mathematics and science, it is also true that if a teacher succeeds in teaching some mathematics and science to some students, he can thereby change an authoritarian structure in the personality. Let those teachers who want to influence their students through the presentation of subject matter take heart, and let those teachers who do not want to upset their students but only to train them in some specialty be aware of the fact that they are living dangerously; for ideas implanted at times when there is special readiness for them can have far-reaching effects.

Just as nothing is truly learned until it has been integrated with the purposes of the individual, so no facts and principles that have been learned can serve any worthy human purpose unless they are restrained and guided by character. Intellect without humane feeling can be monstrous, whereas feeling without intelligence is childish. Intelligence and feeling are at their highest and in the best relation one to the other where there is a taste for art and beauty as well as an appreciation of logic and of knowledge.

We may wonder where some educators and educational spokesmen got the idea of the disembodied intellect that is to be developed through the intake, storing, and reproduction of data. Certainly not from the observation of what happens when learning occurs in college. I am afraid they got it from psychology. Psychologists not only abstract processes such as cognition and learning from their living context but they commonly seek to isolate these processes experimentally, in the hope of obtaining precise information and demonstrating general laws. In consequence there is a vast literature—and even a vast, indigestible undergraduate curriculum—in which perception is treated independently of the perceiver and learning independently of the learner. Apparently this kind of psychology still has influence on education. The abstractions of the psychological experimenter have been reified and are used to rationalize current practices. It is ironic that the vaunted general laws derived from laboratory experiments are not really general. They break down as soon as a new variable is introduced into the situation, and since in real life—in the classroom for example—numerous additional variables are at work, it is impossible to go directly from the laboratory to applications in school.

We should not blame the present generation of psychological experimenters too much, however. They were probably taught by college professors who thought they could train the intellect without touching the rest of the personality. Such professors very probably were under the influence of the know-nothing behaviorism of the 1920's, and this could be understood as an outgrowth of a long tradition in which the narrowly cognitive or mentalistic has dominated in Western approaches to knowledge.

I do not want to suggest that there is no psychology applicable to learning in college; there is a fair amount. Of particular relevance are studies of the modification of belief systems, of attitude change, of development over time of social perception. Indeed I rely on such studies for the argument being made here.

The argument that development in intellectual functioning goes with development in other features of the personality is based on evidence such as the following. When personality tests are given to entering freshmen, and then to sophomores, juniors, and seniors, such basic characteristics as freedom in the expression of impulse, independence of pressures toward conformity, sense of social responsibility, and sensitivity to ethical issues are found to increase on the average with length of time in college—that is, in a good liberal arts college like Vassar. Obviously such changes are far more pronounced in some students than in others. Some actually go backward. If we ask faculty members, as Donald Brown did, to identify those students who most resemble the "ideal" college product, it turns out that, in general, students who are thus singled out are those who stand highest on the measured personality traits. We may be sure that college teachers in expressing their conception of the ideal student put the stress on intellectual characteristics—although not necessarily, as the data show, on the fact of earning high grades.

Again, a great deal of research—at the Institute of Personality Assessment and Research, at Berkeley, and elsewhere—has been directed at the determination of what personality traits are associated with creativity. Creativity in students is rated by their teachers, in professionals by their peers, and personality traits are estimated by a variety of assessment techniques. Here the basic fact is that the traits that distinguish the creative from the noncreative are essentially the same as those that distinguish college seniors from freshmen.

Do graduating seniors who are not creative have any hope of becoming so? It appears that they do, for developmental change *can* occur at any time of life. What in fact happens, as Mervin Freedman has shown, is that those growth curves which show a steady increase in desired qualities during college tend to level off during the four or five years after college. And to stay leveled off.

This makes plain why some of us have been so exercised about what happens, or what does not happen, in college. If college offers a kind of "last chance," if the college years are marked by a degree of openness to change that is not later duplicated, the message to educators seems to be loud and clear.

But these growth curves are based on averages. We know from studies of individual graduates that some fall from grace; they leave college in a spirit of "so much for education," and soon fall back into the patterns that were characteristic of them at the beginning of their freshman years. This means that others contribute more than their share to holding our curves of development on a level. Indeed, individual studies of young alumnae show that some have leaped forward, showing more development during the four or five years after college than most students show during their college careers. If some seniors look back with a certain shame upon what they were like as freshmen, we may be sure that some graduates of four years look with amused tolerance upon their senior selves.

It is clear, then, that not everything depends on college. There are educational stimuli in the larger world. What we see in any alumnus depends in part on what has intervened since graduation. All will agree that education should be life long. There must be a psychology of this education, a developmental psychology that is concerned with the total life span. Anyone who plans, or offers, or takes part in such education should be guided in part by the facts and theories of individual development.

When we think of development—before, during or after college—it is important to consider what might be called its progressive nature. There is some order to the succession of developmental changes. The essential idea is that certain things must happen before other events become possible. The child must walk before he can run. The earlier happening contributes to a state of readiness for change, but it does not make the later happening inevitable; an outside stimulus of the right kind is still necessary.

It is a natural consequence of the progressive nature of development that much education has to be remedial. Such is the continuity of events that failures at early stages lead to distortions in all later ones. If a boy has not learned to read and write by the time he enters college, there is nothing for it but to go back and straighten him out. By the same token, a college freshman who did not have in high school the experience of totally merging himself with a group of his peers, of uncritically accepting the group's goals, and throwing himself into the effort toward their achievement, should be permitted to have the experience now—so that he can get it out of his system and move on to a more reasoned and independent participation in organized activities. A graduating senior who has not been through a phase of ethical relativism must sooner or later have this educational experience, for otherwise it is hard to see how his values can be genuinely his own. A graduating senior who is still caught in authoritarianism and ethnic or racial prejudice has hardly begun to attain a liberal education; he will be handicapped in all future activities requiring a rational approach to human problems; he must start now to achieve the kind of self-understanding without which he cannot become a whole person.

INDIVIDUAL DEVELOPMENT AND OTHER GOALS OF HIGHER EDUCATION

Higher education may be assigned other goals besides that of individual development, and it is possible to debate the relative importance of these goals. I put individual development first because in my view it is the most important goal in its own right. If you were to say it is more important that the individual be adjusted to his society, I would reply that it is more important that he be able to transcend and help to transform society. But I also argue that individual development should have first attention because it is favorable to the achievement of all other legitimate goals. Is it our aim to preserve culture? This can best be done by individuals who have been developed to a point where they can appreciate it. Do we wish to create culture? This is mainly done by highly developed individuals, although there are some important exceptions. Is it our desire to train people for vocations that require technical skills? If this can be done at all in college, it is through the development of qualities that are valuable in a great variety of jobs. Preparation for a high-level profession? Good performance in any profession depends heavily on qualities found only in highly developed individuals. Ask professors of engineering to characterize a good engineer, and they will list such qualities as leadership, capacity to make wise decisions, flexibility of thinking and so on. They ask how such characteristics are to be produced, and, receiving no answer, they go back to teaching mechanics and thermodynamics.

Given the entering college student as he is, a relatively undeveloped human specimen, nearly everything that happens to him in college is relevant to his development, either favoring or hampering it. Deciding on a career or choosing a major field of study may be favorable to the development of a stable personal identity. On the other hand, early specialization can close off sources of developmentally potent stimuli. Losing oneself in the exploration of an academic discipline can be highly favorable to the development of an autonomous self. But note: it is one thing to argue for encouraging this kind of absorption with problems on the ground that it is good for the discipline or academic subject; it is something else to say that it develops the individual. If the latter is being argued, it is necessary to say how the experience does its work, at what stage of development it is most to be desired, and why it is to be preferred to other developmentally potent experiences.

In sum, the scientific study of education means the continuing examination of innumerable means-ends relationships, and of the origins and consequences of ends, so that our means may become increasingly effective and our ends ever more intelligently chosen.

THE PROMOTION OF INDIVIDUAL DEVELOPMENT IN COLLEGE

Once we have decided on individual development as a major goal, we have to think of how all the conditions and processes of the college may be brought into its service. The curriculum, modes of teaching, the social organization of the college community, the behavior of the President—all must be considered as means for the attainment of this goal, and this without neglecting the ways in which these things may promote the achievement of other goals.

With respect to curriculum, let it be stressed that there is nothing in the present approach to suggest that subject matter does not count. On the contrary, students who are to develop need culture in almost the same way that they need food. We should, if necessary, ram it down their throats, or feed it to them in the form of sugar-coated pills. But let us continuously ask ourselves why we use the ingredients we do.

This concern with curriculum applies to disciplines or major subjects as well as to specific materials within them. Happily, it is possible to say that all the major subjects usually taught in colleges can be taught in developmental ways. This includes vocational subjects. Not that any known vocation, at the technical level, can be prepared for in college, but vocational courses might provide the means for introducing students to valuable developmental experiences. The great liberal arts subjects are the easiest to support on the ground of developmental theory. History is a great instrument for showing students, quickly and inexpensively, the joys of more or less independent inquiry; philosophy, and especially ethics, is probably still the standby for challenging unexamined belief systems and for giving the student his necessary introduction to relativity of values; and literature is the great means for acquainting the student with his own feelings—by showing him something of the variety and depth of what is humanly possible; and so on. It would seem to me an interesting exercise for any teacher to ask himself just how his subject, as he teaches it, contributes to the development of the individual.

Nearly everybody agrees that the teacher is the heart and soul of the educational process. But it is not always agreed why this is so, or what the teacher actually does to influence the student, or what are the processes by which students develop under the teacher's guidance. What is it that he does and that cannot be done by machines or by libraries or by TV? The whole phenomenon of the teacher-student relationship needs further study and analysis, with attention to both developmental and antidevelopmental modes of teaching. Let it be said at once that there is nothing in the general theory of personality development in college to suggest that all teachers should be interested in students as persons, or have any special knowledge of them as developing individuals. Indeed teachers—or administrators—who try to be one of the boys, try to participate vicariously in the student's adolescent trials and errors, can be positively harmful. It is usually enough for a teacher to teach his subject and to convey his enthusiasm for it. But if this is the heart of the teacher's work he should not be called upon, or feel called upon, to assign grades, or to teach something just because it appears to be needed to fill out the Department's offerings, or to serve as a prerequisite to something else. A college faculty could be made up very largely of dedicated teachers of subjects. But somebody would have to be responsible for an overall plan in which such teaching had a place. And if a teacher wished to do something more, something that would be very likely to contribute to the students' development, the most fruitful thing for him to do, probably, would be to exhibit for students not just what he knows but also how he seeks to discover truth. This means that he himself must be a student in some sense of the word. He must create situations in which his own learning may be observed. One way to do this might be to let students in on his own research or scholarly activities. Another way to show how he learns would be simply to teach a subject that he knows little about—perhaps in cooperation with a colleague who knows some more about it. This, as Joseph Katz has pointed out, is one of the ways to avoid becoming deadwood. The other major way, of course, is to become intellectually interested in students as developing individuals. Why not? Students are so sadly in need of development and, at the same time, in most cases show so much potential for development, that it is hard to understand how so many teachers can remain essentially indifferent on this score.

When we come to the general social organization of the college our main concern—from the developmental point of view— should be to arrange things so that teachers can get at the students, and vice versa. College graduates a few years out of college tend to remember very little of what was offered in their courses, but they do remember a few of their teachers. In many, perhaps most, of these cases of the remembered teacher not a great deal of the teacher's time was involved. He was not a tutor or counsellor, or companion or a man with a great taste for desserts at fraternity houses. Quite likely he is remembered for some brief encounter, in which something he said or did struck something that was in a special state of readiness in the student. The point is, that in planning campus arrangements to bring faculty and students together in ways that are favorable to the student's development, it is not necessary to assume that a great deal of the teacher's time will be involved. The thing is to have the right kinds of encounters. It is a task of social psychology to discover what these are and how they might be favored by planned arrangements.

With respect to the organization of student life it should be our aim to bring about a maximal integration of living and learning. Students learn from each other, like lightning it seems, and where they live apart, geographically or psychologically, from the academic centers of the college they may actually acquire a culture that is in many respects in opposition to the intellectual culture to which the faculty would like to introduce them. We must find ways to bring the intellectual life of the college into the establishments where students live. We must create campus-wide, student-faculty or faculty-student communities in which the social needs of students, far from being suppressed, are brought into the service of the intellectual aims of the college.

A true community is one where the more advanced people feel some responsibility for helping other people. And a good way for students to learn something of the social and human purposes of intelligence is to create situations in which they can be helpful to others.

It might be proposed, for example, that seniors do a certain amount of teaching of freshmen. I would like to see seniors become expert in the sociology and social psychology of their own colleges and pass this knowledge along to entering freshmen. Seniors, working with faculty and others, should become familiar with all the new literature on college peer groups, student culture, student-faculty relations, what the administration is up against or up to, how the curriculum is made, and so on. Let them be wise men in the eyes of the freshmen, but let this be based in knowledge that comes from systematic study of the college community and from efforts to understand the processes of their own education. If we move far enough in this direction, everything about the college can become the object of intellectual analysis; and the usual barriers between the academic and the other activities of the college can thus be reduced.

Again, we should explore the possibilities of having seniors do some teaching or help with the teaching of academic subjects. Seniors may tutor freshmen, serve as teaching assistants, or participate in seminars or discussions, showing freshmen how educated men conduct themselves in these settings.

I am not thinking here primarily of helping freshmen, nor of helping faculty with their enormous teaching burden; I am thinking rather of helping seniors. If we invite seniors to worry about freshmen, they gain a new awareness of themselves. Like the mother who relives her adolescence through that of her daughter, the senior who works closely with freshmen will recall his own freshman self; he will see it in a new light, and incorporate this new conception in his personality. But probably most important would be a change in the senior's relationships with faculty members. It has often been said that students never understand their teachers until they become teachers themselves. Let us speed the process of understanding. Let us give seniors a taste of colleague-ship, a sense of what it might mean to participate as equals in the activities of the faculty.

I have seen it happen that when seniors were taken on as teaching assistants they immediately began to behave as adults. This is important, but when this happens with just a handful of students at one institution they are put under something of a strain. The movement into adulthood may be too abrupt and may bring alienation from fellow students. It would be better if their teaching activities were institutionalized and performed on a large scale. This would create a student-faculty community in which no student had adulthood too suddenly thrust upon him.

If we could arrange things so that the intellectual activities of students really contribute something to the community in which they live—rather than stand as the means by which they advance themselves at the expense of their friends and neighbors—we would at once promote the intellectual life and the values of decency and social responsibility. The intellectual in our society is much too alienated from his community and consequently much too defensive. Feeling that he is not understood or appreciated, he mutters contemptuously about "togetherness" and sinks more deeply into isolation and meanness. I think this is most likely to happen to a person who has never had an experience in which his best intellectual endeavor became a part of a group enterprise, so that its social meaning and relevance became apparent to him.

It is an odd thing, often commented upon by James Coleman and others, that it is very hard for us to contrive arrangements in which intellectual endeavors are carried out by teams or accompanied by a team spirit. Research work does, of course, often have this aspect, but it is rare that undergraduates are able to take part in activity of this sort. Perhaps those who work on the school paper learn something of intellectual cooperation but, by and large, in hard academic work it is every man for himself. Probably our accent on free enterprise serves our need to evaluate and allocate students better than it serves our purpose of educating them.

This leads me to make just one remark about the fraternity.

Why is it that fraternities are so persistent? Why do they not give up in the face of all the opposition and criticism they encounter? It must be because the fraternities serve some very genuine and legitimate needs of students. It is not all just status and exclusiveness. For many students, surely, the need to have close associates who can be trusted, and for whom sacrifices can be made, is very strong. And today, when in the best colleges academic demands have passed all rational bounds and the adult world wishes to evaluate students solely on the basis of achievement, they have a special need for companions who will accept them as they are.

A visit to the South today will make one very much aware of the clash of cultures in this country. In the South the human community is still very much alive and enormously important; people are accepted and valued unconditionally; the underachiever or ne'r-do-well is not rejected; family solidarity, friendship, fraternity still matter a great deal—often more than success or status. There is still a sharp contrast with Yankee mercantilism, the hard-headed, hard-bargaining, puritanical, competitive system in which people as well as things are evaluated in terms of what they can be exchanged for. Nowhere is the old Yankee spirit more persistent than in Northern colleges and universities—the last of the nineteenth century "enterprises"—where, as Howard Becker has pointed out, grades have for students the functions of money in the larger society and where the marketable professor is the one who publishes. What the Southern states are to the whole body politic, the fraternities are to the colleges and universities. Probably the Civil War is not really going to be won; but we may hope for synthesis that embodies the best elements of the two cultures.

One way to deal with the fraternities is to make them the scenes of our strongest efforts to create intellectual communities. If I were to undertake on an experimental basis the integration of living and learning, I would just as soon start with the fraternity as with any other group. I would win the cooperation of the leadership of a fraternity; I would invite them to help in the education of their younger members and in the turning of the existing social organization into a community of teachers and learners, or teacher-learners.

If students are as resistant to learning as is often said, the success of this experiment would make fraternities so unattractive that they would wither on the vine. If as I am suggesting, fraternities are expressions of pre-industrialized humanity—often abortive, extremist, infantile expressions to be sure—and many students desire learning in proportion as it is integrated with human and social purposes, the success of the experiment would put an end to our worries about our fraternities.

The administration, and particularly the top administration, must not be left out. It has a critical role in the development of the student's personality. College presidents are bound to represent much of what it is that students are supposed to become. As leaders of the whole enterprise, they must embody its aims and ideals, and cannot be merely the engineers who keep the machinery turning. Dr. Robert Hutchins has long been an eloquent spokesman for the great traditional values of liberal education. But rarely has there been a word about how we might achieve these fine things. Hutchins of Chicago did have his method, however, and I know men who feel eternally in his debt. His method was to show in his behavior that he stood for something, that he knew how to make value judgments, and that he had the courage to follow through in action.

Presidents may overlook their role as models for students, and it may appear at times when things are running smoothly that the students are overlooking it too. But let the president make a mistake, act in violation of some ethical norm, compromise once too often with the forces that oppose the true aims of the college, or display some measure of hypocrisy or "phoniness," and the effect on students is immediate and profound. They feel betrayed and lapse into cynicism or passivity. It would be a fine thing if college presidents could be heroes. If they cannot be, what with all the shopping, housekeeping, and trouble shooting they have to do, they must at least behave so consistently with our basic values that they can be ignored or taken for granted by students on the assumption that all is well. College presidents have to be wise and just and good men without expecting, or getting, any credit for it.

If the examples that I have given represent well what must be done in college in order to promote individual development, and if this should be our major aim, it follows that colleges must change many of their practices—perhaps in radical ways.

But how do colleges change? I mean how do they change in desired ways and according to plan? This brings us back to the problem posed in the first chapter of this book. As stated there, the public seems generally satisfied with things as they are, and the colleges—although not many are complacent—are by no means convinced that they should change in the ways here recommended. But there is hope in enlightened public criticism, and I should like to see this encouraged by informing the public about the colleges. Professions benefit from occasional public examination. Probably most college professors would agree that health is too important to be left to the doctors! It is time that college educators had their turn.

There is hope in some of the new and differently conceived institutions that are being founded now and will be founded in the years immediately ahead. We know more about education for individual development than is being applied, and innovation is far easier when we start from the beginning than it is within an existing system.

There is hope of progress in the professional schools. I mean hope that the scientific study of education in these settings will greatly expand our knowledge of means-ends relationships in higher education. These schools are accustomed to applying science to practical problems, and, as compared with the liberal arts colleges, they are clear about what they want to do, for their purposes are explicitly occupational. The liberal arts colleges have unstated, even unrecognized aims, and hence the scientific study of their workings could be quite upsetting, for it could lead to painful revelations.

Where the existing liberal arts colleges are concerned we have to put our faith in the further advance of educational knowledge. The inarticulateness of these colleges about their aims is often baffling, and so is their failure to understand the real sources of their difficulties. In many of these colleges there is grave concern about such problems as raising standards and getting students to work harder. Generally speaking, the liberal arts colleges are certainly trying to do *something*. It is remarkable, as Santayana noted, how we redouble our efforts as we lose sight of our goals.

What the colleges need most of all, it would seem, is knowledge of themselves, of what they do, and of what they should do. They should acquire this knowledge for themselves with help from psychology and the other social sciences. They should study themselves, focusing on goals of individual student development and asking with respect to each practice how it favors or hampers progress toward these goals. Each teacher should ask this question about his own work. There should be continuing and genuine experimentation with new programs, including colleges within colleges, with careful appraisals of results. This can make knowledge of higher education cumulative at last; and the inquiry itself will serve students directly, by displaying for them, and involving them in, the excitement of the quest.

If our colleges would do all these things they would provide inspiration for us all, for they would be acting to further major ideals of the American tradition—the value of the individual as an end in himself, and the belief in the power of intelligent experimentation to improve him and his society.

Index